Archaeology at French Colonial Cahokia

Studies in Illinois Archaeology
Number 3

Thomas Emerson, Series Editor
Evelyn R. Moore, Managing Editor

Archaeology at French Colonial Cahokia

Bonnie L. Gums

with contributions by

George R. Holley, Neal H. Lopinot, Terrance J. Martin,
F. Terry Norris, and John A. Walthall

Illinois Historic Preservation Agency
Springfield, Illinois

ISBN 0-942579-02-X

Illinois Historic Preservation Agency, Springfield, IL 62701
Printed by authority of the State of Illinois
September 1988

This publication was financed in part with federal funds provided by the U.S. Department of the Interior and administered by the Illinois Historic Preservation Agency. However, the contents and opinions do not necessarily reflect the views or policies of the U.S. Department of the Interior and the Illinois Historic Preservation Agency.

CONTENTS

Figures vii

Plates x

Tables xii

Acknowledgments xiii

CHAPTER 1: INTRODUCTION 1
    Environmental Setting 7
    Historical Background 12
    Previous Archaeological Investigations 22
    The Present Condition
       of the Archaeological Record 27

CHAPTER 2: INITIAL ARCHAEOLOGICAL
INVESTIGATIONS 30
    Documentary Evidence 30
    Summary of the Documentary Evidence 43
    Archaeological Investigations and Research 45
    Results of the Initial Investigations 50
    Summary and Conclusions 68

CHAPTER 3: ARCHAEOLOGICAL TEST EXCAVATIONS . . 70
    Test Excavation Methodology 70
    Feature Excavation Methodology 73
    Stratigraphy 75
    Feature Descriptions 77
    Summary and Conclusions 113

CHAPTER 4: ARTIFACT DESCRIPTIONS 115
    Aboriginal Ceramics 116
      by George R. Holley
    Stone Artifacts 117
    Smoking Pipes 125
    Historic Ceramics 134
      by John A. Walthall and Bonnie L. Gums
    Glass Artifacts 158

    Metal Artifacts 176
    Weapons 205
      by F. Terry Norris
    Miscellaneous Artifacts 213

CHAPTER 5: ANIMAL REMAINS FROM THE CAHOKIA WEDGE SITE 221
    by Terrance J. Martin
    Resource Setting 222
    Methods 223
    Discussion 224
    Conclusions 230

CHAPTER 6: BOTANICAL REMAINS FROM THE CAHOKIA WEDGE SITE 235
    by Neal H. Lopinot
    Heavy Fractions 235
    Light Fractions 237
    Summary 243

CHAPTER 7: LIFE IN FRENCH COLONIAL CAHOKIA . . . 244
    Summary of Archaeological Investigations 244
    Historical and Archaeological View
      of French Colonial Life 247
    Concluding Remarks 254

APPENDIX A: FEATURE ARTIFACTS 255

REFERENCES CITED 265

FIGURES

1. Eighteenth-century map of French colonial settlements in American Botton region 2
2. USGS map showing location of the Cahokia Wedge site .. 4
3. Map of the American Bottom region ca. 1800 8
4. Map of village lots from 1766 map 28
5. 1735 map of Cahokia 32
6. Portion of 1766 map of Cahokia by Thomas Hutchins. .. 34
7. 1808 map of common fields of Cahokia (Lowrie and Franklin, eds., 1834) 35
8. Portion of WPA reconstructed map of Cahokia for the years 1790–1826 37
9. Detail of WPA map showing village lots within the Cahokia Wedge site 38
10. Lithograph of Cahokia by J. C. Wild published in 1841 (Wild and Thomas 1841) 40
11. 1956 plat map of the Village of Cahokia 44
12. SIUE topographic map of the Cahokia Wedge site 46
13. Map showing surface structural remains in Areas D and E on the southeast corner of the site 49
14. Detail of surface structural remains in Area E 49
15. Bar graph illustrating percentages of selected surface artifacts 52
16. Distribution map of all collected surface materials 53
17. Map showing location of the six surface artifact concentrations, Areas A-F 53
18. Distribution map of eighteenth-century ceramics 54
19. Distribution map of coarse earthenware ceramics 54
20. Distribution map of creamware and pearlware 55

21.	Distribution map of nineteenth- and twentieth-century ceramics	55
22.	Distribution map of dark green bottle glass	56
23.	Distribution map of clay smoking pipes	56
24.	Distribution map of selected building materials	57
25.	Distribution map of flat glass	57
26.	Distribution map of ordnance group	58
27.	Distribution map of faunal remains	58
28.	Distribution map of lithic debitage	59
29.	Distribution map of historic Indian artifacts and trade goods	59
30.	Piece-plotted surface artifact concentration in Area C	63
31.	Location of test excavation trench on the southwest corner of the site	71
32.	Plan view map of excavation trench	74
33.	Profile map of north balk wall of excavation trench	76
34.	Plan view map of Features 7, 8, and 10 wall trenches	78
35.	Profile maps of Feature 7 wall trench	79
36.	Profile maps of Feature 8 wall trench	83
37.	Profile map of Feature 10 wall trench	86
38.	Plan view map of Feature 2 limestone concentration	90
39.	Plan view and profile maps of Feature 1 pit	93
40.	Plan view map of Feature 4 midden area	98
41.	Profile maps of Feature 4 midden area	99
42.	Plan view map of Feature 3 (unexcavated)	101
43.	Profile map of Feature 11 limestone concentration	103
44.	Plan view map of Features 5 and 6 structural remains	104
45.	Profile map of Features 5 and 6 structural remains	105
46.	Profile map of portion of north balk wall showing Features 7, 8, 9, 12, and 13	111
47.	Stone Artifacts	119
48.	Micmac pipes	126
49.	Kaolin clay pipes	129

50.	Other clay pipes	133
51.	Faience rim border styles represented at the Cahokia Wedge site	136
52.	Faience	140
53.	Faience	142
54.	Faience	143
55.	English delftware	145
56.	Coarse earthenwares	148
57.	Coarse earthenwares	150
58.	Coarse earthenwares	152
59.	Creamware	154
60.	Dark green bottle glass; rim/neck fragments	165
61.	Dark green bottle glass; kick-ups	167
62.	Dark green bottle glass	168
63.	Blue-green bottle glass	171
64.	Brown glass	174
65.	Miscellaneous metal items	177
66.	Manufacturers' marks	187
67.	Buttons and bridle bosses	214

PLATES

1. 1986 aerial photograph of the Cahokia Wedge site .... frontpiece
2. Church of the Holy Family constructed in ca. 1799 and restored in 1949 5
3. Nicholas Jarrot Mansion, completed in ca. 1810, located across the street from the Cahokia Wedge site .. 5
4. Cahokia Courthouse, originally built in ca. 1737 and reconstructed in 1939–1940 by the WPA 6
5. 1927 aerial photograph of Cahokia 42
6. View of excavation trench west toward Illinois Route 3 .. 72
7. View of excavation trench to the east 72
8. Feature 7 wall trench excavation shown in north balk profile 80
9. Feature 8 wall trench lengthwise profile 84
10. Mapping of Feature 2 limestone concentration 91
11. Feature 1 pit profile 94
12. Plan view of Features 5 and 6 structural remains 106
13. View to south of test trench through Features 5 and 6 structural remains. 107
14. Faience 140
15. Faience 142
16. Faience 143
17. English delftware 145
18. Coarse earthenwares 148
19. Coarse earthenwares 150
20. Coarse earthenwares 152
21. Glass beads 160

22.	Dark green bottle glass	163
23.	Metal artifacts	179
24.	Metal artifacts	183
25.	Utensils	185
26.	Trade kettle fragments	189
27.	Furniture hardware	192
28.	Architectural hardware	194
29.	Architectural hardware	196
30.	Metal tools	199
31.	Barrel parts and equestrian items	202
32.	Flintlock gun parts	206
33.	Gunflints	207
34.	Lead	210
35.	Miscellaneous artifacts	218

TABLES

1. Chert Types 118
2. Triangular Point Measurements 120
3. Eighteenth- and Early Nineteenth-Century Ceramics . . . 137
4. Eighteenth Century Ceramic Vessel Form and Function . 138
5. Nineteenth- and Twentieth-Century Ceramics 156
6. Glass Bead Measurements 159
7. Gunflint Types And Percentages 208
8. Lead Balls-Firearms Projectiles 211
9. Comparison of Sizes of Lead Balls from the Cahokia Wedge Site and the Guebert Site 212
10. Species Composition of Animal Remains from Eighteenth-Century Contexts 226
11. Animal Remains from Eighteenth-Century Feature Contexts 228
12. Species Composition of Animal Remains from Nineteenth-Century Contexts 231
13. Animal Remains from Nineteenth-Century Feature Contexts 232
14. Flotation Sample Contents 236
15. Wood Charcoal Identification 238
16. Wood Charcoal Samples 240

Acknowledgments

The preliminary investigations at the Cahokia Wedge site were initiated by the Cahokia French Colonial Committee (CFCC). Funding for the project was contributed by the Cahokia Chamber of Commerce, Cahokia Economic Development Commission, Village of Cahokia, Bank of Cahokia, Cahokia Knights of Columbus, Cahokia Police Benevolent Association, American Legion Memorial Post 784 Auxiliary, Centreville Men's Club, and the Flying Legionnaires. Test excavations were funded by the Illinois Department of Transportation (IDOT) with the support of J. Paul Biggers, Chief of Environment, and Dr. John A. Walthall, Chief Archaeologist.

The controlled surface collection could not have been completed without the help of many willing and interested volunteers, who gave up three consecutive Saturdays in April and May of 1986 to painstakingly collect the thousands of surface artifacts. These persons included members of the CFCC: Larry Turner, President, and his daughter Cindy, Tom Jerome, Jerome Lopinot, Paul McNamara, Terry Osia, John Reed and his son, John Nicholas, and Bernie Thebeau; members of the Kappa Delta Rho fraternity of Parks College in Cahokia: Mike Kazzie, President (Spring 1986), Ken Heckler, President (Fall 1986), Jean Albuquerque, Kurt Bray, Terry Dannenbrink, Bruce Dinopoulos, Rue Flores, Kevin Hendrickson, Tim Hoffman, Brian "Mouse" Jenkins, Dave Koellner, Mike Korell, Dan Mushbarn, Jonas Perez, Rich Scotto, Michael Steiger, Bill Wendel, Neal Westlund, and John Williams. Archaeologists included U.S. Army Corps of Engineers personnel F. Terry Norris and Suzanne Harris, and SIUE personnel Alan Brown, George R. Holley, Mikels Skele, and Christy Wells. Other volunteers included Kevin Gordon of the Cahokia Police force; Dale Goldsmith, Cahokia High School teacher; Jeff Keates; Brian Kleber and his sons Kevin, Chris, and Jack; Jerry Phelan; Annette Simons; Mary Anne Toenjes; and Matt Young. I would also like to thank Noal F. Gruenert of the Public Relations Department of the Village of Cahokia for supplying lunch for the volunteer crew. Aerial photography was completed with the help of pilots Mike Korell and Dave Koellner of Kappa Delta

Rho. Other services were provided by the Cahokia Jaycees and Holy Family Parish.

Work on the November 1986 IDOT excavations was also completed with the help of many people. The SIUE excavation crew consisted of William Woods, Alan Brown, Tina Carter, Jim Collins, Carol DeMott, Rodney DeMott, George R. Holley, Mikels Skele, Christy Wells, and Charles Witty. Dr. John Walthall, Chief Archaeologist for IDOT, also contributed his expertise. A volunteer screening crew on Saturday, November 8, consisted of Carol DeMott, Rodney DeMott, CFCC President Larry Turner, CFCC member John Reed and his son John Nicholas, U.S. Army Corps of Engineers archaeologists Suzanne Harris and F. Terry Norris, and Terry's wife Debbie Dirckx-Norris and their children, Heather and Steven. Backhoe work for the test excavations was completed by Clyde Sweitzer of Collinsville.

Laboratory work was conducted by SIUE personnel Tina Carter, Carol DeMott, Rodney DeMott, George R. Holley, Charles Witty, and Donna Wohlfeil, and SIUE student workers T. Nathan Balakrishnan, Terry Gallagher, and Tim Green. Maps for the report were produced by Mikels Skele. The artifact illustrations and photographs were produced by the author. The draft report was typed by Tina Carter and Karen Carter. Editorial assistance was provided by Evelyn Moore of the Illinois Historic Preservation Agency, Neal H. Lopinot, and Christy Wells.

Specialized artifact analyses were conducted by George R. Holley, SIUE (prehistoric ceramics), Neal H. Lopinot, SIUE (botanical remains), Terrance J. Martin, Illinois State Museum, (faunal remains), F. Terry Norris, (gun furniture and gunflints), and John A. Walthall, (eighteenth-century ceramics). Terry Norris also must be thanked for volunteering to sandblast a large number of metal artifacts.

Other persons who offered assistance and advice include Thomas Emerson, Chief Archaeologist, Illinois Historic Preservation Agency, Springfield; Dr. Vergil E. Noble, Archaeologist, National Park Service, U.S. Department of the Interior; Molly McKenzie, Site Superintendent, Cahokia Courthouse State Historic Site; and Dr. Margaret K. Brown, Site Superintendent, Cahokia Mounds State Historic Site. Many other interested persons contributed in various aspects of these investigations: Parks College President Paul Whelan; Nita Browning of Public Relations; and James Roeder, Director of Plant Operations. Michael Bialas, Renaissance Productions, Cahokia, Illinois, produced a documentary video on the history of Cahokia and the SIUE archaeological investigations for possible local broadcast. He was assisted by Darryl Gregory. I would also like to thank Dr. Rino Cassanelli of the

Foreign Languages Department of SIUE for translating an article on French colonial coins. The late Raymond Hammes assisted in a records search at the Illinois State Archives. The SIUE Graduate School augmented the project funding by providing a grant through the University Supported Projects Program.

The author is especially grateful to Thomas Emerson, George R. Holley, Terry Norris, John Walthall, and Bill Woods, all of whom assisted in various ways toward the completion of this project.

Plate 1. 1986 aerial photograph of the Cahokia Wedge site. Church of the Holy Family (ca. 1799) is shown in bottom right-hand corner

CHAPTER 1:
INTRODUCTION

The historic French village of Cahokia, established in 1699 as a mission among the Tamaroa and Cahokia Indians, is the oldest permanent Euro-American settlement on the Mississippi River. Cahokia was one of several eighteenth-century villages and forts established in the territory known as the Illinois Country (Figure 1). The other French settlements located in the American Bottom region on the eastern side of the Mississippi River included Kaskaskia (1703), Fort de Chartres (ca. 1719), Prairie du Rocher (ca. 1721), and St. Philippe (ca. 1723). Across the Mississippi River in Missouri are the historic French settlements of Ste. Genevieve (ca. 1750) and St. Louis (1764). Throughout most of the eighteenth century, these frontier settlements represented the westernmost outreaches of the French Regime, with governmental headquarters in Quebec, Canada, historically known as New France. The villages played a vital economic role in the fur trade and served as a political connection between New France and settlements to the south, such as New Orleans, along the Mississippi River. The historical remnants of this French network in and around the American Bottom is known today as the French Colonial District.

Historically, the name of the French village originated with a group of historic Indians, the Cahokia, belonging to the Illini Confederacy. Today, the name relates to several other features in the American Bottom including Cahokia Creek and the Cahokia Mounds State Historic Site, a large prehistoric mound complex located nine miles to the north of the Village of Cahokia. Archaeological research at the Cahokia Mounds site has been ongoing for well over a century. Recent discoveries of an historic Cahokia Illini settlement on the First Terrace of the principal mound, Monks Mound (Walthall and Benchley 1987), further complicates the terminology associated with Cahokia. To avoid any possible confusion, it should be underscored that the archaeological research presented in this report was conducted within the eighteenth-century French colonial village, which has been known as Cahokia since 1701 (Schlarman 1929:152).

Fig. 1. Eighteenth-century map of French colonial settlements in American Botton region. (Temple 1975:Plate LXII. Reprinted with permission from the Illinois State Museum)

INTRODUCTION

The four acre project area is located at the intersection of Illinois Routes 3 and 157 in the Village of Cahokia, St. Clair County, Illinois (Figure 2). The study area encompasses a portion of the eighteenth-century French colonial village of Cahokia. The site has been designated as the Cahokia Wedge site (11-S-743) because of local reference to the area as the "Wedge" (Plate 1). The site is surrounded on all sides by Routes 3 and 157, former Route 157 or First Street, and Locust Street. Specifically, the Cahokia Wedge site is located in Section 3, Centreville Township (T1N, R10W). The project area encompasses modern village lot numbers 1, 2, 11, 12, 13, and 14 (see Figure 11).

The Cahokia Wedge site represents approximately 10% of the French colonial village as it appeared in the eighteenth century. The site lies on a sandy ridge above Dead Creek, a lateral side channel of the Mississippi River, formally known as Rigolet Creek. This portion of Dead Creek, oriented northeast-southwest, cuts through the northern edge of the Wedge. Eighteenth-century maps indicate that the village was located on the south side of the creek and, therefore, archaeological investigations were conducted on this portion of the Wedge.

Since the 1930s the Cahokia Wedge has been vacant of structures and in recent years has been used by Cahokia residents as a grassy picnic and recreation area. Directly south of the Cahokia Wedge site, across former Illinois Route 157 or First Street, is the Church of the Holy Family, constructed in ca. 1799 (Plate 2), and the Nicholas Jarrot Mansion, completed in ca. 1810 (Plate 3). The reconstructed Cahokia Courthouse, first built ca. 1737 (Plate 4), is located approximately 250 m west of the project area. These three structures are the only standing remnants of the historic village. The immediate surrounding area includes residential areas to the southeast, commercial/industrial complexes to the west, and the campus of Parks College of St. Louis University to the east.

The present archaeological research at Cahokia is the result of a convergence of vested interests between the state, the local community, and concerned persons. Investigations at the Cahokia Wedge site were initiated by a small group of Cahokia residents who recently formed the Cahokia French Colonial Committee (CFCC). The interests of the CFCC lie in the possible reconstruction of French colonial structures on the Cahokia Wedge site to promote and develop tourism for the Village of Cahokia. The committee recognized that archaeological fieldwork and historical research is necessary for the historical accuracy of these proposed reconstructions. The CFCC, supported by funds donated by various local and civic groups, contracted with the Contract Archaeology Program (CAP) of Southern Illinois University at Edwardsville

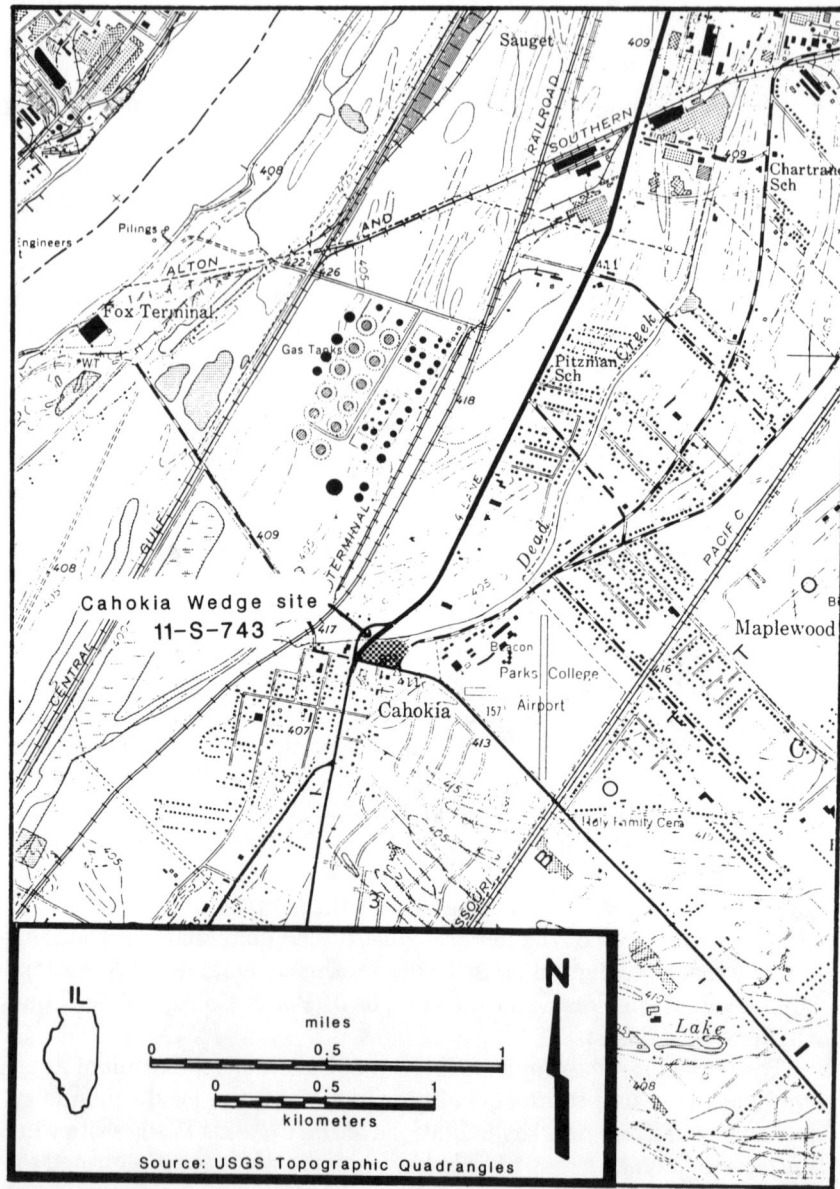

Fig. 2. USGS map showing location of the Cahokia Wedge site

Plate 2. Church of the Holy Family constructed in ca. 1799 and restored in 1949. This structure is located across the street from the Cahokia Wedge site.

Plate 3. Nicholas Jarrot Mansion, completed in ca. 1810, located across the street from the Cahokia Wedge site

Plate 4. Cahokia Courthouse, originally built in ca. 1737 and reconstructed in 1939-1940 by the Works Progress Administration (WPA). This structure is located approximately 250 meters west of the Cahokia Wedge site.

(SIUE) for the initial investigations, which included topographic mapping, aerial photography, and a controlled surface collection.

The presence of abundant eighteenth-century artifacts in the surface collection led to limited test excavations funded by the Illinois Department of Transportation (IDOT) under contract with SIUE. A test excavation trench consisting of 132.24 square meters was excavated on the southwest corner of the Cahokia Wedge within the IDOT R.O.W. of former Route 157 or First Street. The test excavation trench represents less than 1% of the site. These excavations uncovered 13 cultural features, including two structural remains dating to the eighteenth and nineteenth centuries.

The primary intent of archaeological investigations at the Cahokia Wedge site was the identification of materials dating to the historic eighteenth-century French village. Therefore, artifact analysis and this descriptive report have focused on cultural remains dating to this period. Unlike the other French forts and villages that were abandoned in the eighteenth or early nineteenth centuries, Cahokia has continued to exist, resulting in the collection of abundant materials dating to the nineteenth and twentieth centuries. The artifact collections postdating the eighteenth century have been curated for future research by interested scholars. All of the materials collected from the Cahokia Wedge site will be curated at SIUE. The archaeological investigations were conducted under the direction of CAP-SIUE personnel, Dr. William I. Woods, Principal Investigator, and Bonnie L. Gums, Project Director.

Environmental Setting

The Village of Cahokia is located in the north central portion of the American Bottom near the southern end of the broadest portion of the floodplain (Figure 3). To the north of Cahokia, the American Bottom expands to its maximum width of approximately 17.7 kilometers or 11 miles, adjacent to the prehistoric Cahokia Mounds site, which is approximately 14.5 kilometers or nine miles from the Village of Cahokia. The other historic French villages and forts were situated approximately 64.4 km or 40 miles south of Cahokia village, within the narrow expanse of the American Bottom.

In prehistoric times and the early historic period, the American Bottom region of the Central Mississippi Valley was an area consisting of diverse environments and abundant natural resources (Chmurny 1973; Gregg 1975; White et al. 1984). The American Bottom, extending from Alton in the north to Chester in the south, is approximately 980 square

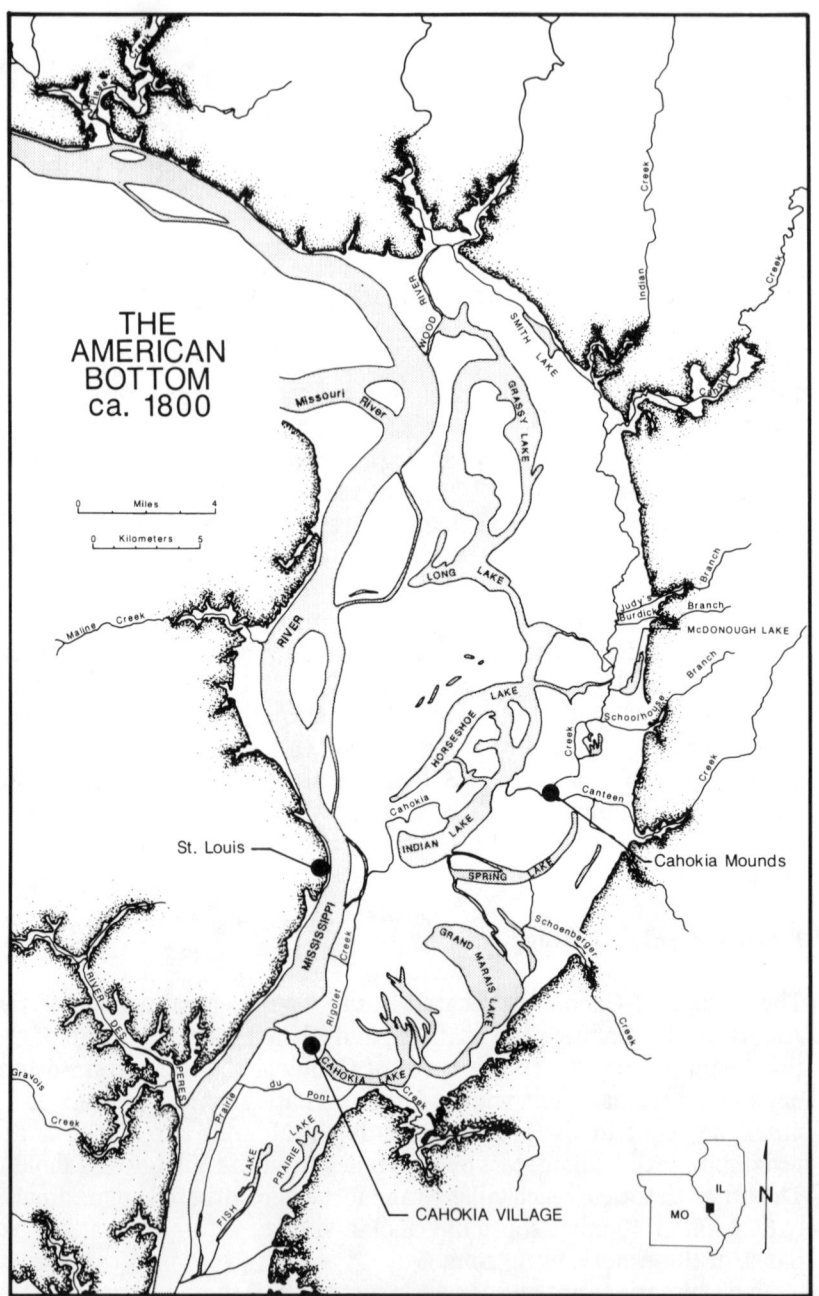

Fig. 3. Map of the American Bottom region ca. 1800

kilometers of rich alluvial floodplain encircled by limestone bluffs created by the Mississippi River during the Pleistocene Epoch (Chmurny 1973:73). The floodplain surface was formed primarily over the last 10,000 years by the deposition of sediment from the flooding of the Mississippi River and its tributaries (Gregg 1975:13). Migrations and channeling of the Mississippi River have resulted in the creation of at least thirteen meander scars forming oxbow lakes, backwater sloughs, or marshes within the American Bottom (Chmurny 1973:83).

The Cahokia Wedge site is located on a sandy ridge directly south of Dead Creek, formerly an active channel of the Mississippi River. The slough, known in the eighteenth century as Rigolet Creek, was cut off prior to A.D. 1800 (Chmurny 1973:88). Elevations at the site range from 405 to 415 feet above sea level. Cahokia is within the physical region, adjacent to the Mississippi River, referred to as the Ridge and Swale Region. This region, previously an area of swamps, partially filled-in water courses, and active sloughs with natural levees and sand bars, is today the area of most recent cutting and filling-in action by the Mississippi River (Yarbrough 1974:19). Soils at the Cahokia Wedge site are of the Landes-Riley association characterized by nearly level to sloping, well-drained to somewhat poorly drained soils that are formed in loamy and sandy alluvial sediments under forests and grasslands (Wallace 1978:9). Landes-Riley soils occur in a nearly unbroken band along both shorelines of the Mississippi River for the extent of the American Bottom (Chmurny 1973:74).

The area to the east of Cahokia, which would encompass the common fields of the eighteenth-century French village, is within the physical region termed the Lake Region. This region is characterized by large, low areas that were previously marshes, sloughs, or oxbow lakes resulting from the meandering of the Mississippi River (Yarbrough 1974:22). In this area are several remnants or scars of Mississippi River channels known as Goose (Cahokia) Lake, Lily Lake, Labras Lake, and Grand Marais (Pittsburg Lake).

Ninety percent of the floodplain in the American Bottom lies below a flood recorded at 35 feet above low water (Chmurny 1973:91) indicating the potential frequency of most of the American Bottom to be at flood stage. Between the recorded 154 years from 1785 to 1939, the Mississippi River was at flood stage a total of 48 times or an average of once every three years (Chmurny 1973:91). The flood of 1844 was reported to have covered the entire American Bottom, and steamboats were able to float over to the eastern bluff line (Wilderman and Wilderman 1907:709).

Many of the eighteenth-century letters and accounts written by the French settlers attest to the natural beauty, the fertility of the soils, and the abundance and diversity of floral and faunal resources. In 1723, Diron d'Artaguiette, Inspector General of Louisiana, wrote:

> The climate of the Illinois is very temperate and healthy, being 38 degrees in latitude. The soil is very rich and fertile. It has never yet failed to produce anything which has been planted in it. It is to be remarked that winter is very severe, since the Mississippy [sic] freezes over and one has to cross it on the ice to go to hunt on the other side. The stone there is very good for building and very common . . . The fruits which I have seen are some red plums which are very good. There also some apples the size of an egg, but very acid to taste, and some currants which do not differ in the least from those of France. There are some walnut trees which bear nuts, but of a very bad taste. There is another kind of nut tree which bears fruits just like a walnut but much smaller. The shell is very thin and the inside is exactly like our French walnut. They call this fruit the paguannes [pecans]. There is another tree which does not grow any larger than a leg which bears a fruit called the asmine [paw-paw] which is almost like the banana. The inside is entirely filled with little seeds or nuts which are the shape of a marsh bean and very hard. They taste very good.
>
> The wood which I have seen is very fine and suitable for building, especially the walnut and the paquanier. The mulberry trees here bear fruit similar to those in Europe. The wood of the mulberry tree lasts for thirty years in the ground without rotting. There are two kinds of elms which are very beautiful and two kinds of oak. The white oak can be worked up very easily, but the other, which is red, is hard as iron. There are also some grapes, which are very good and plentiful. Their vines climb to the top of the highest trees, and when one wished to get the grapes it is necessary to cut down the tree which is why one says commonly that they make the vintage with a hatchet (Mereness, ed., 1916:74–75).

Another description of the American Bottom region was recorded in 1750 by Jesuit Father Vivier, residing at the French village of Kaskaskia:

INTRODUCTION

> Wild cattle, deer, elk, bears and wild turkeys abound everywhere, in all seasons, except near the inhabited portions. It is usually necessary to go one or two leagues to find deer, and seven or eight to find oxen. During a portion of autumn, through the winter, and during a portion of spring, the country is overrun with swans, bustards, geese, ducks of three kinds, wild pigeons and teal. There are also certain birds as large as hens [prairie chickens], which are called pheasants in this country . . . I speak not of partridges or hares, because no one descends to shoot at them (Kenton, ed., 1927:468).

Based on the United States General Land Office (GLO) data collected in the early 1800s, researchers have reconstructed the environmental setting of the American Bottom (Chmurny 1973; Gregg 1975). These data present a reasonably unaltered view of the environment as it appeared when the French settled the area in the early 1700s. The Cahokia Wedge site is located in the Bottomland Prairie Zone, characterized by floodland prairies and wet or sedge prairies with a wide variety of grasses and sedges (Gregg 1975:32). The adjacent area along Rigolet Creek has been characterized as the Cottonwood-Willow-Deposition Zone (Gregg 1975:24). Another historical account by Father Mercier in 1735 describes this setting:

> The island of the Holy Family, which conceals the view of the Mississippi from the French settlement as well as from the Indian village of the Kaokia [sic], measures one league or more in length by nearly one half of a league in width [and] is completely covered with a forest of full grown trees good for building purposes or for fuel, especially quantities of cottonwoods but very few walnuts and mulberry trees. It is almost everywhere covered with rushes, which our horses seek greedily. When the waters of the Missouri and Mississippi rise very high, the greater part of the island is flooded . . . (Donnelly 1949:75).

Today very little of the natural environment remains in the American Bottom. Extensive flood and drainage control, predominantly in the twentieth century, has resulted in the construction of levees, drainage ditches, and the canalization of many creeks and streams. Many of the lakes and sloughs created by the Mississippi River have been drained for agricultural use, and the prairies and forests have given way to modern farms and urban centers.

Historical Background

Cahokia is located within the vast territory known in the seventeenth and eighteenth centuries as the Illinois Country. The Illinois Country was named after the Algonquian-speaking Illini or Illiniwek Indian groups. The Illini Confederacy included the Kaskaskia, Peoria, Tamaroa, Cahokia, Michigamea, and several smaller groups. During the early period of European contact, 1670s and 1680s, the Kaskaskia were located on the Illinois River, the Peoria were living at the confluence of the Iowa and Mississippi rivers, the Tamaroa were within the interior at the headwaters of the Sangamon and Kaskaskia rivers, the Cahokia were located at the confluence of the Illinois, Missouri and Mississippi rivers, and the Michigamea were living on the Mississippi in northeast Arkansas (Bauxer 1973:47). During the protohistoric period the population of the Illini groups has been estimated at 10,500 (Blasingham 1956:372).

The first recorded account of Euro-Americans within the Illinois Country described the explorations of Jesuit Father Jacques Marquette and Frenchman Louis Jolliet in 1672 and 1673. Their voyage took them down the Illinois River to the Mississippi River and as far south as the Arkansas River, where they encountered a village of the Michigamea (Temple 1966:18). The map of the expedition attributed to Marquette, does not illustrate any Illini Indian villages along the Mississippi River from the Illinois River to the Ohio River (Tucker 1942:Plate V).

The next recorded European contact took place with the voyage of Robert Cavelier LaSalle and Henri de Tonti from 1679 to 1683 on the Illinois and Mississippi rivers. The expedition reportedly reached a village of Tamaroa located six to seven leagues below the mouth of the Missouri River on the east side of the Mississippi River (Temple 1966:25). The approximate location of the Tamaroa village suggests the vicinity of the French mission site established in 1699 and known today as Cahokia (Sauer 1980:152; Temple 1966:25). In 1680, Father Louis Hennepin, a Recollect with the LaSalle expedition, reported at least 200 families at the Tamaroa village (Blasingham 1956:364). Two years later, Henri de Tonti wrote that the Tamaroa had reoccupied this former village of 180 cabins after an Iroquois raid in 1680; although at the time of Tonti's visit the Indians were apparently away on a hunt (Temple 1966:25). In 1687, this village was reported to be occupied by the Cahokia and Tamaroa and consisted of more than sixty cabins (Pease and Werner, eds., 1934:341–342). By 1697, two more villages of the Tamaroa were reported in the southern end of the American Bottom (Temple 1966:32).

INTRODUCTION

When first contacted by the early French explorers and fur traders, the Illini groups were primarily located on the Illinois River and on the Mississippi River at the confluence of the Illinois and Missouri rivers. By the end of the seventeenth century, several groups, in particular the Cahokia and Tamaroa, had migrated to the southern end of the American Bottom (Blasingham 1956:193; Bauxer 1973:48). By 1700, after approximately thirty years of contact with Europeans, the population of the Illini Indian groups had decreased by approximately 40% to an estimated population of 6,000 (Blasingham 1956:372).

The first permanent Euro-American settlement on the Mississippi River, known as Cahokia, was a mission established at a village of the Tamaroa and Cahokia Indians in 1699. The official "Letters Patent" written in 1698 by the Bishop of the Seminary of Foreign Missions in Quebec, stated:

> ... by virtue of Letters Patent heretofore granted them by us conferring exclusive right to establish and found missions among the savages call Tamaroa, who are between the Illinois and Arkansas ... considering that the location of the above Tamaroa is as it were the key and necessary passageway to the nations beyond ...
> (Donnelly 1949:57).

The mission site was chosen primarily for two reasons:(1) to bring Christianity to the relatively large population of Illini groups in the area; and (2) to establish a strategic position for travel and communications between New France, with governmental headquarters at Quebec, and mission sites and French settlements along the Mississippi River to the Gulf of Mexico (Schlarman 1929:131-132).

The expedition left Quebec on July 16, 1698, in eight canoes, with Henri de Tonti as guide. The group, led by Reverend Francois Jolliet de Montigny, included Seminary priests Jean Francois Buisson de St. Cosme and Antoine Davion, layman Thaumur de LaSource, three lay assistants, two blacksmiths, and about a dozen *voyageurs* (Donnelly 1949:60-61). Traveling through the Great Lakes region, down the Illinois River to the Mississippi River, the party set up camp on the west side of the Mississippi River across from the Tamaroa and Cahokia village. On December 8, the missionaries visited the village, and St. Cosme recorded this initial contact:

> The Indians had been early notified of our coming ...
> As they had given trouble to some of Mr. de Tonty's men
> a year before, they were afraid, and all the women and

> children fled from the village . . . Mr. de Tonty went to the village, and having assured then a little, he brought us the chief who begged us to go and see him in his village. We promised to do so and next day, Feast of the Conception, after saying our Masses we went with Mr. de Tonty and seven of our men well armed. They came to receive us and took us to the chief's cabin. All the women and children were there, and we were no sooner there than the young folks and women broke in a part to be able to see us . . . They gave us a meal, and we made them a little present as we had done to the Carrechias. We told them that is was to show them that we had a well made heart, and that we wished to contract an alliance with them, so that they should kindly receive our people who often passed there, and that they should give them food . . . The Tamarois were cabined on an island lower down than their village, perhaps to get wood more easily, from which their village, which is on the edge of a prairie, is somewhat distant; perhaps too for fear of their enemies. We could no well see whether they were very numerous. They seemed to us quite so, although the greater part of their people were hunting. There was wherewith to form a fine mission by bringing here the Kavvchias [Cahokia] who are quite near, and the Michiagamias, who are a little lower down on the Mississippi, and said to be quite numerous. We did not see them as they had gone inland to hunt. The three villages speak Illinois (Shea, ed., 1861:66–67).

After this visit to the Indian village, the expedition continued down the Mississippi River to search out and establish other mission sites. On the return voyage, Father St. Cosme and several workmen remained at the Cahokia and Tamaroa village and the mission was formally established. The first French structures built at the mission site included a lodging for Father St. Cosme and a chapel (Peterson 1949:10). Completion of the chapel and the raising of the cross occurred prior to May 20 in 1699 (Fortier 1909:33). Father de Montigny described the ceremony:

> [The chapel] being finished we planted a cross with the greatest possible ceremony. All the Indians were in attendance; they showed a great desire to be instructed and become Christians and brought their little children

that we might baptize them and give them a name (Garraghan 1928:109).

An estimated 2,000 Indians were living in the mission area, including the Cahokia, Tamaroa, Michigamea, and Peoria (McDermott 1949b:9). During the first few years at the mission site, the Indian population fluctuated due to seasonal migrations and relocation of various groups caused by continual raids by the hostile Fox, Sioux, and Iroquois. In a letter dated February 1700, Father Bergier, who had taken over the mission after the departure of St. Cosme to Natchez, wrote the Bishop in Quebec:

> The village is composed of Tamarois, Cahokia, some Michigans and Peorias. There are also some Missouri cabins, and shortly, there are to come about thirty-five cabins of this last named nation who are winterquartering some ten or fifteen leagues from here below the village on the river ... The Tamarois and Cahokias are the only ones that really form part of this mission. The Tamarois have about thirty cabins and the Cahokias have nearly twice that number. Although the Tamarois are at present less numerous than the Cahokias, the village is still called Tamaroa, gallicized "Des Tamarois," because the Tamarois have been the first and are still the oldest inhabitants and have first lit a fire there, to use the Indian expression (Fortier 1909:236–237).

Another letter of Father Bergier in June of 1700 tells of an attack on the Illini village by a small party of Sioux, which prompted the building of a fort (Fortier 1909:237–238). In 1700, the Kaskaskia, having abandoned their village on the Illinois River, settled west of the Mississippi River on the Des Pere River (Temple 1966:34–35). In 1701, approximately one-third of the Tamaroa relocated at the Kaskaskia village. The Cahokia Illini remained at the mission site, and it was probably at this time that the settlement became known as Cahokia (Schlarman 1929:152).

Within a year after the establishment of the mission, Canadian fur traders had settled in the Illinois Country, with a reported 19 Frenchmen living on the Illinois River or at the mission site at Cahokia (Alvord 1922:128).

Shortly after the establishment of the mission by the Seminary of Foreign Missions, Jesuit Father Pinet arrived at Cahokia. A dispute had developed because the Jesuits contended that the Seminarians had intruded into their mission field, for the Jesuits had been proselytizing in the area for 20 years prior to the arrival of the Seminary missionaries. At the Cahokia mission, Father Pinet, who was familiar with the language of the Illini, administered to the spiritual needs of the Indians, and Father Bergier was in charge of the French inhabitants (Shea, ed., 1861:117). The dispute was settled by a 1701 Royal Decree from Paris, which gave the mission claim to the Seminarians; however, the official letter did not arrive at Cahokia until one year later (Garraghan 1928:125). After resolution, Father Pinet left the Cahokia mission to be among the Kaskaskia across the Mississippi River on the Des Pere River (Thwaites, ed., 1959:LXIV:278). In 1703, this village moved back to the Illinois side, thus establishing the settlement known as Kaskaskia.

In the early years, the Cahokia mission served as the frontier outpost for the fluctuating populations of the *coureurs de bois, voyageurs*, and merchants. Cahokia slowly evolved into a traditional French village with the parish as the focal point of town life (Donnelly 1949:55). An early description of the settlement was recorded in 1710 by an Englishman named Joseph Kellogg, who was traveling with six Frenchmen to the Gulf of Mexico:

> They raise Excellent wheat, very good Indian corn,
> have a Wind Mill, and had Stock of Cattle, make a very
> good Sort of wine ... The land produces Excellent
> mellons, good beans, turnips and all Sorts of Garden
> Erbs; the Woods, oak and Several sorts of Walnuts
> (Stearns 1936:354).

Beginning in 1718, the Fox Indians from the north invaded the Illinois Country regularly, and for several decades continually attacked the Illini Indians, as well as disrupting the peace at the French settlements. In 1722, the Fox attacked the remaining Peoria villages on the Illinois River, which led to the abandonment of this area and the migration of the Peoria to the American Bottom, some settling at the Illini village at Cahokia (Palm 1931:69).

In the early years Cahokia was under the government of Quebec, with administration headquarters at Fort St. Louis on the Illinois River (Peterson 1949:12–13). In 1717, the Illinois Country was reallocated to the administration of Louisiana. By 1720, a wooden fort was constructed in the Mississippi floodplain approximately 40 miles south of Cahokia. This fort, Fort de Chartres, was to serve as the district command post under the new Company of the Indies (Alvord 1922:153; Schlarman 1929:193).

In 1721, a description of the village at Cahokia was written by Pierre Charlevoix:

> The same Day we went to lay in a Village of the Caoquias [sic], and the Tamarouas: These are two Nations of Illinois, which are united and who do not together make a very numerous Village. It is situated on a little River, which comes from the East, and which has no Water but in the Spring Season; so that we were forced to walk a good half League to the Cabins. I was surprised that they had chosen such an inconvenient Situation, as they might have found a much better; but they told me that the Missisippi washed the Foot of the Village when it was built, and that in three Years it had lost half a League of Ground, and that they were thinking of looking for another Settlement (McDermott 1949b:13).

In the first few decades of the 1700s, the permanent French population at Cahokia grew very slowly, overshadowed by the increasing populations at Kaskaskia and Fort de Chartres. Among the eighteenth-century French settlements in the American Bottom, Cahokia evolved as the major trading center, the village at Kaskaskia became an agricultural community, and Fort de Chartres served as the governmental headquarters for the Illinois Country. The villages near Fort de Chartres included Prairie du Rocher (ca. 1721) and St. Philippe (ca. 1723).

In June of 1722, the Seminary of Foreign Missions received a concession of four leagues square from the commandant at Fort de Chartres. This concession encompassed the area above the Cahokia Illini village and extended along the Mississippi River for twelve miles (Schlarman 1929:279). To encourage settlement, the missionaries offered free building lots to anyone wishing to settle, but often the *habitants* would "take land today and leave it tomorrow" preferring the adventurous life of itinerant fur traders (Peterson 1949:22). In 1731, the missionaries purchased an additional thirty arpents of frontage land above the 1722 land concession from the Cahokia Illini. This land was set up as the village common fields, laid out in the traditional feudal land tenure system of long, narrow strip tracts (Peterson 1949:20).

The first official census of the population in the Illinois Country was made by Diron d'Artaguiette in 1723. The recorded population at Cahokia included seven *habitants*, one white laborer, one married woman, and three children (Belting 1948:13). This census, however, included only permanent residents of the village and did not mention transient merchants and fur traders, or the priests, laymen, and slaves associated with the mission (McDermott 1949b:14). In the same census, Kaskaskia had a reported 196 *habitants* and at the relatively new village at Fort de Chartres were 126 *habitants* (Belting 1948:15). Diron d'Artaguiette also mentioned the newly built fort at Cahokia as being a "wretched fort of piles" with a garrison of six soldiers (McDermott 1949b:13).

A 1732 census of Cahokia only mentioned persons at the mission—the priests, Messrs. Mercier and Courier, lay brother Le Mieux, engage Le Flament, and three *habitants* Louis Gaut, Capucin, and La Source (McDermott 1949b:14–15). A letter from Father Mercier, dated August 3, 1732 and sent to the Seminary at Quebec, alludes to the relatively few French *habitants* at the village:

> If only twenty families would come down from Canada, that would start a parish. More than two hundred *habitans* [sic] could be wonderfully placed, and in a very short time they could live as comfortably as they do in Canada (Schlarman 1929:290).

Also inventoried as the Cahokia mission property were two houses, one barn, four Negroes, five Indian slaves, 30 pigs, 10 horses, seven cows, and three oxen (Belting 1948:38). In the same year, the Cahokia and Peoria Indians at Cahokia numbered between 300 and 400 individuals (Palm 1931:72).

A 1734 map of the Illinois Country by Ignace Francois Broutin shows Cahokia as a village of seven or eight French houses and the Cahokia Illini settlement with 130 males located to the north of the French village (Tucker 1942:Plate XXII).

In 1735, an ink and watercolor map (see Figure 5) of the village at Cahokia and the surrounding area was drawn by missionaries Mercier and Courier (Tucker 1942:Plate XXIII). The map identifies 15 dwellings including the houses of two Negro families and one Indian family who served at the mission, the fort built in the previous year, the mill at St. Michaels Bluff (Falling Springs), the common fields to the east of the village, and the road from the floodplain to the bluffs, which connected with Fort de Chartres. Also identified is the Cahokia Illini village a short distance north of the French village. A small insert at the upper left of the map shows a detailed layout of the mission property, including the church, quarters for the priests, slave cabins, the orchards and gardens, barns, and latrine.

The 1735 map also shows a former establishment of the French, now abandoned, located a short distance to the southeast and closer to the

Mississippi River. This appears to be the first settlement described in 1721 by Charlevoix who reported that the French were looking for a new settlement further away from the flooding waters of the Mississippi River (Peterson 1949:215).

By 1735, the increasing French population and the need for agricultural land precipitated hostilities between the French villagers and the Cahokia Illini (Palm 1931:70–71; Walthall and Benchley 1987:9). More than half of the Cahokia were relocated three and a half leagues to the north, where fields were plowed for them and a chapel was built on the First Terrace of Monks Mound (Donnelly 1949:79; Walthall and Benchley 1987). The Cahokia remained at the new mission site until 1752 (Walthall and Benchley 1987:10). In this year, the Fox attacked the Illini village while the Cahokia French were attending a Corpus Christi celebration at Fort de Chartres. As the Fox traveled up the river with their Illini prisoners, they fired a salute at the Cahokia fort (Bossu 1771:132–134).

Macarty's 1752 census of the population, mission properties, and agricultural resources of Cahokia was reported in detail (Peterson 1949:22). The population consisted of the priest at the mission, 13 married couples with 42 children, four unmarried men, one widow, and 15 *volontaires* (landless inhabitants). This population was broken down racially as 89 whites, 24 Negroes, and four Indians. Other resources of the village were 33 arpents of land, 224 head of cattle, 83 horses and mules, and 100 hogs.

Beginning in 1763, several events led to rapid changes at Cahokia and the other French villages in the American Bottom. After the defeat of the French in the Seven Years War, the British gained control of all land east of the Mississippi River with the Treaty of Paris. Not wishing to live under British rule, many French villagers fled across the Mississippi River to Spanish-controlled territory. The founding of St. Louis in 1764 further encouraged flight to the western side of the river. Many of the Illinois French abandoned their homes and resettled in St. Louis or Ste. Genevieve, often fleeing in the middle of the night with their cattle, grain, and even parts of their houses (Peterson 1949:26). The British banished the Jesuits from the Illinois Country and Father Forget du Verger, fearing the same persecution, sold the mission property and fled from Cahokia, leaving the village without a priest. The mission property was not restored to parish ownership until 1786 (McDermott 1949b:25).

In October 1765, British troops arrived in the Illinois Country and peacefully occupied Fort de Chartres and Cahokia, with the remaining French inhabitants pledging allegiance to the government of King

George III (Carter 1910:49). Initial plans of the British included removing the French from their villages and sending them back to Canada (Alvord 1907:xxv).

In August 1766, British Captain Henry Gordon described Cahokia:

> Here are 43 Families of French who live well and so might three times the number as there is a great Quantity of arable clear land of the best soil near it. There is likewise 20 Cabbins of Peoria Indians left here (Alvord and Carter 1916:299).

Forty warriors of the Cahokia Illini were also reported living near the Cahokia village (Temple 1966:4). In the same year, Philip Pittman recorded 65 families remaining at Kaskaskia, 12 families at Prairie du Rocher, three to four families at Fort de Chartres, and only one inhabitant at St. Philippe, although 16 houses were still standing (Pittman 1770:43–47).

A map of the village at Cahokia (see Figure 6) was drawn in 1766 by British army cartographer Thomas Hutchins (Peterson 1949:200–201). It illustrates village lots with houses and barns and the surrounding area. Pittman (1770:48) described the village as:

> ... long and straggling, being three quarters of a mile from one end to the other; it contains forty-five dwelling-houses, and a church near its center. The situation is not well chosen, as in the floods it is generally overflowed by two or three feet ... What is called the fort is a small house standing in the center of the village; it differs in nothing from the other houses except in being one of the poorest; it was formerly enclosed with high palisades, but these were torn down and burnt. Indeed a fort at this place could be of little use.

A noteworthy event occurred at Cahokia in April of 1769. Ottawa Indian chief Pontiac, the leader of an Indian uprising against the British known as Pontiac's Conspiracy, was murdered in the streets of Cahokia. He was allegedly beaten and stabbed to death by Peoria Indians after leaving the store of Baynton, Wharton, and Morgan (Peckman 1947:310-311), which was located across the street from the present day Cahokia Courthouse State Historic Site.

With the Quebec Act of 1774, the Illinois Country once again was united with the government represented in Canada, and many of the British left the area (Alvord 1907:xxvii-xxxi).

The next political period was the result of the Revolutionary War. The villages in the Illinois Country had remained relatively unaffected during the first few years of the Revolution (Peterson 1949:193). In July of 1778, George Rogers Clark and his American troops occupied Kaskaskia and Cahokia, and the Illinois French were drawn into the war. Local government was set up in Cahokia under the command of Captain Joseph Bowman, who had occupied a stone building on the mission property, which was to become known as Fort Bowman (Peterson 1949:196). In the winter of 1779, with the British occupation of Vincennes on the Wabash River, George Rogers Clark led an epic march, including many Illinois Frenchmen, across the frozen bottomlands to attack the British and recapture Vincennes (Peterson 1949:198). In May of 1780, the war came even closer with the failed British attack on Cahokia and Spanish-controlled St. Louis (Peterson 1949:203).

With the end of the American Revolution in 1783 and the Americanization of the region, the period of French domination was over. The remaining villages at Cahokia, Kaskaskia, and Prairie du Rocher having survived both the British and American invasions, settled into a relatively peaceful way of life. An observance of Moses Austin (1900:534) described Cahokia at this time:

> [Cahokia had] been and place of wealth and did When under the English government command an Extensive Indian Trade. It is not the case now. Since the Americans have held the Country it has been Shamefully Neglected and that many of the best families have cross.d [sic] the Missisipi [sic] and with them the Indian trade . . . there is not a building in the Place that can be call.d [sic] Elegant. there may be about 200 Houses in all, but not more then half of the[m] Inhabited. there is little or no Trade and the people are poor.

With the Northwest Ordinance of 1787, the Illinois Country became part of the Northwest Territory under the United States government. In the same year, a census recorded 239 male inhabitants at Cahokia and 191 male inhabitants at Kaskaskia (Alvord 1907:624–632). These were two of the remaining French settlements, Fort de Chartres, having been abandoned by the British in 1772 because of the encroaching Mississippi River.

In 1795, Cahokia became the county seat for St. Clair County when Kaskaskia was made the county seat for the newly formed Randolph County. At this time, St. Clair County extended as far north as the Canadian border. The county government was set up in the building known today as the Cahokia Courthouse State Historic Site. A jail was constructed on the courthouse lot and a stockade was emplaced (Peterson 1949:328–329). In 1800, a census recorded 719 individuals living at Cahokia and 467 individuals at Kaskaskia (Alvord 1907:405). Within the early years of the nineteenth century, the French began to settle away from the village at Cahokia. The first incursion by French settlers outside the limits of the Cahokia village proper occurred when a house was constructed in the northern section of the commons in what is now East St. Louis (Wilderman and Wilderman 1907:709). A string of houses was constructed along or near Rock Road (formerly Vincennes Road), which ran east from East St. Louis to Belleville (Brink 1881:323–324; Wilderman and Wilderman 1907:711). The settlement of Little French Village, to the northeast of Cahokia, was founded by Cahokia residents around 1800 (Wilderman and Wilderman 1907:712).

The first American settlements were established within the western portion of St. Clair County around 1800 (Puckett 1979:20). An influx of American settlers into the American Bottom region was precipitated by the Pre-Emption Act established by the United States Congress in 1813, which made these lands available for settlement.

In 1812, the boundaries of St. Clair County were again divided, this time to its present day borders. In 1814, the county seat was officially moved from Cahokia to Belleville due to the continual flooding problems at Cahokia and because Belleville was more centrally located within the county. With this administrative move to Belleville, Cahokia lost its prominence in the political matters of the county.

Further contributing to the virtual stagnation of the village at Cahokia was the increasing importance of St. Louis as a commercial center and the development of the town of East St. Louis, originally founded as Illinoistown in 1817, across the river from St. Louis. Cahokia remained a small, semi-rural community throughout the nineteenth century. In 1841, the village had "a convent, courthouse, post office, catholic church, three taverns, five or six groceries, one general store, and between 60 and 70 houses" (Wild and Thomas 1841:106). One observer, Lewis Thomas, wrote that "the lapse of nearly two centuries has not entirely destroyed the original impress upon this people of the manners, customs, and the language of Old France" (Wild and Thomas 1841:103).

Previous Archaeological Investigations

The Village of Cahokia is located in a rich archaeological district, highlighted by the prehistoric Cahokia Mounds complex and surrounding smaller mound groups. The earliest prehistoric period, known as the Paleo-Indian, dates from approximately 10,000 B.C. to 8000 B.C. Archaeological evidence for this occupation is limited to isolated finds of diagnostic projectile points (Munson 1971:4). Extensive excavation at the Modoc Rock Shelter, in the southern end of the American Bottom near Fort de Chartres, has provided much information concerning prehistoric adaptations during the Archaic period, beginning ca. 8000 B.C. (Fowler 1959). Based on recent archaeological investigations by the FAI-270 project, a substantial prehistoric occupation in the American Bottom has been identified for the Late Archaic period dating from ca. 3000 B.C. to 600 B.C. (McElrath et al. 1984:34).

The introduction of ceramic technology characterizes the beginning of the Woodland period. By the Late Woodland period, ca. A.D. 300 to A.D. 900, there was a greater dependency on cultivated plants, leading to increased populations and sedentary villages. The Emergent Mississippian period, beginning in ca. A.D. 900, and the Mississippian period mark the culmination of prehistoric cultural and societal development in the American Bottom. The emergence of the Cahokia Mounds complex as a major ceremonial center was highlighted by extensive mound construction, including Monks Mound, the largest prehistoric earthen mound in North America. By ca. A.D. 1400, the Mississippian society had declined, marked by a depopulation of the American Bottom. This period, known as the Oneota, is characterized by small, temporary settlements. Archaeologically, this period had been relatively unknown until the recent work by the FAI-270 project, which has identified Oneota cultural affiliations with populations to the north (Milner et al. 1984:186).

Archaeological investigations of protohistoric/historic Indian and colonial sites in the American Bottom are relatively few in comparison to the extensive studies of the prehistoric sites. This is due somewhat to the more widely scattered and less intensive occupation during these times, in particular, the protohistoric Indian period. Colonial archaeology has tended to focus on the more spectacular aspects of the French Colonial period associated with the military sites at Fort de Chartres (Brown 1976; Keene 1986) and Fort Kaskaskia (Orser 1977; Orser and Karamanski 1977). Excavations at these sites have concentrated on the fortifications and structures within the forts. Investigations at Fort de Chartres have primarily been at the site of the third fort, which was constructed of stone in ca. 1752. This fort has been partially reconstructed and is within the Fort de Chartres State Historic Site. Excavations have been conducted at the Laurens site, the first Fort de Chartres constructed of wood and dating from ca. 1719 to 1729 (Jelks and Ekberg

1984; Weymouth and Woods 1984). More recently investigated was a portion of the original village site of Prairie du Rocher (Safiran 1987), which was established in the 1720s.

Archaeological investigations have also focused on the historic Indian villages associated with the French forts; the Guebert site, village of the Kaskaskia Indians from 1719 to 1833 (Good 1972), and two Michigamea villages near Fort de Chartres; the Kolmer site, dating 1720 to 1753 (Orser 1975), and the Waterman site (Brown n.d.).

French colonial archaeology on the Missouri side of the Mississippi River has focused on the Krelich site at the Saline Springs (Keslin 1964; Michael Trimble, personal communication, 1987) and the original site of the town of Ste. Genevieve dating from ca. 1750 to 1785 (Norris 1979). Early investigations at the Krelich site concentrated on the prehistoric Mississippian occupation at the site; however, the presence of historic artifacts was noted and it was suggested that the area had been occupied by the Kaskaskia Indians (Keslin 1964:67-69). Investigations in 1986 at the Krelich site resulted in the excavation of a French colonial *poteaux-en-terre* (posts in the earth) structure dating to the late eighteenth century (Michael Trimble, personal communication, 1987). Archaeological survey at the original town of Ste. Genevieve, which over the last century has been severely damaged by the migration of the Mississippi River, revealed the remains of at least eight structural features (Norris 1979:10).

Archaeological surveys and excavations in the immediate vicinity of Cahokia have been conducted prior to the Blue Water Ditch alignment (Denny 1974) and the construction of FAI-270 (Kelly et al. 1979; Bareis and Porter, eds., 1984). These studies have investigated numerous prehistoric and historic sites in the areas to the south, east, and northeast of Cahokia.

Evidence of historic trade goods has been reported at several archaeological sites in the American Bottom and the adjacent uplands. During the initial survey for the FAI-270 project, historic artifacts, including trade pipes, gunflints, leadshot, and porcelain, possibly dating to the eighteenth century, were among surface debris at sites located on ridges along the abandoned channels of the Mississippi River known as Goose Lake, Prairie Lake, and Grand Marais (Kelly et al. 1979). Glass trade beads were reported from the prehistoric Adler Mound site (Williams and Lacampagne 1982) and a catlinite pipe, possibly dating to the Early Historic period, was recovered from the Florence Street site (Emerson et al. 1983:215). These sites are located in the American Bottom region within a short distance from Cahokia.

Historic materials, including gunflints and clay pipe fragments, were reported in the surface collection of the Ramey Field, east of Monks Mound at the Cahokia Mounds site (Benchley 1981:55). The First Terrace of Monks Mound and the surrounding areas were the sites of a French mission and a Cahokia Illini settlement from 1735 to 1752, a trading post from 1776 to 1784 known as the Cantine, and an 1804 settlement of French farmers from Prairie du Pont (Walthall and Benchley 1987). Perhaps the most relevant archaeological investigations regarding the French village at Cahokia have been the excavations on the First Terrace of Monks Mound. The remains of a French colonial chapel and an aboriginal cemetery are the first documented site that can be associated with the Cahokia Illini, who were relocated from Cahokia to Monks Mound by the French in 1735 (Benchley 1974; Walthall and Benchley 1987).

Eighteenth-century trade goods have also been reported in the uplands at the Emerald Mound site near the town of Lebanon (Wray 1952:160; Koldehoff 1980:8). An early historic account by John Francis Snyder indicated that a heavily worn path from the Cahokia Mounds site in the Bottom, up the bluffs to the Emerald Mound site, was still visible in the early nineteenth century (Walton, ed., 1962:259).

Isolated historic Indian burials have also been reported at prehistoric sites within the American Bottom and the upland area. A single historic Indian burial was excavated on the upland bluffs in Madison County. Artifacts associated with the burial included two silver medallions of French Canadian manufacture dating from 1778 to 1786, silver tinklers and pendants, a copper pot lid and handle, and white glass trade beads (Sidney Denny, personal communication, 1987). Intrusive historic Indian burials with trade goods were found within the Powell Mound at the Cahokia Mound site (Wray 1952:160) and within a mound of the East St. Louis mound group (Walton, ed., 1962:249). Historic burials were also excavated on Mound 66 or Rattlesnake Mound at the Cahokia Mounds State Historic Site. Several burials with traces of wooden coffins associated with nails, metal buttons, and buckles were thought to be of early European, possibly French, settlers (Moorehead 1929:74–75).

Eleven historic sites were excavated by the FAI-270 project. The earliest historic site investigated, the Robert Watts site, was a portion of the first American settlement in the American Bottom, established in 1783 and known as Grand Run or Grand Ruisseau (Philippe and Esarey 1983). The Robert Watts site is located at the base of the bluffs 12 kilometers south of Cahokia. The other FAI-270 historic sites were mid-nineteenth century farmsteads, including the Alorton site located a short distance east of Cahokia, and several late nineteenth-century coal miner residences (Esarey 1984).

Specifically, archaeological investigations within the Village of Cahokia have been limited. In 1938–1939, the Works Progress Administration (WPA) excavated the original site of the Cahokia Courthouse State Historic Site. This structure, built ca. 1737 (Plate 4), was used as the St. Clair County courthouse from 1793 to 1814. The structure was dismantled in 1903 and put on exhibit at the Louisiana Purchase Exposition in St. Louis, Missouri. After the fair, the structure was purchased by the Chicago Historical Society and moved to Jackson Park in Chicago, where it remained until the late 1930s when Cahokia residents regained ownership of the historic structure. Prior to the reconstruction of the Cahokia Courthouse, members of the WPA project and the Illinois State Museum excavated the original foundation of the courthouse (Report on file at the Cahokia Courthouse State Historic Site). Archaeological excavations were also conducted on the courthouse lot prior to the construction of the administration building for the Cahokia Courthouse State Historic Site (Jelks and Shun 1975).

Two eighteenth-century house sites within the Village of Cahokia have been identified as surface scatters in a plowed field west of the Cahokia Courthouse State Historic Site. These house sites can be identified on the 1766 Hutchins map of Cahokia as the Boudriau-Gammon residence (11-S-725) and the Jacquet/Germain residence (11-S-726) (Norris 1984:4). These house sites represent the westernmost remains of the eighteenth-century village that survived the 1866 migration of the Mississippi River (Norris 1984:16).

Concurrent with SIUE investigations at the Cahokia Wedge site, archaeological monitoring was conducted during road construction activities along Illinois Route 3 from Fifth Street to Illinois Route 157 in Cahokia (Walitschek 1986). The construction work included the excavation of a drainage ditch along the western edge of the Cahokia Wedge site. Although French colonial artifacts were recovered during the monitoring, these apparently were from previously disturbed areas (Walitschek 1986:27).

Unlike most of the French colonial sites, which were abandoned in the eighteenth and early nineteenth centuries, the village at Cahokia has continued to exist and today is a flourishing urban center within the Metro East area. The Cahokia Wedge site represents a relatively undisturbed archaeological resource having been protected by city and county ownership for several decades. The importance of the present archaeological investigations at the Cahokia Wedge lies in the recovery of data relating to domestic activities of French colonial life.

The Present Condition of the Archaeological Record

The site of colonial Cahokia has not been spared from various forms of alteration and destruction. Specifically, urban and commercial development within this century has played the greatest role, with other damage occurring from the migration of the Mississippi River in the late nineteenth century. An extensive study and assessment of the archaeological remains of the historic French village was conducted by F. Terry Norris (1984). By identifying common reference points on a map of the village drawn in 1766 by British army cartographer Thomas E. Hutchins and a modern USGS map, Norris was able to superimpose the two maps (Figure 4) and speculate on the condition of the archaeological remains of structures identified on the 1766 map (Norris 1984:4).

The lateral movement of the Mississippi River in the 1860s to a point 175 m west of the location of the CahokiaCourthouse State Historic Site resulted in the destruction of the western portion of the French colonial village and the remains of the "Indian Village and burying ground" as identified on the 1766 Hutchins map (Norris 1984:8–9). Other late nineteenth- and twentieth-century impacts included Illinois State Highway construction and expansion, development of the East St. Louis Carondelet Railroad, the expansion of the facilities of the Holy Family Parish, the construction and development of Parks College of St. Louis University, and the development of subdivisions and residential areas. In summarizing Norris's interpretations, possible preserved structural remains have been identified and the destruction of other house sites by urbanization, industrial/commercial development, and natural causes has been assessed. Norris (1984:15) concludes that the archaeological remains of 21 structures or 20% of the structures identified on the 1766 Hutchins map appear to have survived major alterations or damage. The virtual stagnation of the village and its population in the nineteenth century, which occurred subsequent to the removal of the St. Clair County seat from Cahokia to Belleville, was important in the preservation of the archaeological remains throughout the nineteenth century. Unfortunately, most of the destruction of the archaeological remains of the village has occurred in the twentieth century.

A 1927 aerial photograph (see Plate 5) of the Cahokia Wedge and surrounding areas to the south and southwest shows the sparsity of standing houses within the community at this time. The area shown in this photograph represents the core or center of the eighteenth-century village, and probably at the time of this photograph many archaeological house sites were still undisturbed. The photograph also shows most

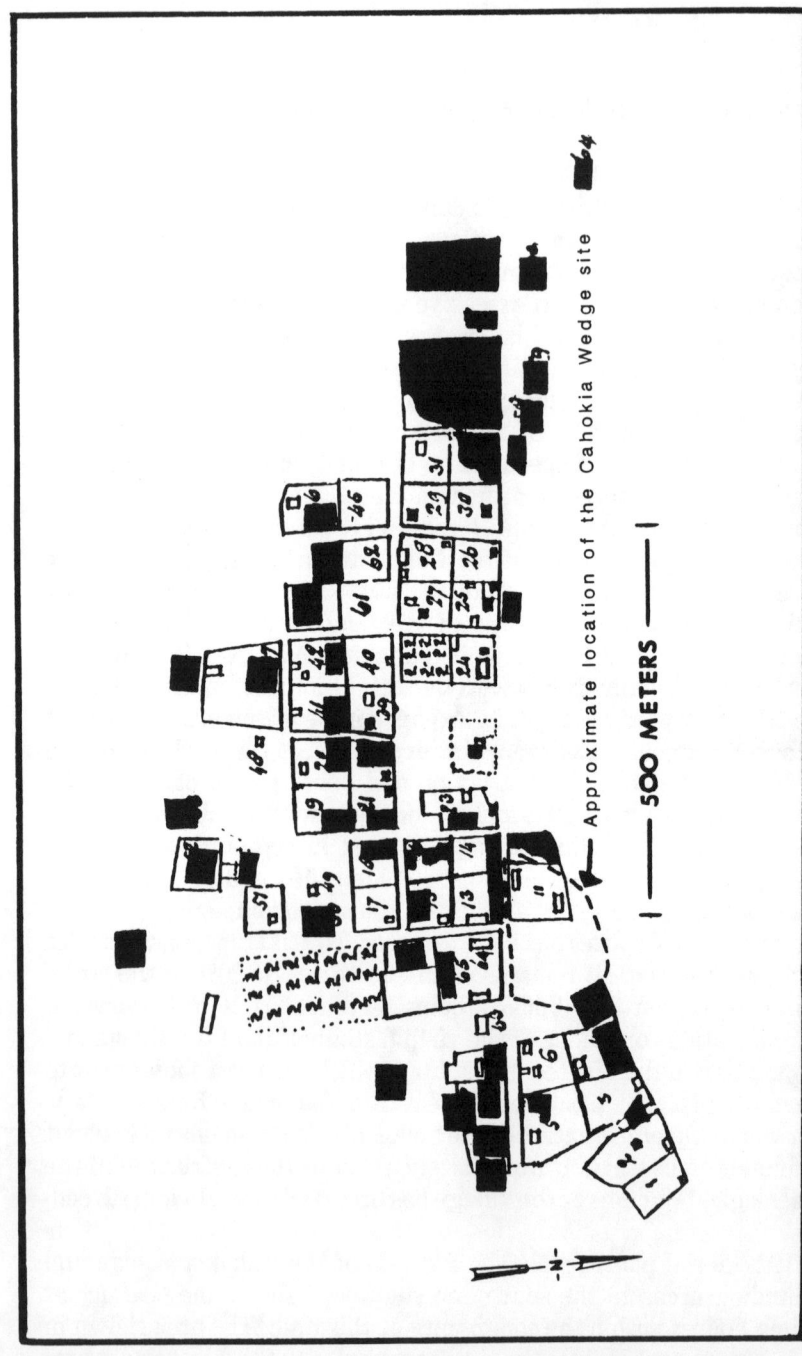

Fig. 4. Map of village lots from 1766 map (see Plate 6). Shaded areas denote structural sites probably destroyed, based on superimposed 1766 map and USGS map. Two structures owned by Etienne Nicolle (#11) are located within the Cahokia Wedge site. (Adapted from Norris 1984)

of the Cahokia Wedge site. Fieldwork done by the WPA in 1938–1939 on a project named the Cahokia Memorial Survey recorded only five historic log structures still standing, four of which were within the village proper (Illinois State Archives n.d.). The largest impact has occurred in the last 20–40 years with the industrial developments to the north of Cahokia, at Sauget. The influx of heavy industry has led to an increased population and subsequent construction of residential areas and subdivisions in Cahokia, as well as the expansion of the state highway system.

Today the Cahokia Wedge site represents one of the largest and least disturbed tracts of land within the present day town of Cahokia. The site encompasses approximately 10% of the original eighteenth-century village as it appeared on the 1766 map. The only modern alterations that have occurred at the site have been the expansion of the surrounding streets, in particular, Illinois Route 3 on the western edge. The historical significance of the Cahokia Wedge site was first noted in 1938–1939 with the Cahokia Memorial Survey of the Works Progress Administration (Illinois State Archives n.d.). At this time Lots 13 and 14 had been privately deeded to St. Clair County for use as an historical park. A 1956 plat map (see Figure 11) has the Wedge labeled as "Proposed State Park-St. Clair County Property" (St. Clair Title Company 1956:128).

A 1969 letter to the Illinois Department of Conservation from the Cahokia Historical Commission expressed interest in developing the Wedge into an historical park. The Wedge apparently had recently been acquired by the commission (Illinois State Archives n.d.). In 1972, interest in this type of project still existed, yet no actual results had yet occurred. This proposal, which included a map of the Historic District in Cahokia, outlined the development of a walking tour pathway from the Cahokia Courthouse to the historic Church of the Holy Family and the Jarrot Mansion, and included the Wedge, now identified as "Proposed Historic Park owned by City" (Illinois State Archives n.d.).

However, not all proposals concerning the Cahokia Wedge have been based on the historical and archaeological significance of the site. More recently, the Wedge was proposed as the site for the construction of a new Fire Department facility for the Village of Cahokia. One of the original proposals of the Cahokia French Colonial Committee and the Cahokia Chamber of Commerce was the relocation of the reconstructed Cahokia Courthouse to a more visible location at the Cahokia Wedge for tourism enhancement. Fortunately, for the sake of the preservation of archaeological remains and historical accuracy, neither of these proposals was carried out.

CHAPTER 2: INITIAL ARCHAEOLOGICAL INVESTIGATIONS

The primary purpose of archaeological investigations at the Cahokia Wedge site was to identify cultural remains dating to the eighteenth-century French village. A controlled surface collection was proposed to answer two questions: (1) were eighteenth-century cultural remains present; and (2) if present, did these artifact types appear in spatially discrete concentrations, which would indicate possible subsurface archaeological remains?

The analysis of the spatial distribution of cultural materials on the Wedge was utilized in interpreting site structure and function. Correlating these results with field reconnaissance and documentary evidence, the locations of possible structural remains dating to the eighteenth century have been identified. The later nineteenth- and early-twentieth-century habitation areas at the site have also been determined.

Documentary Evidence

Documentary evidence utilized in this research encompassed a variety of resources relevant to the history of Cahokia and the Wedge proper. These resources included:

1) eighteenth- and nineteenth-century maps of Cahokia that depict the evolution of the village plan through time;
2) a ca. 1841 lithograph of the village that includes the Wedge (Wild and Thomas 1841);
3) published historical documents (Alvord 1907; Lowrie and Franklin, eds., 1834) and St. Clair County land records;
4) previous historical research, in particular, the Cahokia Memorial Survey of the Works Progress Administration (WPA) in 1938–1939, and research conducted in commemoration of the 250th anniversary of the founding of Cahokia (McDermott, ed., 1949; Peterson 1949); and

5) an early-twentieth-century aerial photograph of a portion of the village including the Cahokia Wedge.

The WPA research contributed greatly to these investigations in providing a reconstruction of the village plan, as it appeared from 1790 to 1826. The map was reconstructed based on the early land titles and property descriptions from Deed Books B-F. Village lot owners were identified and when property descriptions were available, structures and other features within each lot were illustrated. The original translations from French into English by WPA researchers, which would provide a complete chain of ownership for village lots from 1783 to 1939, have not been relocated and could not be incorporated into this research. The summary report of the Cahokia Memorial Survey (Boylan n.d.) and weekly narrative reports (Illinois State Archives n.d.) have provided some information as to the succession of property ownership on the Cahokia Wedge site; however, gaps do occur. It was not feasible or practical during the current research to duplicate the WPA research; therefore, available WPA documents were utilized as a primary source.

Since 1872, the village lots within Cahokia have been identified with lot numbers that are still used today. The Cahokia Wedge site encompasses Lots 1, 2, 11, 12, 13, and 14 (see Figure 11). For convenience and understanding, these lot numbers will be used in the discussion of the documentary evidence and in the interpretations of the controlled surface collection.

1735 MAP

A map of the French village of Cahokia (Figure 5) drawn by missionaries Mercier and Courier was sent to the Seminary of Foreign Missions in Quebec in 1735 (Tucker 1942:Plate XXIII). This map places the eighteenth-century French settlement within the present day boundaries of Cahokia. The map is a sketch and therefore is of little value in terms of identifying the Cahokia Wedge site; however, it does have a few notable features. An area to the south of the village is identified as the former French establishment, which apparently is the original mission site founded in 1699 among the Tamaroa and Cahokia. This is probably the village that Charlevoix visited in 1721, commenting that the French were looking for a new place to settle because of flooding problems. This would indicate that the village location on the 1735 map was established sometime between 1721 and 1735. This map also shows that the Cahokia Illini village was located a short distance north of the French settlement.

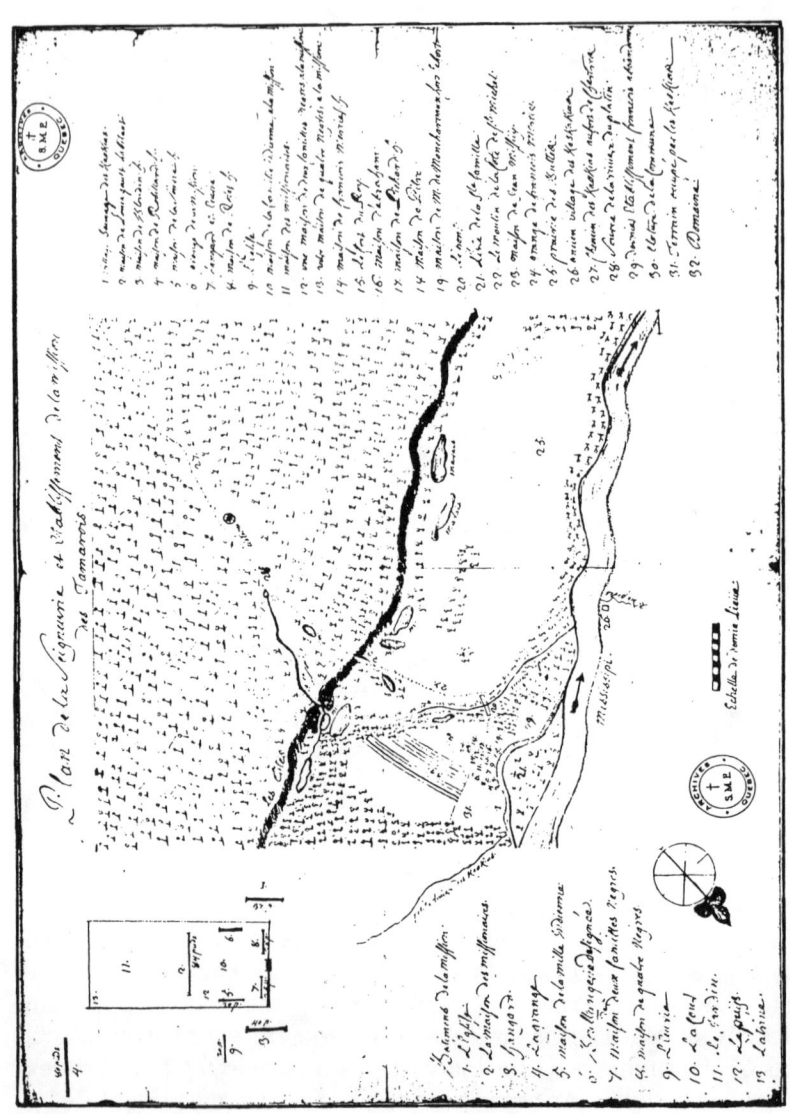

Fig. 5. 1735 map of Cahokia. (Tucker 1942:Plate XXIII. Reprinted with permission from the Illinois State Museum)

INITIAL ARCHEOLOGICAL INVESTIGATIONS 33

1766 MAP

A map of Cahokia (Figure 6) drawn in 1766 by British army cartographer Thomas Hutchins was rediscovered in the 1940s by Charles E. Peterson (1949). This map appears to be fairly accurate based on the presence of a scale in English feet (Peterson 1949:200). Village lots are illustrated with residential structures, barns, and other outbuildings, and the owners are identified. Utilizing common reference points on the 1766 map and a modern USGS map, F. Terry Norris (1984) superimposed these two maps and assessed the archaeological remains of the eighteenth-century village. According to Norris, the Cahokia Wedge site is located within the east central portion of the eighteenth-century village. The superimposed maps show that two structures owned by Nicolt (Etienne Nicolle) are within the western portion of the Wedge, and the eastern portion of the Wedge was unoccupied in 1766 (Norris 1984:6). The Nicolle property is identified as number 11 on the 1766 map; however, this number does not correspond to the modern lot number, Lot 13.

WPA RESEARCH—1783 OWNERSHIP

At the time of the WPA research, the 1766 map of Cahokia had not yet been rediscovered. With the exception of personal letters and documents from the early eighteenth century that were sent to other places, such as Quebec, many documents and parish records were destroyed in a fire in the Church of the Holy Family in 1783. The earliest land titles available appear to date to 1783 (Lowrie and Franklin, eds., 1834:195–202).

In reconstructing the succession of land ownership for properties within Cahokia, using Book of Deeds B-F and the American State Papers, Public Lands Series (Lowrie and Franklin, eds., 1834;195–202), WPA researchers recorded village lot owners in 1783, including the lots within the Cahokia Wedge (Boylan n.d.:61–63). Lots that are presently identified as 1, 2, 11, and 12 were owned by Pierre Lize, Thomas Brady, and Dutrimble. Lot 14 was owned by Baptiste Allary and Lot 13 was owned by Greater Comsal (?). However, no information was provided in the WPA research about what existed on these properties in 1783.

COMMON FIELD MAP OF 1808

An 1808 map of Cahokia (Figure 7) was prepared by Wm. Rector for the United States Land Commission (Lowrie and Franklin, eds., 1834).

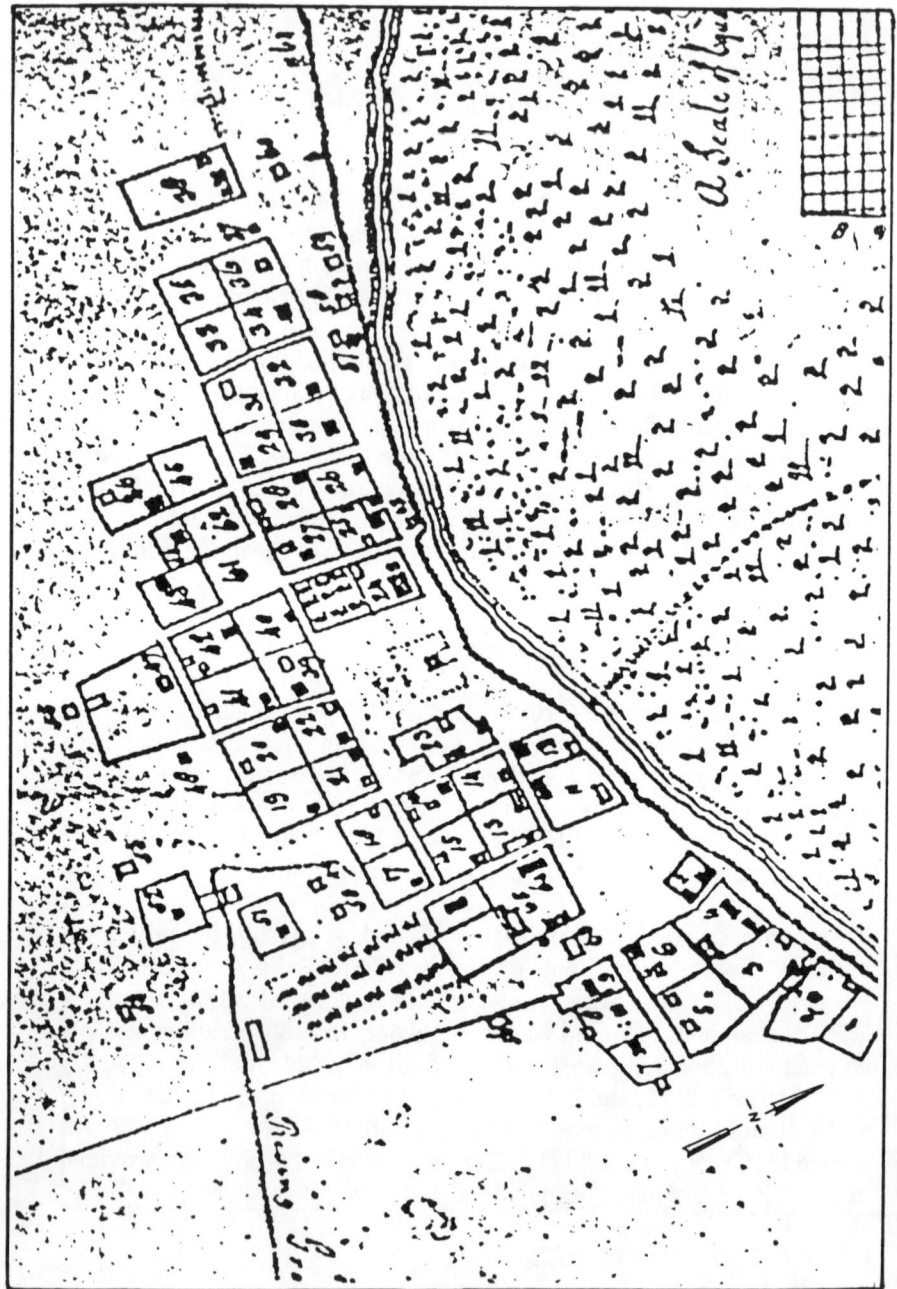

Fig. 6. Portion of 1766 map of Cahokia by Thomas Hutchins. (Peterson 1949:200. Reprinted with permission from the Illinois State Historical Library)

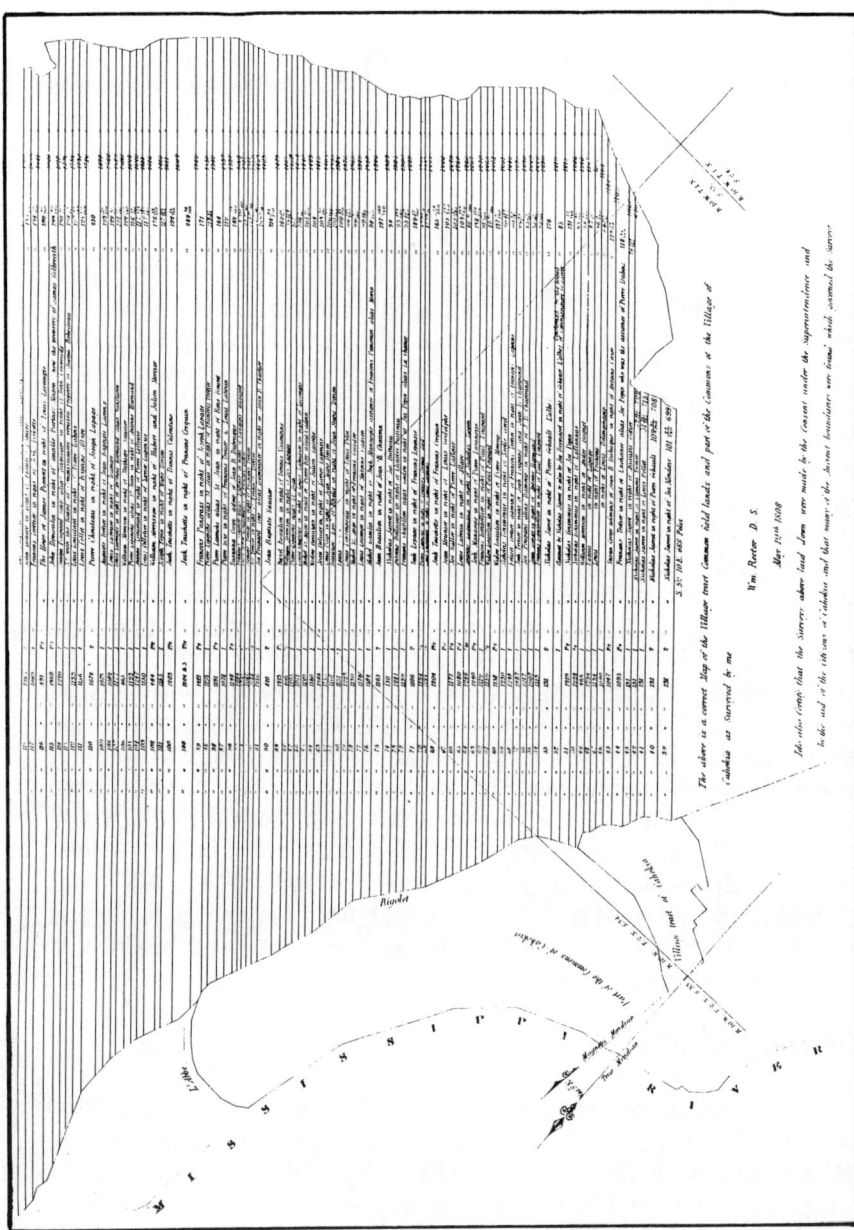

Fig. 7. 1808 map of common fields of Cahokia (Lowrie and Franklin, eds., 1834)

This map identified the owners of the tracts within the common fields and illustrated the village boundaries. Unfortunately, the village was shown as a blank area. It is noteworthy that the village boundaries on this map may have been one source used for the WPA reconstructed map from 1790 to 1826.

WPA Reconstructed Map for 1790–1826

One of the projects in the WPA Cahokia Memorial Survey was the reconstruction of a map of the village for the period dating from 1790 to 1826 (Figures 8 and 9). The 1872 plat map of Cahokia appears to be the source for the layout of the streets and village lots on the reconstructed map. Utilizing the translated property descriptions in Deed Books B-F, in conjunction with field surveys, "pictoral representations of buildings [were] placed as nearly as possible in their relative positions" (Illinois State Archives n.d.).

By superimposing the WPA map and the SIUE topographic map, using the Church of the Holy Family and the Jarrot Mansion represented on both maps as reference points, properties within the Cahokia Wedge can be identified. The western portion of the Wedge has the reconstructed properties of J. Meunier (1798) on Lot 13 and J. Dehai (1804) on Lot 14. Most of the Dehai property has been destroyed by the expansion and realignment of Illinois Route 3 in the last few decades; however, the Meunier property is completely within the Wedge. Shown on the Meunier property are a house, a barn, two sheds, a stable, a mill, and a well. The eastern portion of the Wedge is divided into three lots, two of which are identified by the owners, P. Lize Dit Mimi (1795), Lot 1, and L. Pinconneau (1801), Lot 2. Lots 11 and 12 are not identified as to ownership. None of these lots on the eastern portion of the Cahokia Wedge were reconstructed by the WPA researchers.

WPA Research–1809 Ownership

WPA researchers identified lot owners for the village, including the Cahokia Wedge, using a list of land claims for Cahokia and the common fields recorded for 1809 (Lowrie and Franklin, eds., 1834;195–202). In this year, Lots 13 and 14 were still owned by J. Meunier and J. Dehai, respectively, as indicated on the WPA reconstructed map. Lots 1, 2, 11, and 12 were now owned by Francois Bouthellier and a house was reported on one of the lots; however, no further details as to the actual location of the structure were provided (Boylan n.d.:61–63). The WPA reconstructed map does not show F. Bouthellier as a property owner on

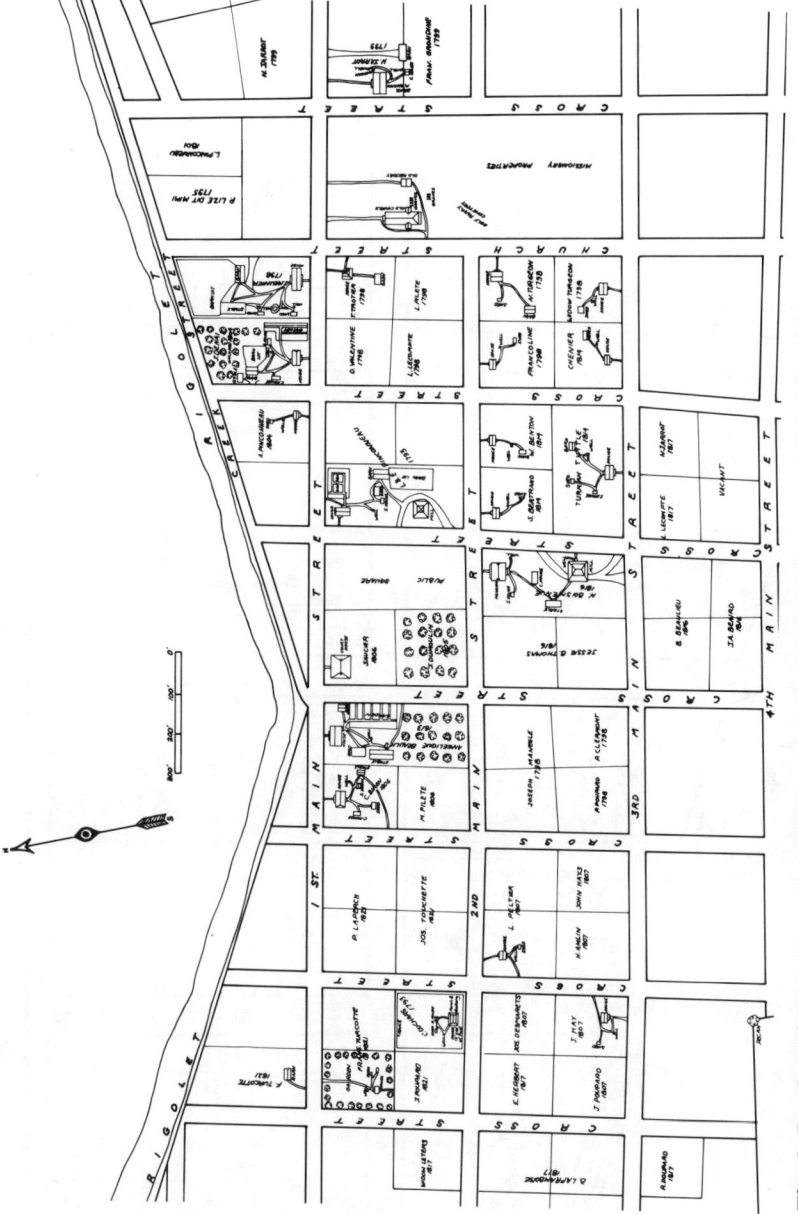

Fig. 8. Portion of WPA reconstructed map of Cahokia for the years 1790–1826. (Redrawn from original blueprint in Cahokia Courthouse Archives)

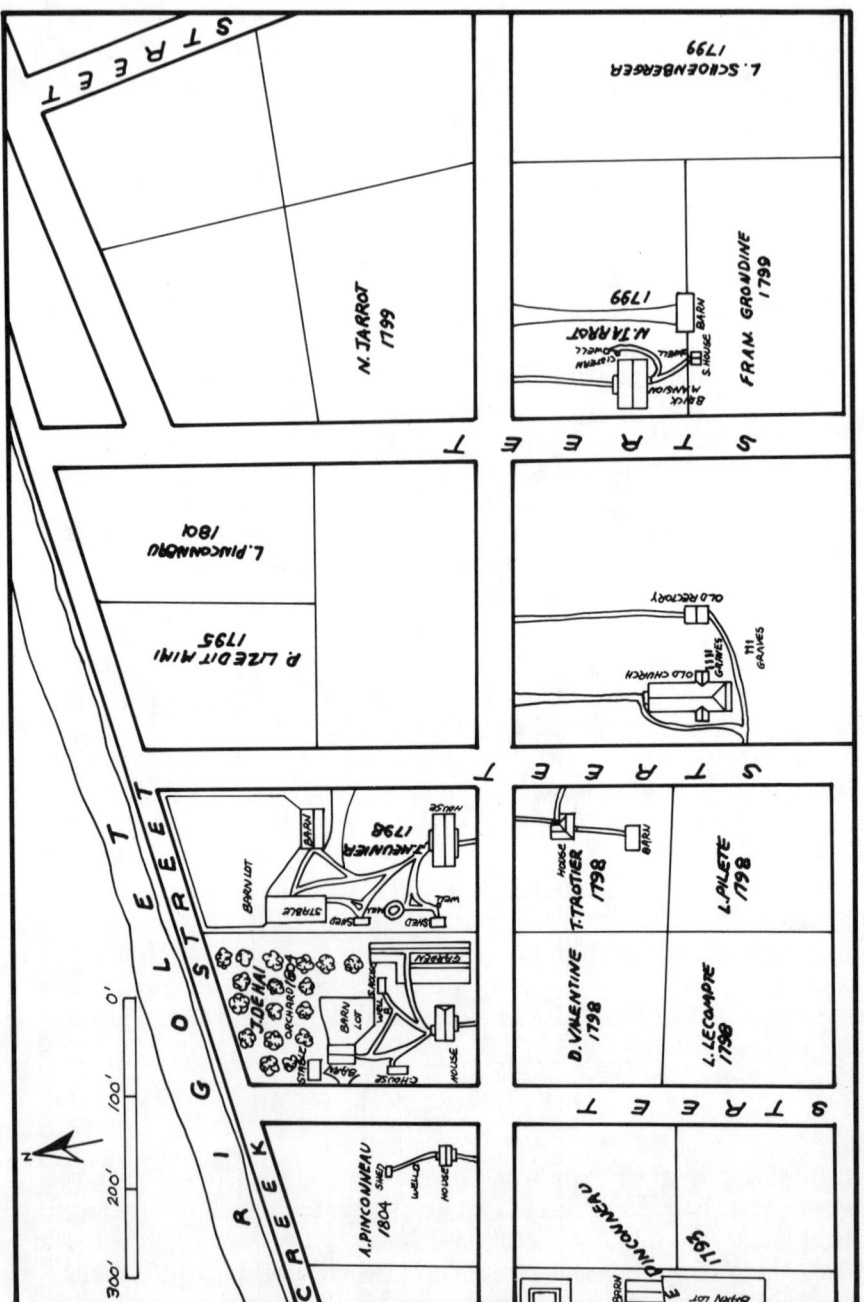

Fig. 9. Detail of WPA map showing village lots within the Cahokia Wedge site. (Redrawn from original blueprint in Cahokia Courthouse Archives)

the Cahokia Wedge, so it may be assumed that no further information was found.

LITHOGRAPH OF CAHOKIA (CA. 1841)

A lithograph of a winter scene in Cahokia (Figure 10) was illustrated by J. C. Wild in the 1841 publication *The Valley of the Mississippi Illustrated* (Wild and Thomas 1841). This view, to the south-southeast from present day Illinois Route 3, shows Dead Creek, the Cahokia Wedge, and a row of structures, including the Church of the Holy Family and the Jarrot Mansion, facing the Wedge. Based on the quality of this illustration, the perspective and depth of the scene, and with the Church and the Jarrot Mansion as reference points, this illustration is of some value as an historical document in assessing occupation on the Wedge in 1841.

The lithograph does show that the western portion of the Wedge (Lots 13 and 14) was vacant of structures. This documents that the Nicolle/Meunier structures were no longer in existence. There are several structures, a two-story house and one or two outbuildings, which may have been located within Lot 11 on the southeast corner of the Wedge. The depth of the illustration is somewhat confusing in that these structures, in relation to the Church of the Holy Family, appear to be in the correct location for Lot 11; however, in relation to the Jarrot Mansion, the structures seem to be across the street from the mansion, and therefore not on the Cahokia Wedge. In the lithograph, the distance between the church and the mansion appears distorted; they are not as close as illustrated. This, therefore, creates a problem in assessing the exact location of the structures as on Lot 11 on the Wedge or across the street from the Jarrot Mansion. It may be postulated, keeping in mind that this is an artist's perspective, that these structures were on the Wedge and possibly represent the house and outbuildings owned by F. Bouthellier in 1809.

PLAT MAP OF 1872

A plat map of Cahokia was prepared by the St. Clair County surveyor, F.G. Hilgard, in 1872. This plat shows for the first time the village lot numbers that are still used today. As previously stated, the Cahokia Wedge site encompasses lot numbers 1, 2, 11, 12, 13, and 14. In 1872, Lots 1, 2, 11, and 12 were owned by J. R. Trottier, and Lots 13 and 14 were owned by Henry Labuxier (Labusier). This plat map, however, does not illustrate structures within the village, with the ex-

Fig. 10. Lithograph of Cahokia by J. C. Wild published in 1841 (Wild and Thomas 1841). The Church of the Holy Family is the structure with the steeple and the Nicholas Jarrot Mansion is to the left of the church. The Cahokia Wedge site is located in the central portion of the illustration

ception of the log Church of the Holy Family and a structure that probably is the Cahokia Courthouse. This plat does show Church Street extending north from First Street through the Cahokia Wedge site. The street system shown on this plat map was probably the source for the WPA reconstructed map. Many of these streets may not have existed during the period (1790–1826) represented by the WPA map, which may explain many vacant lots shown on the WPA reconstructed map.

AERIAL PHOTOGRAPH OF 1927

An aerial photograph dated 1927 (Plate 5) shows the Cahokia Wedge and the surrounding areas to the south and southwest. The western and central portions of the Wedge are vacant of structures and within cultivation or pasture at this time. In the northeastern corner of the Wedge, Lot 2, is a small, rectangular structure facing Locust Street, a short street connecting Route 157 and First Street. It is a one-story building of frame construction and appears to be a domestic dwelling.

Five structures are shown on the southeast corner of the Wedge. Two of these structures, both facing First Street on Lot 11, are domestic dwellings: a two-story frame building and a one-story building of French colonial style with a porch or gallery on all four sides. The former structure, with some alterations, is reminiscent of the structure in the ca. 1841 lithograph by J. C. Wild, which would indicate it to be at least eighty-six years old in 1927. As postulated, if this structure was that owned by F. Bouthellier in 1809, it would be well over one hundred years old at the time of this photograph. The latter structure was probably of *poteaux-en-terre* or *poteaux-sur-solle* (posts on sill) construction that appears to be covered by a horizontal board frame. Most of the archaeological remains of this structure may have been destroyed by the expansion of First and Locust streets and associated drainage ditches. A smaller structure that resembles a shed is located in back of these residences. Two other outbuildings or sheds are located on Lot 12.

This photograph shows the surrounding streets as being fairly narrow. Abbey Street or State Highway 10 had not been extended through the Wedge and the north extension of Church Street, recorded on the 1872 map, was no longer present on the Wedge.

Plate 5. 1927 aerial photograph of Cahokia. This view is to the southwest, and the Cahokia Wedge site is located in the lower half of the photograph. Two residential dwellings, including one of French colonial style and several outbuildings are shown on the southeast corner of the site. (Photograph courtesy of Parks College, St. Louis University.)

WPA RESEARCH—1938 OWNERSHIP

There were no standing structures on the Cahokia Wedge by 1938, based on WPA research, which indicated that all lots within the Wedge were owned by St. Clair County (Boylan n.d.:61–63). Lots 1, 1A, 2, 2A, 12, and 13 were identified as the former property of Prosper J. Soucy taken by condemnation in County Court. The subdivisions of Lots 1 and 2 indicate that Abbey Street or State Highway 10 was now present on the east side of the Wedge. Lots 13 and 14 had been deeded to the county for use as an historical park by Charles and Barbara Idoux, descendants of Nicholas Jarrot.

PLAT MAP OF 1956

A plat map of Cahokia from 1956 (Figure 11) has the Wedge labeled "Proposed State Park-St. Clair County" (St. Clair Title Company 1956:128). This map also shows Abbey Street or State Highway 10 running diagonally on the ridge crest through the Cahokia Wedge site.

THE WEDGE—1986

Alterations to the Cahokia Wedge over the last few decades primarily involved the expansion of the surrounding streets. Illinois Route 3 has been widened to a four-lane highway and realigned, curving to the northeast. This has resulted in the destruction of most of the western edge of the site and the Dehai property on Lot 14. First Street (former Illinois Route 157) and Locust Street have also been widened. The expansion of Locust Street probably destroyed much of Lot 11 and the archaeological remains of the French colonial style structure seen in the 1927 photograph. Abbey Street (State Highway 10) had been abandoned sometime after 1956, although its remnants are visible on the Wedge. Drainage ditches running parallel to the streets have cut through the edges of the site, and possibly destroyed subsurface archaeological deposits.

Summary of Documentary Evidence

A review of the documentary evidence has revealed that the Cahokia Wedge site was within the boundaries of the second village illustrated in the 1735 map. Actual occupation of the Wedge cannot be determined until the 1766 map. Two structures owned by Etienne Nicolle were present in the southwest corner (Lot 13), the only occupation of the

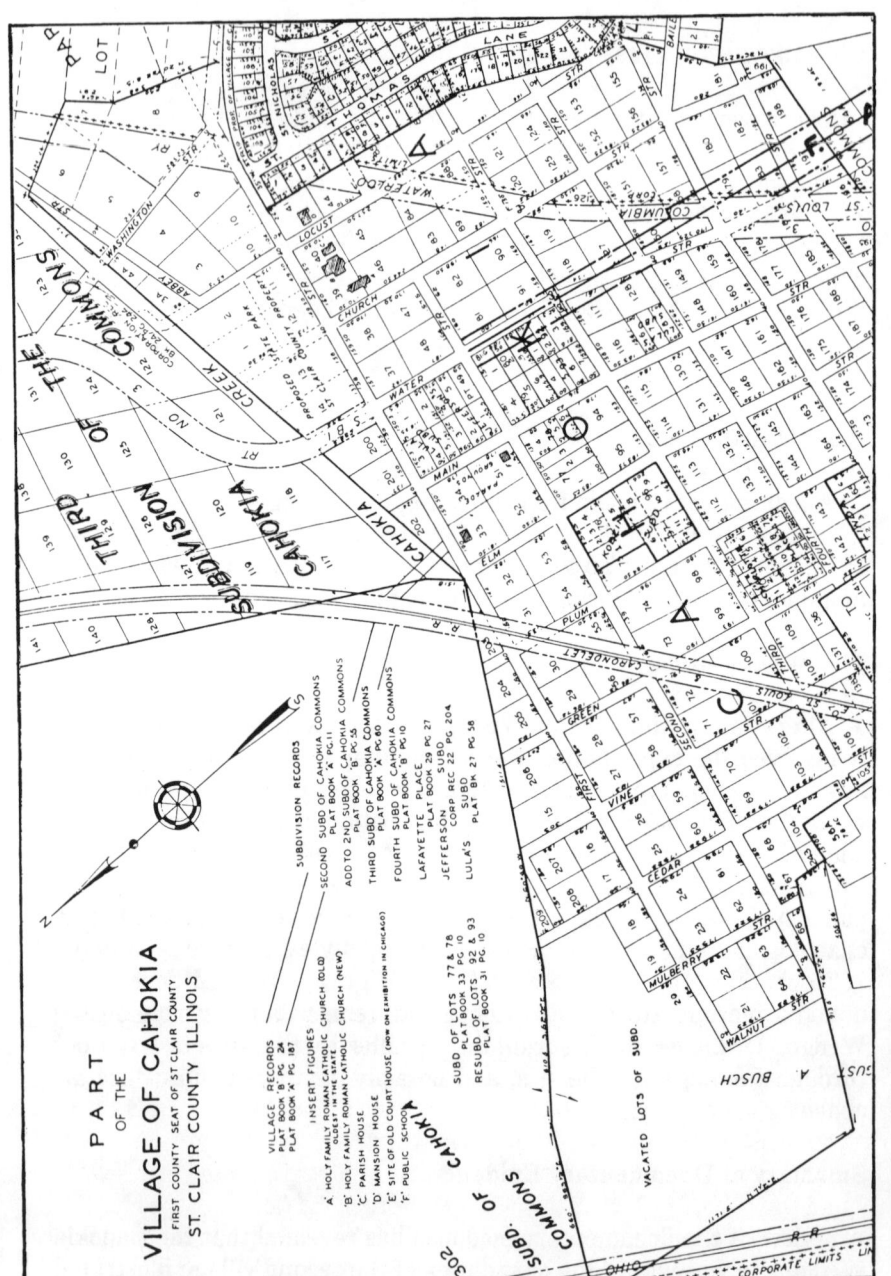

Fig. 11. 1956 plat map of the Village of Cahokia with the Cahokia Wedge site labeled "Proposed State Park-St. Clair County Property" (St. Clair County Title Company 1956)

INITIAL ARCHEOLOGICAL INVESTIGATIONS 45

Wedge at this time. The structures at this location existed at least until 1809 and based on the J. C. Wild lithograph were gone by 1841.

Another structural complex owned by Francois Bouthellier may have been constructed prior to 1809 on the southeast corner (Lot 11) of the Wedge. The 1841 illustration depicts a substantial two-story house with associated outbuildings. This structure is possibly the same as the one shown in the 1927 aerial photograph. However, there is a discrepancy among the sources concerning the actual number of houses constructed in the southeast corner of the Wedge. According to the available documentary evidence, there is only one domestic structure in this area; however, the 1927 photograph reveals two domestic structures. This could be accounted for in the gap of documentary coverage for structures from 1841 to 1927.

Archaeological Investigations and Research

The initial field investigations involved the following: preparation of a topographic map, plowing the site, aerial photography, the establishment of a permanent grid system, field reconnaissance of surface features, and a controlled surface collection. Laboratory work included initial washing and labeling of artifacts, generalized and specialized analyses, and the preparation of artifact distribution maps. Utilizing the artifact distribution maps in correlation with documentary research, interpretations of the archaeological remains at the Wedge were postulated. Six discrete clusters of surface artifacts were defined and interpreted in terms of content and function. These areas have been designated as Areas A through F (see Figure 17).

METHODOLOGY

A topographic map was prepared prior to the plowing of the site for the surface collection (Figure 12). All natural (i.e., contours, trees, creek) and cultural features (i.e., utility poles, abandoned road, gravel turn-around, existing streets) were mapped, including a structural depression located in the southeastern corner of the Wedge. Also tied into this map are the locations of the historic Church of the Holy Family and the Nicholas Jarrot Mansion. The smaller triangular area to the east of the Wedge and separated by Locust Street was also mapped because this area was initially considered for archaeological investigations; however after a wealth of data was recovered from the Wedge, plans to investigate this triangular area were temporarily put on hold.

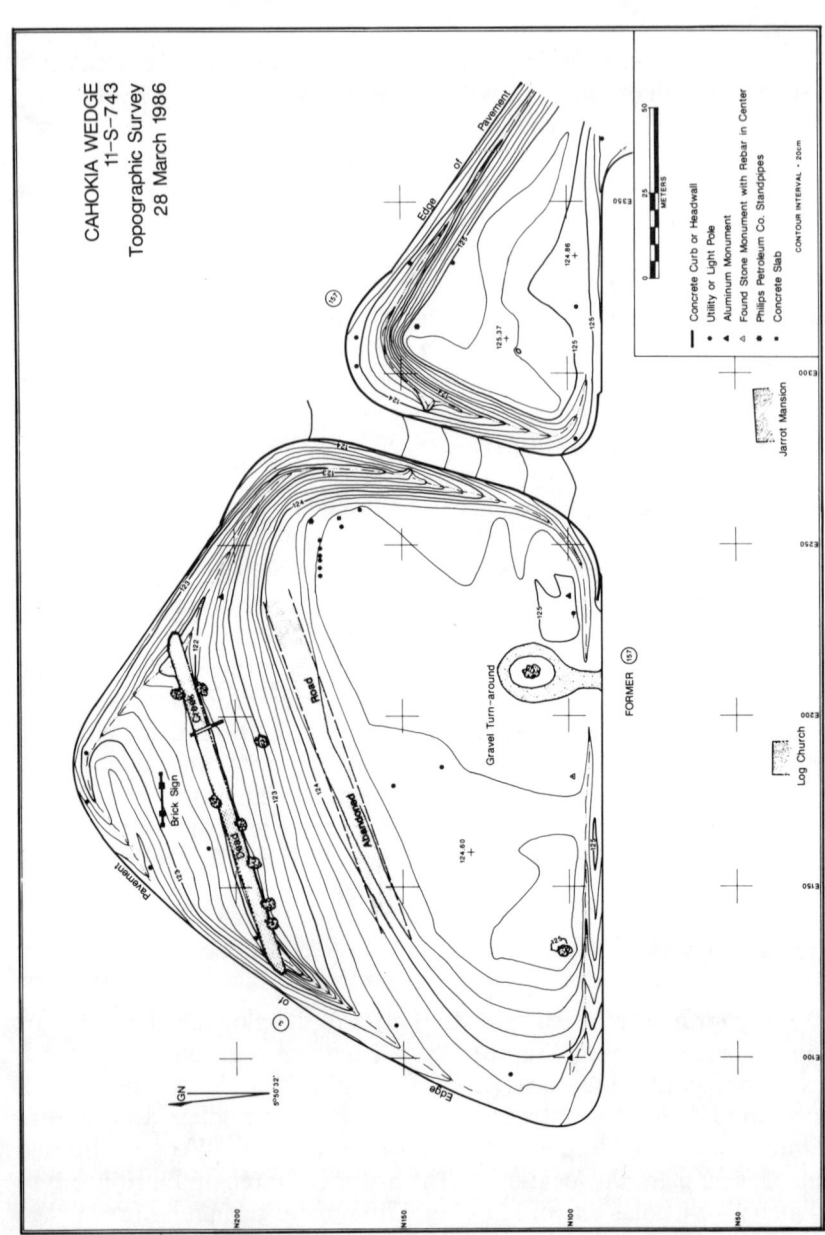

Fig. 12. SIUE topographic map of the Cahokia Wedge site

The site was then plowed to a depth of approximately 10–12 inches. The 1927 aerial photograph of the Cahokia Wedge showed that most of the site was within cultivation and therefore no further damage to possible archaeological deposits occurred. The extent of the plowed areas was defined by the presence of drainage ditches for the streets along the southern, eastern, and western edges. A small area in the northeast corner of the site was not plowed, and therefore not collected, due to the presence of utility poles, a concrete slab, and standpipes. The northern edge of the plowed area was defined by the edge of Dead Creek. A few isolated utility poles and trees within the site area were plowed around and these units were collected. Immediately after plowing, color, infrared, and black and white aerial photographs were taken from a height of approximately 500 feet. Photographs were taken on several occasions; immediately after plowing, and twice after moderate rainfalls.

Three permanent aluminum markers were emplaced on the periphery of the site: southwest corner at N100 E100, southeast corner at N100 E235, and northeast corner at N205 E235. A 5 m interval grid was emplaced for the controlled surface collection using flags and flagging tape labeled with the appropriate north and east coordinates. After patiently waiting for rain for several weeks, the controlled surface collection was begun after a few light to moderate rainfalls. Surface visibility ranged from approximately 50% to 80%.

A total of 570 five-meter-square units were collected. No time limit was set for collection within each unit. Each collection unit was identified by the coordinates of the southwest corner of the respective unit. Due to the abundance and non-portability of various materials such as flagstone, limestone gravel, brick, asphalt, and cinders, these materials were not collected. Notes were made on each unit bag concerning the presence and amounts of these types of materials. Unit bags were labeled with consecutive numbers as the bags were collected from the field.

Surface Observations

The SIUE aerial photographs (see Plate 1) revealed dark soil stains along the south edge of the Wedge parallel to First Street, which dates to the eighteenth-century village when it was known as "la rue du Rigolet." Dark soils are also present on the eastern edge of the site parallel to Locust Street, which was indicated for the first time on the 1872 plat map. The darker soils possibly representing midden accumulation suggest that the major occupations at the site occurred near these streets. A curved band of dark soil is also observed on the eastern side of the Wedge at the ridge crest. Light yellow, sandy soils are located on the gentle slope of the western edge of the site, and these soils appear to be the result of natural processes.

A narrow band of lighter-colored soils, oriented north-south and extending from the south edge and through the Wedge, appears to identify the extension of Church Street. The presence of this street on the Wedge was first documented on the 1872 plat map, and by the time of the 1927 photograph this road had been abandoned and the area was under cultivation. This band of soil is much narrower than the present day Church Street and is located slightly further to the east.

Also documented in the SIUE aerial photographs are more recent disturbances including the concrete/asphalt remains of Abbey Street or State Highway 10, running diagonally northeast-southwest through the Wedge at the ridge crest. This street was abandoned sometime after 1956. Located on the northern edge of the site is an area of yellow soils. Field reconnaissance identified this area as being heavily disturbed and the result of introduced fill.

Two limestone foundations were plowed to the surface on the southeast corner of the site, Lot 11 (Figures 13 and 14). These foundations were first noted as surface depressions prior to plowing the site. After plowing, the locations of the walls of these structures were well-defined by large slabs of limestone and brick rubble. These structural remains correspond to buildings seen in the 1927 aerial photograph. The foundation at the edge of the street is probably the one-story extension attached to the rear of the two-story building. The second foundation, set behind the two-story house, is shown in the 1927 photograph as a shed. One small surface concentration of limestone located directly north and east of these foundations may represent an associated outbuilding. No structure at this location is visible in the 1927 photograph, although it may be hidden by a tree.

The remains of another possible structure were defined on the surface by the presence of several large displaced limestone blocks and limestone and brick rubble. This area is along the south edge of the site, directly west of the two limestone foundations, within Lot 12. These structural remnants correspond to two outbuildings shown in the 1927 photograph.

Several areas on the site have modern disturbances, which may have affected the presence and patterning of artifacts on the surface. The plow churned up large pieces of the asphalt remains of Abbey Street or State Highway 10. The area of disturbed, yellow soils north of the remains of Abbey Street was littered with large pieces of concrete, ap-

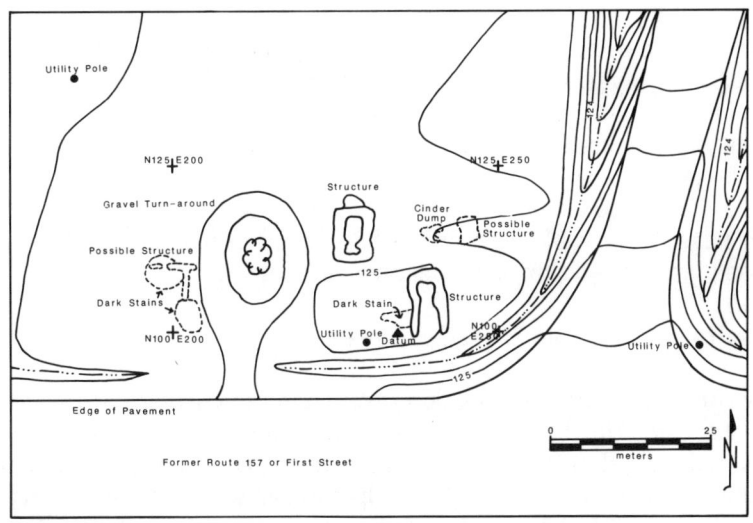

Fig. 13. Map showing surface structural remains in Areas D and E on the southeast corner of the site

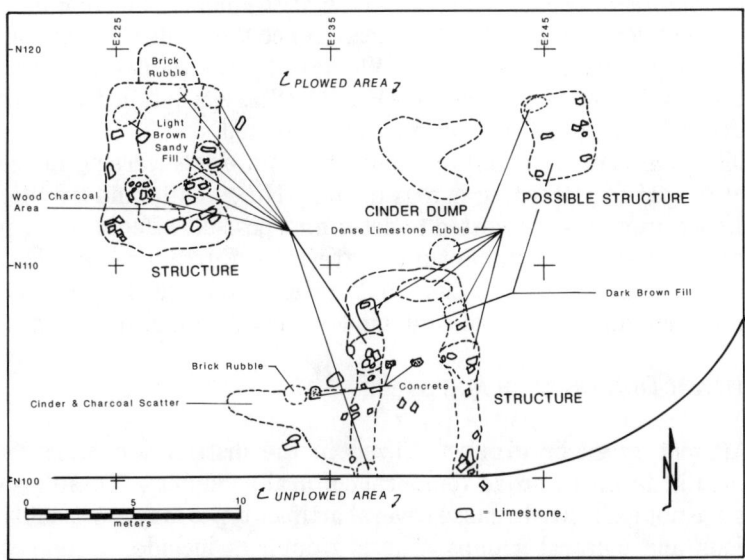

Fig. 14. Detail of surface structural remains in Area E. Two of these structures can be seen in the 1927 aerial photograph (see Plate 5).

parently the discarded remains of surrounding road construction. A limestone gravel turn-around that encircled a tree on the southeast corner of the site was also plowed up. Surface visibility in these three areas was hindered by the abundance of asphalt, concrete, and gravel.

The presence and abundance of uncollected materials, such as limestone, limestone gravel, bricks, and cinders, were noted on collection unit bags. Observable clusters of these types of materials will be discussed later in relation to artifact distributions.

Results of the Initial Investigations

The controlled surface collection resulted in the recovery of 15,986 artifacts from the 570 five-meter-square units. This total includes materials that date to the twentieth century. The numbers of artifacts within units ranged from 0 to 366. The total area covered in the surface collection was 14,250 square meters.

Laboratory work included a general analysis of all controlled surface collection materials. To summarize, the cultural materials from the surface of the Cahokia Wedge site are abundant and diverse. Identified cultural components include prehistoric Emergent Mississippian/Mississippian (A.D. 900–1150), protohistoric/historic Indian and trade goods, eighteenth-century French and British colonial, and nineteenth- and early twentieth-century American. Since the focus of archaeological investigations at the Cahokia Wedge site was to identify cultural remains of the eighteenth-century French village, a detailed analysis of artifacts diagnostic of this period was conducted.

Distribution maps of eighteenth-century materials were produced to identify spatial patterning across the site. Nineteenth- and twentieth-century ceramics were plotted to determine possible effects on the patterning of eighteenth-century materials. Furthermore, certain artifacts sensitive to function and/or time, such as lithics, faunal remains, building hardware, and window glass, were also plotted.

Artifact Distribution Maps

Artifact types or groups utilized in the distribution maps were defined in terms of broad temporal/cultural groupings. These groupings are not exclusive because several artifact types may cross-cut time periods and cultural groups. These groupings include: a composite prehistoric, protohistoric, and historic Indian; historic Indian and trade goods; French colonial; materials dating to the eighteenth or nineteenth century that could relate to French, British, or American occupations; and nineteenth- and twentieth-century American artifacts. Figure 15 illustrates the percentages of selected artifact types within the six defined areas, Areas A-F, and the remaining portion of the site.

Since the artifacts were collected from the surface, it is somewhat difficult to identify temporal and cultural associations. For example, many of these artifact types, such as Micmac pipes, mouth harp frames, and clasp knives, may have been used by the historic Indians and/or by the French. Artifacts that may range throughout the historic period include blue-green bottle glass, unidentified and other metal, building hardware, flat glass, and unidentified nails. In addition, faunal remains cannot be temporally placed.

Two types of distribution maps were produced: (1) diagnostic artifact types that were infrequent were plotted individually, and (2) artifact types that were frequent and could be plotted in terms of relative density. To create the second type of maps the numerical data for each artifact type were broken into intervals based on discontinuities in the frequency distribution.

As indicated on the distribution map of all collected surface materials (Figure 16), artifact densities are greater on the ridge crest with a lower density occurring on the northern slope towards Dead Creek, and on the western edge of the site. On the ridge crest, artifacts were more abundant along the south and east edges of the site, adjacent to present day streets; on the south edge is First Street or former Illinois Route 157, which originated in the eighteenth century. The existence of Locust Street on the east side of the site was first documented on the 1872 plat map.

INTERPRETATIONS

Six concentrations designated Areas A through F (Figure 17), have been identified by the relative densities and co-occurrences of selected artifact types and groups as illustrated on the distribution and frequency maps (Figures 18–29). Utilizing relative temporal dating of artifact groups in correlation with historical maps and documents, land records, and previous research, the period of occupation and the functions of identified structural remains within five of the six areas can be postulated.

By reproducing the various maps, the WPA reconstructed map, and the SIUE topographic map to approximately the same scale, and utilizing these data with previous research by F. Terry Norris (1984), it was possible to superimpose all maps dating from 1766 to the present. With the exception of the 1766 map, the location of the Church of the Holy

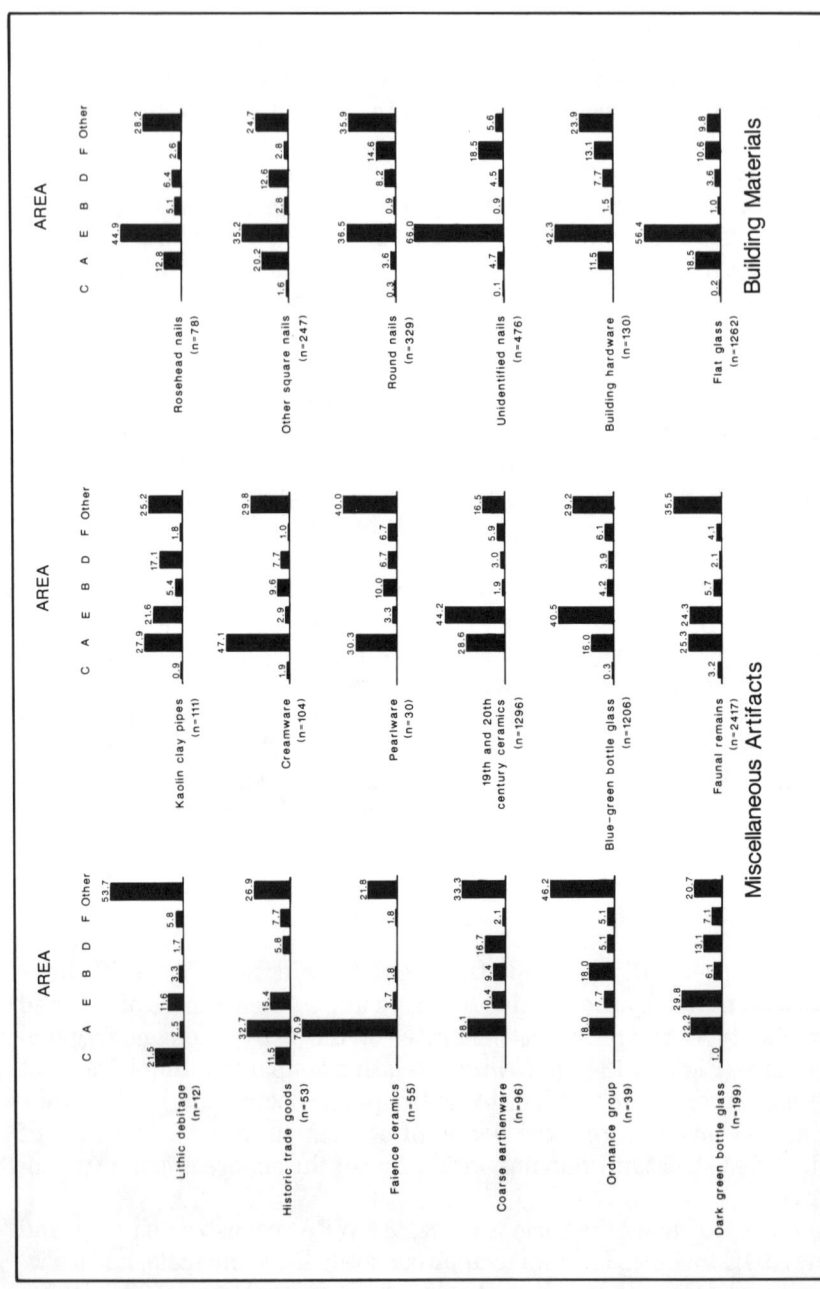

Fig. 15. Bar graph illustrating percentages of selected surface artifacts

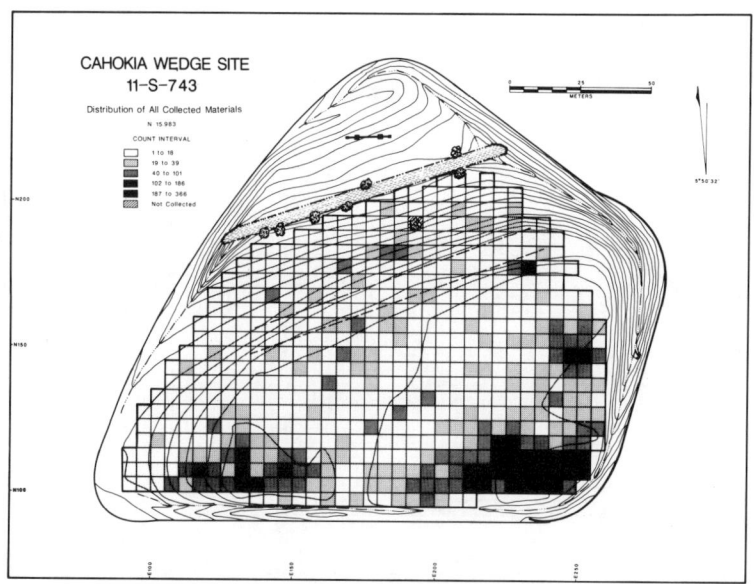

Fig. 16. Distribution map of all collected surface materials

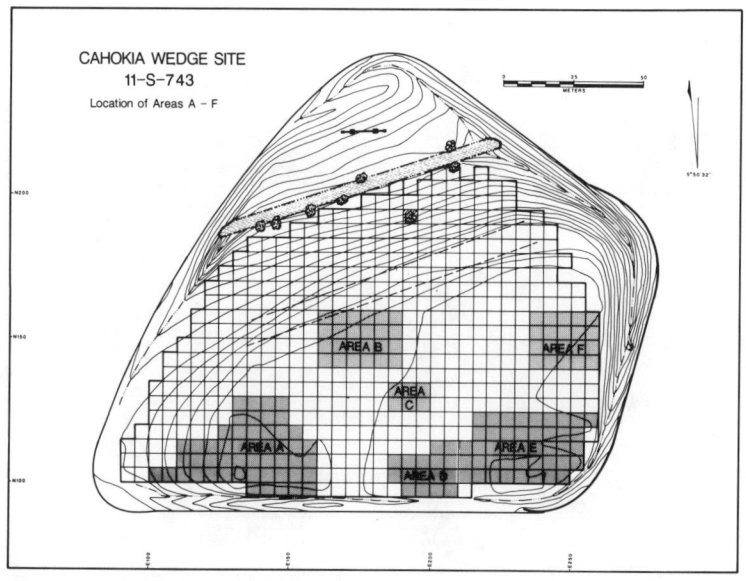

Fig. 17. Map showing location of the six surface artifact concentrations, Areas A-F

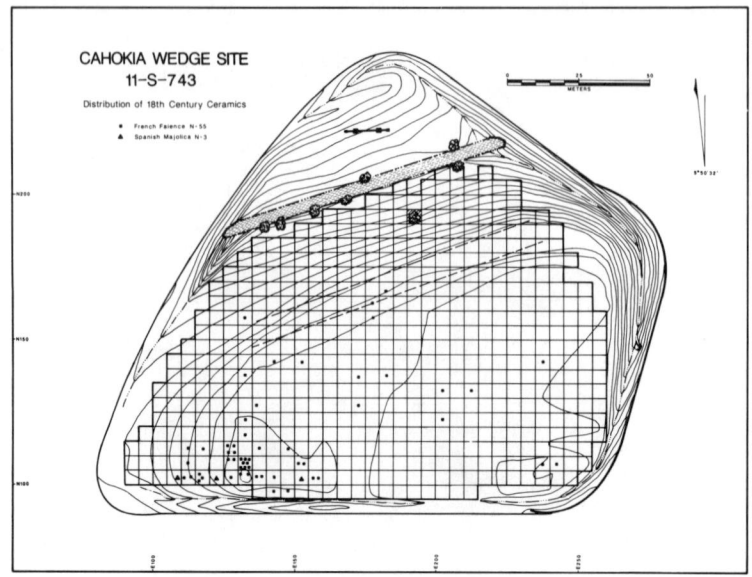

Fig. 18. Distribution map of eighteenth-century ceramics

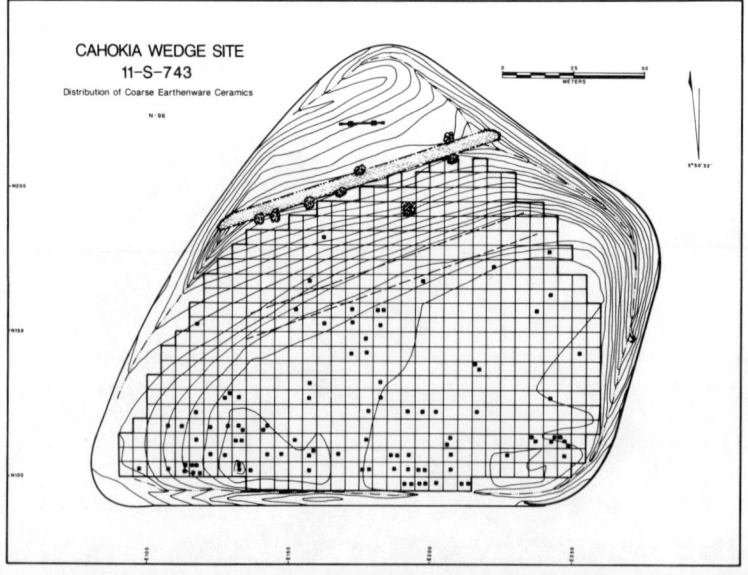

Fig. 19. Distribution map of coarse earthenware ceramics

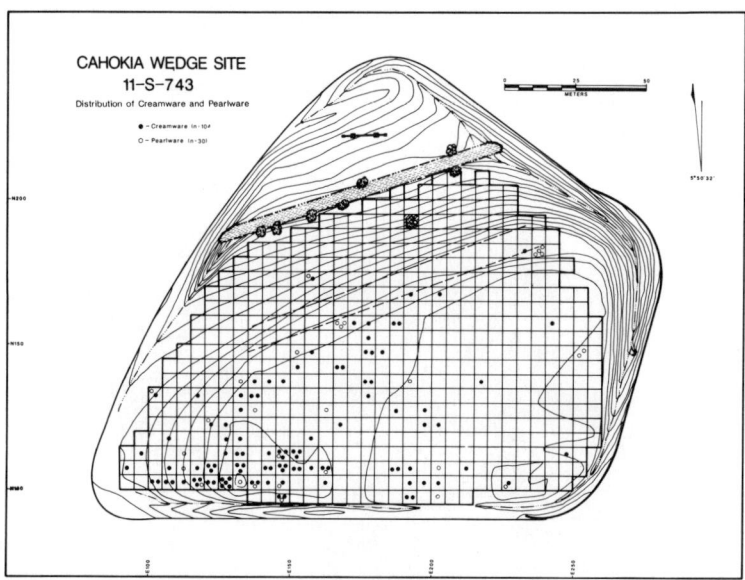

Fig. 20. Distribution map of creamware and pearlware

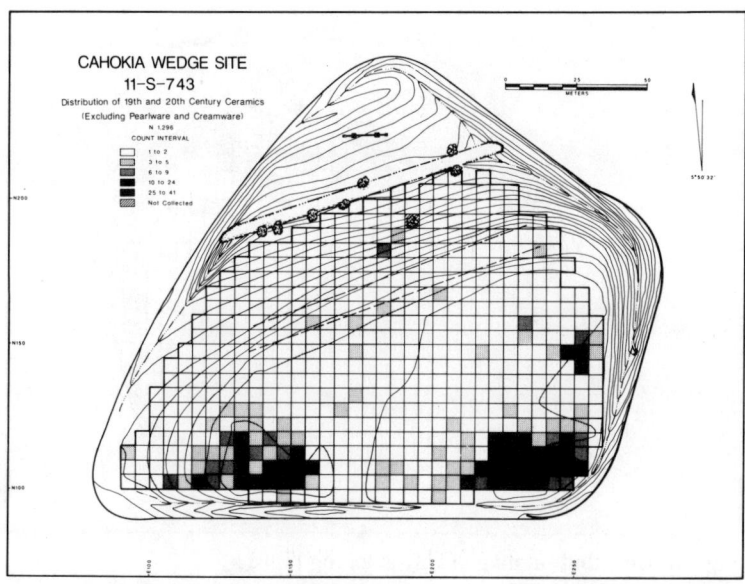

Fig. 21. Distribution map of nineteenth- and twentieth-century ceramics

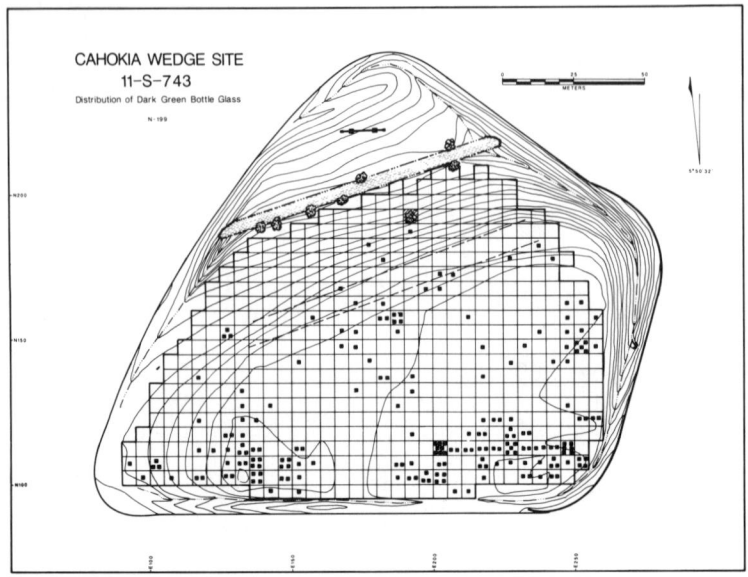

Fig. 22. Distribution map of dark green bottle glass

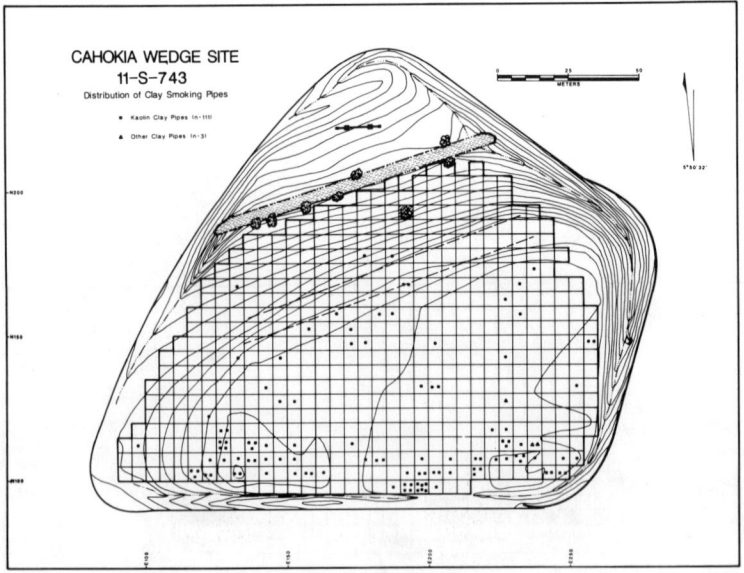

Fig. 23. Distribution map of clay smoking pipes

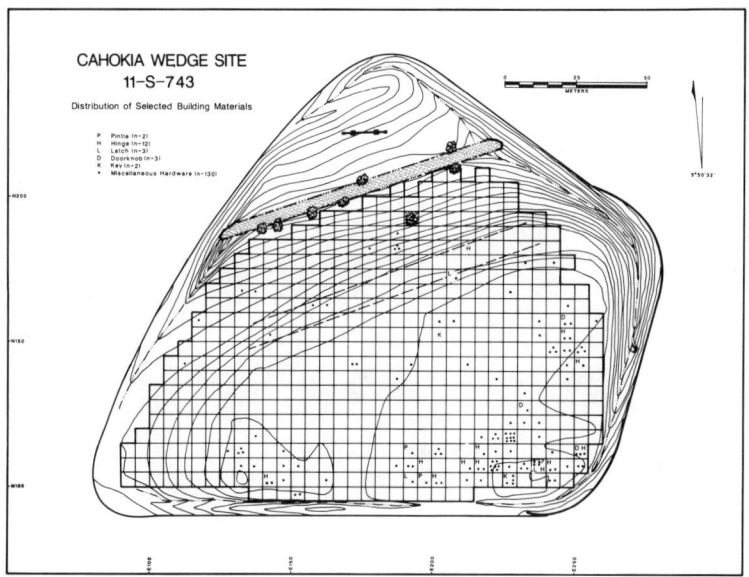

Fig. 24. Distribution map of selected building materials

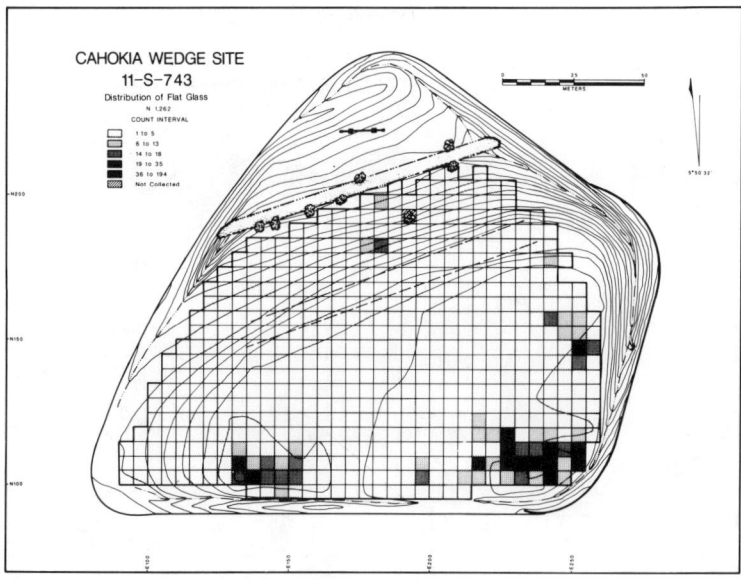

Fig. 25. Distribution map of flat glass

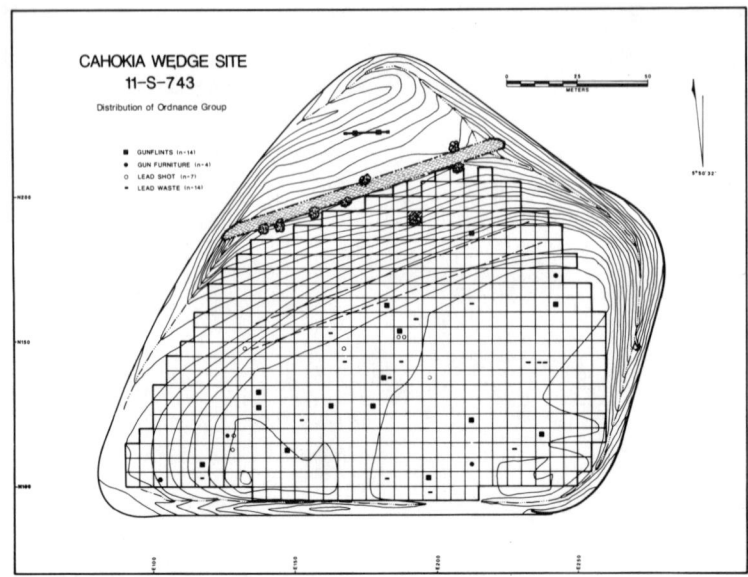

Fig. 26. Distribution map of ordnance group

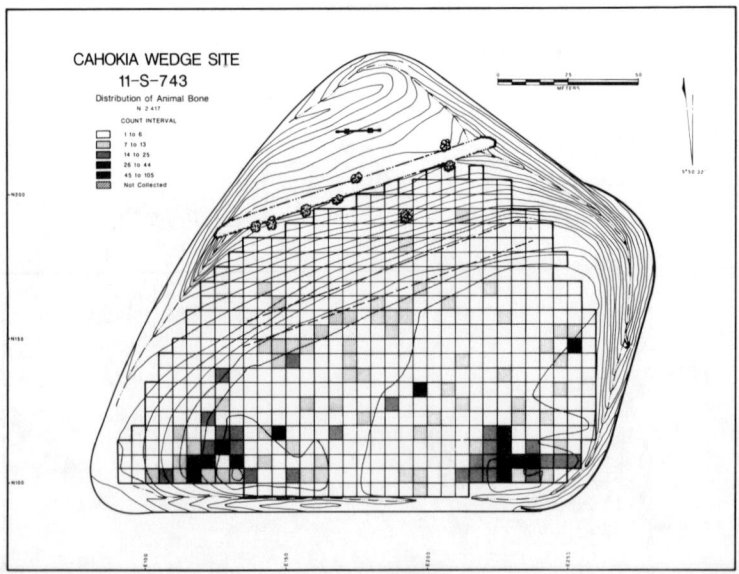

Fig. 27. Distribution map of faunal remains

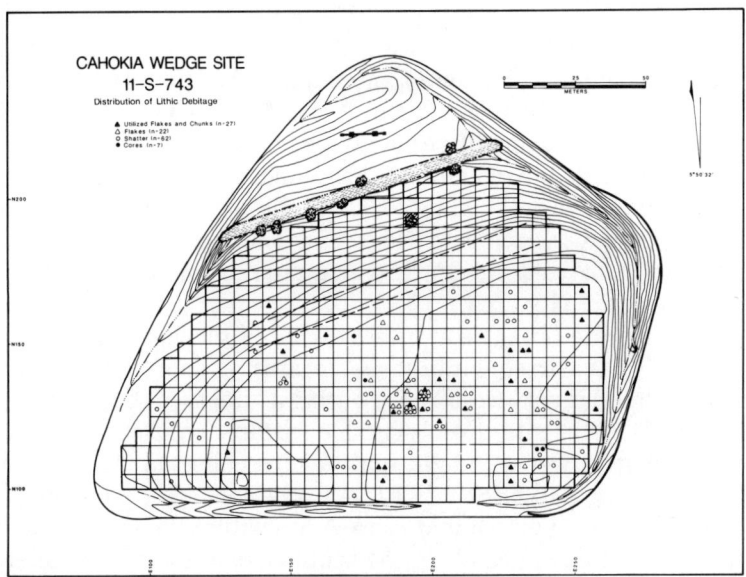

Fig. 28. Distribution map of lithic debitage

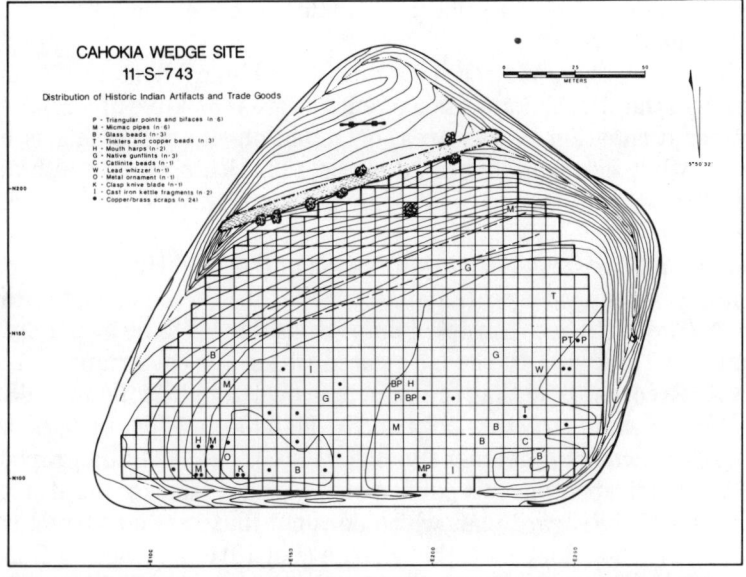

Fig. 29. Distribution map of historic Indian artifacts and trade goods

Family and the Jarrot Mansion were also utilized as reference points. This allowed the identification of approximate locations of structures on the Wedge. Three concentrations, Areas A, E, and F, have been interpreted as the remains of residential/domestic structures. Area B probably represents the remains of a barn, and Area D can be identified as the remains of two outbuildings or sheds. The remaining artifact concentration, Area C, which cannot be referenced to historical maps or documentation, is being interpreted as a protohistoric/historic Indian habitational or activity area.

Area A is located in the southwest corner of the site within Lot 13 (see Figure 17). It is irregular in shape, measuring approximately 35 m north-south by 60 m east-west, representing a total area of 1,275 square meters or 9% of the site. No observable surface features were noted before plowing, however, a light scatter of uncollected materials, including limestone and brick rubble, was observed after plowing. The aerial photographs indicate that Area A lies within the broad band of darker soils that extended along the south edge of the site parallel to First Street.

Area A was the largest of the defined concentrations, although the artifact density was less than the second largest defined concentration, Area B. Although materials reflecting all temporal/cultural groups were represented in Area A, the predominance of eighteenth-century artifacts (of the 55 faience sherds, 39 or 70.9% were recovered from Area A) suggests this area was the location of the earliest French occupation on the Wedge.

It is noteworthy that Area A contained the highest density of faunal remains at the site. Whether these remains are indicative of a relatively longer occupation in this area, or actual on-site processing is unknown. A butcher shop identified in the 1927 photograph, south and across First Street from Area A, may account for some of the faunal remains (Walitschek 1986:23).

Based on Norris's (1984) interpretation of the 1766 Hutchins map, a structure owned by Nicolt (Etienne Nicolle) should be located within Area A. The WPA reconstructed map shows this lot to be owned by J. Meunier in 1798, with the house located within the eastern portion of Area A. Records show that the structure owned by Nicolle in 1766 is probably the same structure occupied by Meunier in 1798. In 1809, the lot was still owned by Meunier (Boylan n.d.:63). The 1841 lithograph by J. C. Wild indicates that this portion of the Wedge was vacant of structures. The 1872 Hilgard plat, which does not illustrate any structures within the village, does show that Area A (Lot 13) was owned by Henry Labuxier (Labusier). In 1874, Lots 13 and 14 were sold by Melanie, Angelica, and Louis Labusier to John B. DeLorme. The 1927 aerial photograph shows Area A vacant of structures and within cultivation or pasture.

Based on documentary evidence, a structure was located in Area A in 1766 to at least 1809 and was no longer present based on the 1841 lithograph. The abundance of artifact types representing domestic activities, particularly ceramics, suggests that the structure in Area A functioned as a residential dwelling. The predominance of eighteenth-century artifacts substantiates that the earliest structure to be identified at the Cahokia Wedge site was located in Area A.

Test excavations, to be discussed in Chapter 3, were conducted in Area A because of the clustering of eighteenth-century artifacts and the location of Area A within the IDOT R.O.W of former Illinois Route 157 or First Street. Test excavations did uncover a portion of an eighteenth-century French colonial *poteaux-en-terre* (posts in the earth) structure interpreted as the Nicolle/Meunier house.

Area B is located centrally on the Wedge near the ridge crest above Dead Creek and cross-cutting Lots 12 and 13 (see Figure 17). Area B is rectangular in shape, measuring 20 m north-south by 30 m east-west, representing a total area of 600 square meters or 4.2% of the site. Surface features were not observed before plowing. On the aerial photographs taken after plowing, the band of lighter-colored soil interpreted as the extension of Church Street goes through the center of Area B. This portion of Church Street existed as early as 1872 and was abandoned by 1927. Field reconnaissance identified a light scatter of uncollected materials including limestone and brick rubble in Area B.

Compared to the other areas that can be identified as residential (Areas A, E, and F), Area B had a relatively light density of surface artifacts. Documentary research indicates that a structure owned by Nicolle in 1766, was located within Area B. The WPA reconstructed map identifies a barn owned by J. Meunier in 1798; however, the barn was illustrated directly north of the Meunier house and therefore not within but west of Area B. Records show that the structure owned by Nicolle in 1766 is probably the same structure owned by Meunier in 1809 (Boylan n.d.:63) and identified as a barn. This would indicate that the structure served the same function during the Nicolle occupation. This suggests a possible error in the WPA reconstructed map that shows the barn directly north of the Nicolle/Meunier house. The 1841 lithograph of the Cahokia Wedge shows that the barn was not present and Area B was vacant of structures. The 1872 Hilgard plat map shows Lot 13 belonging to Henry Labuxier, but it is not known what existed on the property.

Based on documentary evidence a barn was located near or within Area B as early as 1766 and at least until 1809; however, this structure was apparently not present in 1841. The presence of Church Street through Area B on the 1872 map indicates the area was still vacant of structures in 1872. The 1927 photograph shows Area B within cultivation or pasture.

The lighter density of surface artifacts compared to the other areas may substantiate that the postulated structure in Area B was a barn and not residential. There was a light concentration of eighteenth-century coarse earthenwares, which possibly served a more utilitarian function than tablewares such as faience, which were rare in Area B. Building materials were present within Area B; however, these were not abundant. A low frequency of nails may also support the interpretation of Area B as a barn. An eighteenth-century account indicates that nails were "the most rare and precious items" (Peterson 1949:11) and probably were used primarily in domestic dwellings. Wooden pegs were probably substituted for iron nails in barns and other outbuildings. Flat glass was uncommon in Area B, which also suggests a non-residential structure. The interpretation of a barn can be further substantiated by the map of 1766 and the WPA map, which show that residences were often located very close to the edges of streets and that barns and other outbuildings were usually located within the lots and set back from the streets.

Area C is located approximately in the center of the site within Lot 12 (see Figure 17). It is a relatively small, rectangular area measuring 10 m north-south by 15 m east-west. It represents a total area of 150 square meters or 1.1% of the site. Area C is unique compared to the other five areas in that it is defined primarily by the abundance of lithics and the presence of materials assumed to be protohistoric/historic Indian artifacts and trade goods. Included in this concentration were three triangular points, four utilized flakes, lithic debitage, two glass trade beads, and a brass mouth harp frame. This concentration was noted during field reconnaissance and many of the artifacts were piece-plotted (Figure 30). No other observable surface phenomena were noted in the aerial photographs or during the field reconnaissance.

Within this small concentration of culturally specific artifacts there was a virtual lack of materials identified as historic Euro-American. A cluster of human bone, including fragments of an ulna, a radius, and a vertebrae, was identified 15 m to 20 m to the north and northwest of Area C, within and around Area B. This concentration of human bone suggests the presence of an aboriginal burial or cemetery, possibly associated with Area C.

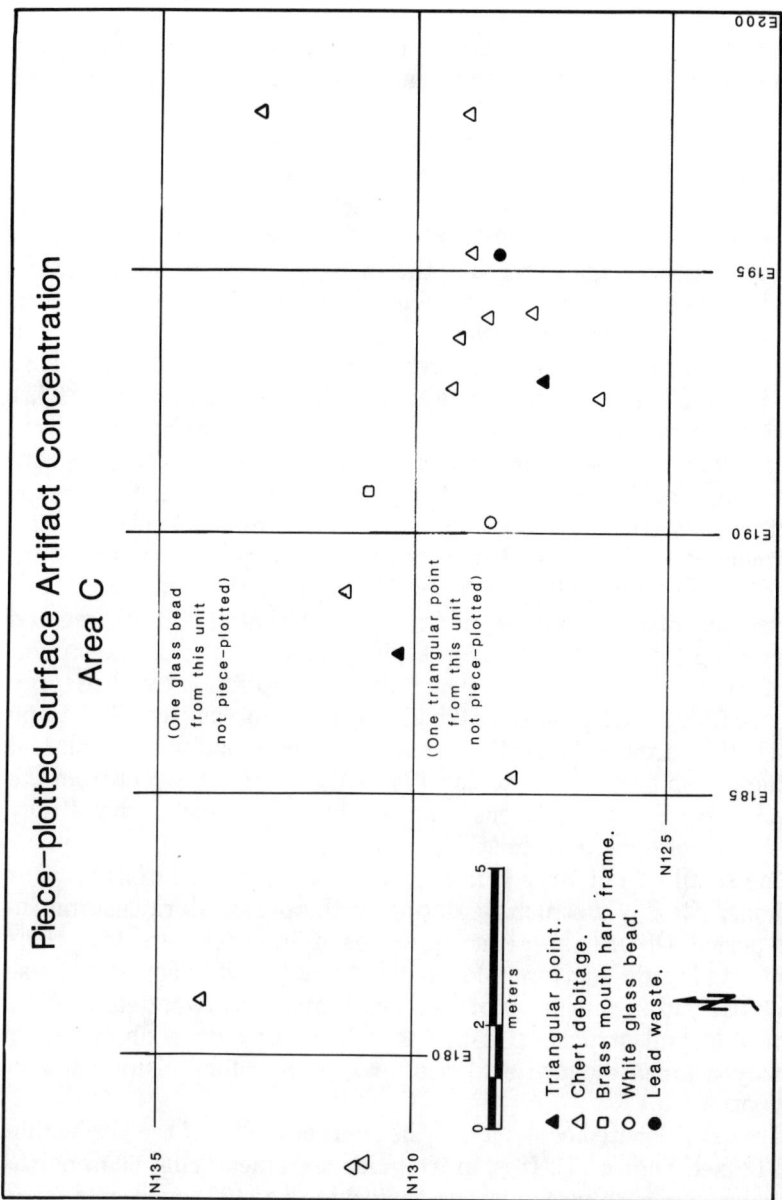

Fig. 30. Piece-plotted surface artifact concentration in Area C

There is a lack of documentation and archaeological evidence for protohistoric/historic Indian settlements in the immediate vicinity of Cahokia. The sketch map of 1735 does show the relative position of the Cahokia Illini village on Rigolet Creek to the north of the French settlement. The 1766 Hutchins map also illustrates the "Indian Village and Burying Ground" to the south of the French village, which actually may represent the original site of the mission founded in 1699. Unfortunately, it appears that the remains of the 1699 mission site and Indian village have been destroyed by the migration of the Mississippi River in the late nineteenth century (Norris 1984).

It may be assumed that the French settlement shown on the 1735 map is actually the second village site, settled sometime between 1721 and 1735. A protohistoric/historic Indian occupation, although undocumented, may have been present at the Cahokia Wedge site. This concentration could represent an occupation of Illini Indians, perhaps brief, who settled in close proximity to the original mission site. Another interpretation is that these artifacts may be the result of Indians visiting and trading with the French after the establishment of the second village at the present day town of Cahokia. It is documented that during the fall of 1778 several Illini groups camped on the property of Thomas Brady during peace treaty negotiations with George Rogers Clark (McDermott 1949b:29). This camp was reported to be within 100 yards of the British commanding post that was established on the parish property (Peterson 1949:201) across the street from the Cahokia Wedge site. Records from the 1780s do indicate that Brady owned one of the lots on the Cahokia Wedge.

The small size of Area C may indicate the presence of subsurface remains, possibly a structure, dating to the protohistoric/historic Indian period. Other lighter concentrations of lithic debitage, triangular points, and trade items were located in Areas E and F; however, these areas also had an abundance of nineteenth- and early twentieth-century materials and structural remains, which may have obscured or destroyed archaeological evidence for a protohistoric/historic Indian occupation.

Area D is located centrally on the southern edge of the site within Lot 12 (see Figure 17). It is an irregular area measuring 20 m north-south by 25 m east-west and represents a total of 400 square meters or 2.8% of the site. Area D is directly north and across First Street from the historic Church of the Holy Family. Although the east edge of Area D adjoins the west edge of Area E, the separation of these two was based on an observed difference in the number of nineteenth- and twentieth-century artifacts, with Area E containing an abundance of later materials.

After plowing, several large blocks of cut limestone were noted on the surface within Area D suggesting structural remains. An abundance of other uncollected materials, such as limestone and brick rubble, and cinders was also observed. Area D is located within the band of dark soils along First Street as indicated on the aerial photographs.

With the notable exception of French faience, Area D had a light scatter of eighteenth- and early nineteenth-century artifacts, particularly coarse earthenwares, creamware, dark green bottle glass, and kaolin pipes. An abundance of all types of nails, flat glass, hardware, and building rubble suggests the presence of structural remains. There was a paucity of mid- to late-nineteenth-century and early-twentieth-century ceramics in Area D.

Eighteenth-century documentary evidence does not identify structures within Area D. The 1766 map shows Area D as a large, unoccupied area within the village. The WPA map from 1790 to 1826 also documents Area D as unoccupied, although it is now represented as a village lot. The 1841 lithograph, although questionable as discussed previously, shows a two-story house in the relative vicinity of Area D. This structure may have been present as early as 1809 when it was owned by F. Bouthellier. This could account for the presence of late eighteenth- and early nineteenth-century artifacts. The 1872 plat map has Area D in Lot 12 within a larger tract including Lots 1, 2, and 11, owned by J. R. Trottier, although it is not known what existed on the property. The 1927 photograph clearly shows two outbuildings, probably sheds, as part of a structural complex associated with the two houses in Lot 11.

Area E encompasses the southeast corner of the site within Lot 11 (see Figure 17). It is approximately rectangular in shape, measuring 25 m north-south by 50 m east-west. Area E represents a total of 1,075 square meters or 7.5% of the site. As noted above, Area E is adjoined to Area D but differs in the overwhelming abundance of later materials. Area E, although the second largest of the six defined areas, contained the highest density of surface artifacts, particularly nineteenth- and early-twentieth-century materials. Depressions were noted when mapping the area, and after plowing the site, two limestone foundations were identified (Figures 13 and 14). An abundance of limestone and brick rubble, and cinders was scattered throughout Area E, but these materials were not collected. Aerial photography reveals dark soils within Area E.

Eighteenth- and early-nineteenth-century materials, such as faience, coarse earthenwares, creamware, and pearlware were uncommon. The predominant ceramic types in Area E were later nineteenth- and twentieth-century decorated and undecorated whitewares with a total of 572 sherds or 44.2% of this ceramic assemblage. Area D also had an abundance of dark green bottle glass, blue-green bottle glass, and kaolin pipes, artifact types that may date to the eighteenth and/or nineteenth century. Faunal remains and all types of building materials including nails, flat glass, and hardware were also densely concentrated in Area E.

The 1766 map and the reconstructed WPA map from 1790 to 1826 indicate that Area E was vacant. WPA researchers recorded that Lots 1, 2, 11, and 12 were owned by Bouthellier in 1809. A house was reported within the property, although the exact location is unknown. The 1841 lithograph suggests that a two-story residential structure may be within the vicinity of Area E, which could represent the structure owned by Bouthellier in 1809. The 1872 plat map identifies Lots 1, 2, 11, and 12 as owned by J. R. Trottier. In the 1927 aerial photograph, two houses are seen in Area E: a two-story frame building and a one-story French colonial style house with a gallery on all four sides.

As discussed previously (see description of 1927 photograph) the former structure is similar to that illustrated by Wild in 1841. The latter structure of French colonial style, may date as early as 1855. A photograph made from an ambrotype dated between 1855 and 1865 shows a portion of a structure similar to that in the 1927 photograph in front of the Jarrot Mansion (Hess et al. 1982:186–187). The two residential structures and associated outbuildings in Areas D and E were demolished in the 1930s. The remains of most of the two-story structure are probably within the Wedge and probably extend underneath the drainage ditch for First Street. Most of the remains of the French colonial style house now lie underneath or may have been destroyed by the expansion of First and Locust streets.

Area F is located on the east edge of the site, adjacent to Locust Street within Lot 2 (see Figure 17). It is a rectangular area, measuring 20 m north-south by 25 m east-west, representing a total area of 500 square meters or 3.5% of the site. Although artifacts from all cultural periods were present within Area F, there was a notable abundance of late nineteenth- and early twentieth-century materials. After plowing, a light scatter of limestone and brick rubble was observed but not collected. Also noted on the surface was a relatively small, circular depression, which may indicate the presence of a cistern, well, or other type of feature. Aerial photography indicated that relatively dark soils are present along the east edge of the site including Area F.

Compared to the other identified residential areas, Areas A and E, Area F is relatively small in size. Area F contained a light scatter of artifacts dating to the eighteenth century. However, nineteenth- and early twentieth-century artifacts were predominant, particularly later ceramics and round nails. Other artifact types abundant in Area F were blue-green glass, unidentified nails, and flat glass. A light concentration of lithics and historic Indian artifacts, including two triangular points and one copper tinkler, was within Area F and may identify a possible protohistoric/historic Indian activity area similar to Area C. Additional evidence for a protohistoric/historic occupation may have been masked by the dense concentration of artifacts of the nineteenth- and twentieth-century occupation.

The 1766 map shows Area F within a large, vacant area of the village. In 1783, Lots 1, 2, 11, and 12 were owned by Pierre Lize, Thomas Brady, and Dutrimble, although no further information is available. The WPA map shows Lot 2 as vacant and owned by L. Pinconneau in 1801. In 1809, Lots 1, 2, 11, and 12 were owned by F. Bouthellier, and in 1872, the same properties were owned by J. R. Trottier. Documentary evidence for structures in Area F is seen only on the 1927 aerial photograph. A small, rectangular, wood frame house faces Locust Street; the street appears for the first time on the 1872 plat map. Based on the artifact types, the structure probably was constructed in the latter half of the nineteenth century. This structure was demolished in the 1930s.

Discussion of Miscellaneous Artifact Distributions

The prehistoric or possible protohistoric components at the Cahokia Wedge site can only be identified by the presence of four limestone- or shell-tempered body sherds from the surface collection, three of which were located on the southwest corner of the site, in and around Area A. The few pieces of modified rock, hematite ($n=4$), limestone ($n=1$), sandstone ($n=1$), and catlinite ($n=1$), which cannot be temporally placed, were located in three areas of the site; however, an adequate interpretation of cultural affiliation cannot be made.

One hundred twenty-one lithics were recovered in the controlled surface collection (Figure 28). With the exception of five small triangular points, which are interpreted as dating to the protohistoric/historic Indian period, the remaining lithics cannot be temporally placed. However, the three lithic concentrations associated with triangular points and historic trade goods (Figure 29), such as glass beads, are noteworthy. The spatial distribution of lithics occurs primarily on the higher elevations at the site, on the ridge above Dead Creek.

One of the more abundant materials collected from the surface was faunal remains (Figure 27), with a total of 2,417 specimens. Although dense concentrations were identified within Areas A, B, E, and F, faunal remains were also widely scattered across the site, indicating disposal of animal bones in both habitational and non-habitational areas. Several isolated collection units with large amounts of faunal remains may represent activity areas and/or the presence of subsurface remains, possibly refuse pits.

SUMMARY AND CONCLUSIONS

The prehistoric or protohistoric/historic Indian period at the Cahokia Wedge site appears to be minimal, and interpretations based only on surface collection data are inadequate. One concentration, Area C, may be interpreted as dating to the protohistoric/historic Indian period; this concentration of culturally specific artifacts may indicate the presence of subsurface remains. Two other lighter concentrations of these types of materials were recorded in Areas E and F. Further evidence for earlier occupations may have been concealed by the density of later historic materials.

Historical research and the controlled surface collection data have defined three Euro-American habitational areas (Areas A, E, and F identified as houses) and two areas with specialized functions (Area B as a barn and Area D as outbuildings or sheds).

Documentary and archaeological evidence indicates that the major habitational areas, Areas A, E, and F, occur along the south and east edges of the site adjacent to present day streets that originated in the eighteenth and nineteenth centuries. The central portion of the Wedge, as interpreted from these sources, encompasses the non-habitational areas, such as yards, orchards, gardens, etc. of the individual house lots. Within these non-habitational areas, several small concentrations of surface materials, such as faunal remains, may suggest the presence of subsurface features, possibly the remains of outbuildings, refuse pits, or other types of cultural features or activity areas.

The historic habitational areas contained abundant ceramics and all types of building materials including nails, hardware, and flat glass. Artifacts which also had dense concentrations within the habitational areas, as well as lighter densities across the site in non-habitational areas, include kaolin pipes, the ordnance group, faunal remains, unidentified and other metal artifacts, and bottle glass. There was no one type of artifact or artifact group that was found primarily outside of the six defined areas.

Correlations of the controlled surface collection data with historical documentation indicate that Areas A and B (Lot 13) were occupied from as early as 1766, when the property was owned by Etienne Nicolle, to at least 1809 when it was owned by Jean Meunier. Comparisons of the distributions of the eighteenth-century artifacts with the later nineteenth- and twentieth-century materials indicate a shift of habitational areas from Area A (Lot 13) to the southeast corner, Area E (Lot 11) and the east side of the site, Area F (Lot 2). This is documented by the 1766 Hutchins map, the WPA reconstructed map from 1790 to 1826, and the 1927 aerial photograph.

In conclusion, the identification of Areas A and B as representing cultural remains dating to the eighteenth-century French village fulfilled the primary purpose of the initial archaeological investigations at the Cahokia Wedge site. It is important to underscore that the identification of numerous eighteenth-century artifacts recovered merely from the surface of the site indicates the archaeological significance of the Cahokia Wedge.

CHAPTER 3:
ARCHAEOLOGICAL TEST EXCAVATIONS

Test Excavation Methodology

The purpose of the test excavations was to determine the presence and condition of subsurface archaeological deposits and to assess the potential significance of cultural remains relating to the eighteenth-century village. The southwest corner was chosen for three reasons: (1) surface collection artifact distribution maps indicated a relatively high density of eighteenth-century materials in this area; (2) this location was within the IDOT R.O.W. of First Street; and (3) because First Street is a side street which has probably has not been extensively altered during construction activities in comparison with Route 3. The test excavations were located within and along the southern edge of the Area A concentration as defined by the controlled surface collection analysis.

Test excavations were funded by the Illinois Department of Transportation (IDOT). Concurrent archaeological investigations (Walitschek 1986), also funded by IDOT, were conducted on the west edge of the Cahokia Wedge site during construction work within the R.O.W. of Illinois Route 3. These investigations revealed that this portion of the Wedge was disturbed by construction activities in the realignment of Route 3, a major thoroughfare through the Village of Cahokia. Concerned interest on the part of IDOT, with the support of Dr. John A. Walthall, Chief Archaeologist, led to test excavations within the R.O.W. of former Illinois Route 157 or First Street, on the southwest corner of the Wedge.

Utilizing the permanent grid system that was emplaced for the controlled surface collection, an east-west oriented trench was excavated with a backhoe (Figure 31; Plates 6 and 7). The initial test excavation trench was 2 m in width (N98 to N100) and ca. 45 m in length (E105 to E150). In two areas, the excavation trench was extended 2 m further to the south to expose larger portions of defined features. Plowzone and midden soils were removed by the backhoe to the level at which cultural

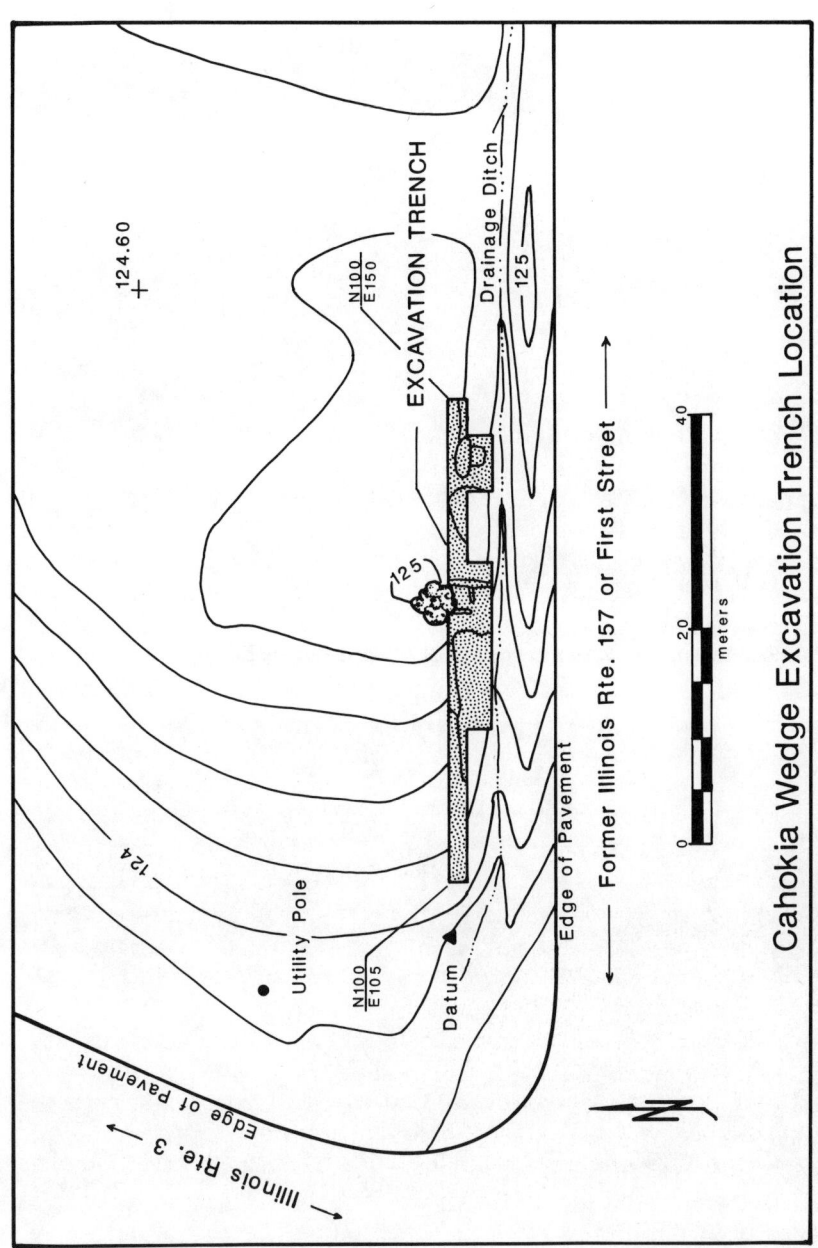

Fig. 31. Location of test excavation trench on the southwest corner of the site

Plate 6. View of excavation trench west toward Illinois Route 3

Plate 7. View of excavation trench to the east. Test trench through Features 5 and 6 shown in foreground and excavated Feature 7 wall trench shown in background

features were defined. Generally, this occurred within the sterile sand. Using the established grid, the soil removed by machine excavation was screened (1/2") and bagged separately according to the respective 5-by-2 m unit coordinates.

After the completion of feature excavations, the north balk profile wall was troweled, photographed, and mapped. Black plastic tarp was then laid on the bottom of the excavation trench and the soils from the excavation units were screened back into the trench. The use of heavy equipment completed the backfilling process and restored the excavation area to its original ground contours.

Feature Excavation Methodology

The excavation of cultural features entailed several methods, based on various factors, including time restrictions and the size and location of the features. Features were defined in three different contexts: (1) completely within the test excavation trench; (2) partially within the test excavation trench; and (3) in profile within the north balk wall of the test excavation trench.

Thirteen feature numbers were assigned to 12 cultural features (Figure 32). Feature types included pits (n = 4), eighteenth-century wall trenches (n = 3), a nineteenth-century structural foundation basin (n = 1; assigned 2 feature numbers), limestone concentrations (n = 2); and unidentified features (n = 2). Cultural periods represented by these features included eighteenth-century French colonial and nineteenth-century American.

Feature excavation and recording methods included the following:

- Features located completely within the excavation trench were completely excavated (Feature 1).
- If only a portion of feature was located within the excavation trench, only this portion was completely excavated (Features 7 and 8).
- Large features partially located within the excavation trench were sampled with a test trench (Features 4, 5, and 6)
- Features defined in plan view within the excavation trench, recorded but not excavated (Features 2, 3, and 10).
- Features defined in profile in the north balk wall of the excavation trench were recorded, but not excavated (Features 9, 11, 12, and 13).

Specifically, feature excavation included mapping in plan view; length and/or width profile cuts which were mapped and photographed;

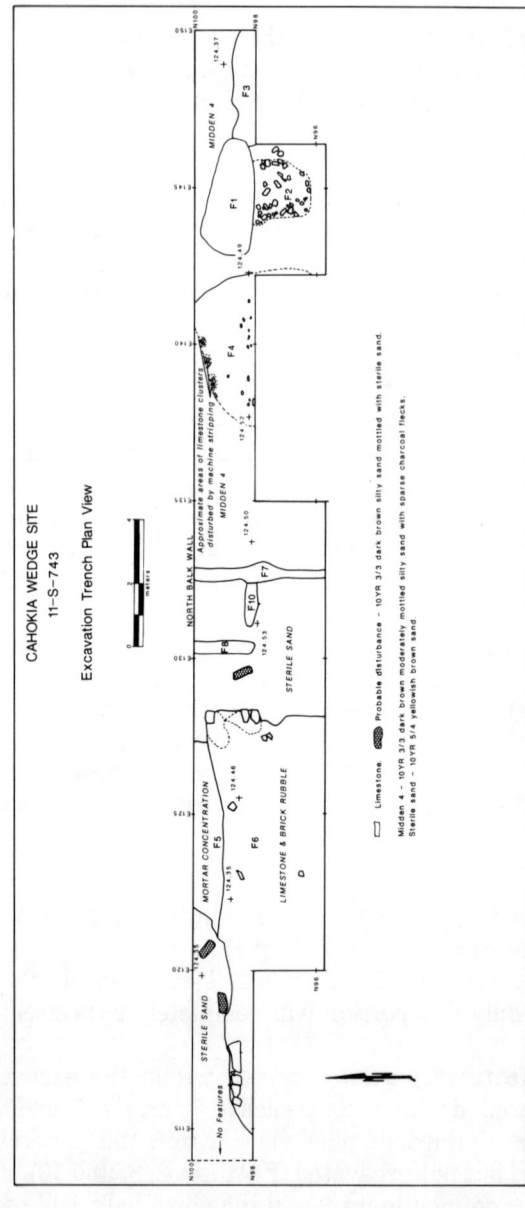

Fig. 32. Plan view map of excavation trench

1/2" screening of removed feature fill; and, when appropriate the collection of other samples, such as flotation, soil, and Carbon-14.

Stratigraphy

Prior to the description of features, a discussion of the soil stratigraphy in the test excavation trench will provide an understanding of the feature contexts. The complete length of the north balk wall was troweled and mapped (Figure 33). The north balk wall (N100) extended from E105.4 to E150.2, a total length of 44.8 m. The exposed soil profile ranged in depth from 0.27 m below ground surface at the western end of the trench to 1.24 m below surface in the area of Feature 8 excavation. The depth of the eastern portion of the excavation trench generally ranged from 0.55 m to 0.65 m below surface.

Viewing the profile from west to east, the westernmost 15 m, which is on a gentle slope, exhibits a plowzone/sod level and a leached zone on top of sterile sand. With the exception of an isolated, thin lens of cultural debris (K in Figure 33), the area is devoid of midden accumulation and cultural features. The remainder of the trench profile is characterized by complex stratigraphy and abundant features.

The small segment of the profile bracketed by the dense concentrations of Features 7, 8, 9, 12, and 13 and the Feature 5 structural remains has two midden levels, identified as Middens 1A and 2A. These midden soils are lighter in color, and cultural debris was less abundant when compared to the dense midden area to the east.

The dense midden area is located predominantly to the east of the feature concentration (Features 7, 8, 9, 12, and 13) in the soil profile. This midden area is on the highest elevation of the ridge crest. Middens 1 through 4 were identified by differences in soil color and the amounts of wood charcoal and cultural debris. Midden 4, the earliest deposit representing the eighteenth-century occupation, rests on sterile sand. Features 1, 2, 3, and 11 were defined within Midden 4. Midden 3 is a discontinuous, thin lens that lies on top of Midden 4. Midden 2 is a relatively thick, homogeneous zone that overlies the eighteenth-century Nicolle/Meunier structure (Features 7, 8, and 10) and probably dates to the nineteenth century. Finally, Midden 1, the latest deposit, is a thin zone that contains abundant limestone and recent cultural materials. Above Midden 1 is a relict plowzone and sod level.

The eastern portion of the excavation trench was not stripped completely to sterile sand due to the presence of features located within Midden 4. At various intervals along the profile in this midden area, test trenches measuring 35 cm to 40 cm in width were excavated to ex-

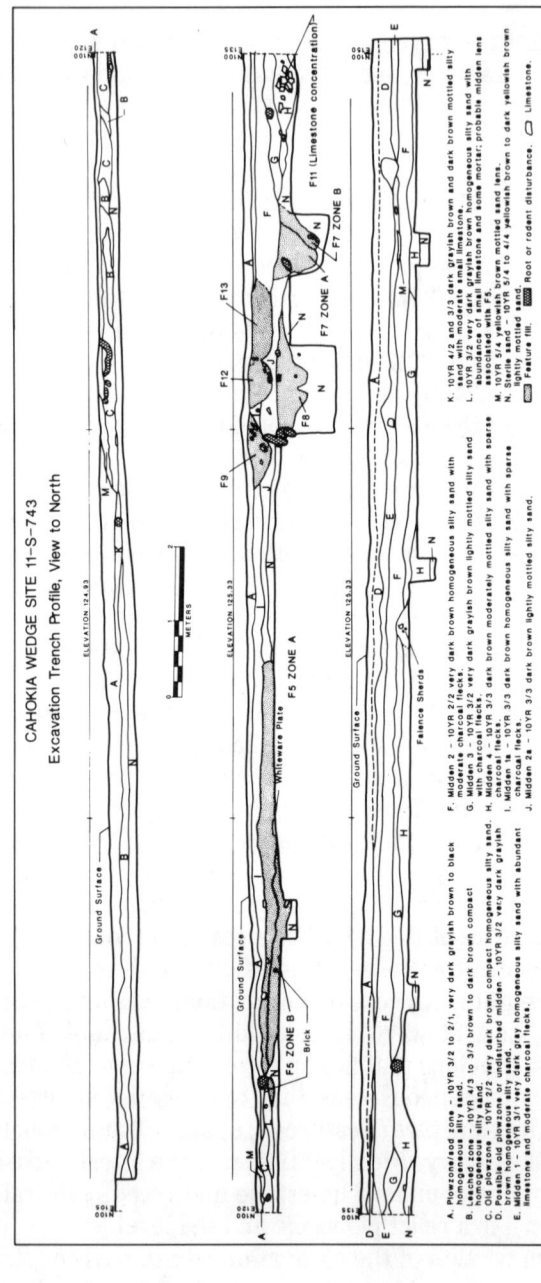

Fig. 33. Profile map of north balk wall of excavation trench

tend the soil profile into sterile sand. Three pit features, Features 9, 12, and 13, and a limestone concentration, Feature 11, were defined in the north balk profile wall. These features were not noted during machine excavation of the trench. Features 5, 7, and 8, which were defined and excavated within the trench, were also shown in the north balk wall profile.

Based on various factors including topography, soil stratigraphy within the trench, and surface artifact distribution maps, it is probable that midden deposits occur along the length of the south edge of the site, parallel to First Street, which originated to the eighteenth-century village.

Feature Descriptions

Feature descriptions will be presented in terms of association, feature type, and/or chronology. Diagnostics and other artifacts are listed with the feature descriptions to provide information regarding temporal and functional interpretations. A complete listing of artifact counts and weights from all features is presented in Appendix A. Analyses of faunal and botanical remains are presented in Chapters 5 and 6, respectively.

Features 7, 8, and 10 (Figure 34) are the three wall trench features representing a portion of an eighteenth-century French colonial *poteaux-en-terre* (posts in the earth) structure. This typical style of French colonial construction consisted of large, upright posts set into an excavated trench, with the crevices between the posts filled in with *boussilage*, a limestone mortar mixed with grasses. The wall trench features were defined at approximately the same elevation and were clustered in an area measuring approximately 2.5 m by 4.0 m. The configuration of the wall trenches in relation to each other suggests that the features represent separate elements of one structure. These features will be described individually and then discussed and interpreted as one structural feature.

Based on documentary evidence, this structure is interpreted as the domestic dwelling first identified on the 1766 Hutchins map as belonging to Etienne Nicolle. A chain of ownership of this structure has been identified through 1809, but by 1841 the structure was apparently gone.

Feature 7 (Figure 35; Plate 8), a linear wall trench oriented north-south, was defined at the bottom of the excavation trench at an elevation of 124.67 m. Feature 7 was the midsection portion of a wall trench, which extended between the north and south balk walls of the excavation trench for a maximum exposed length of 4.30 m. The actual length

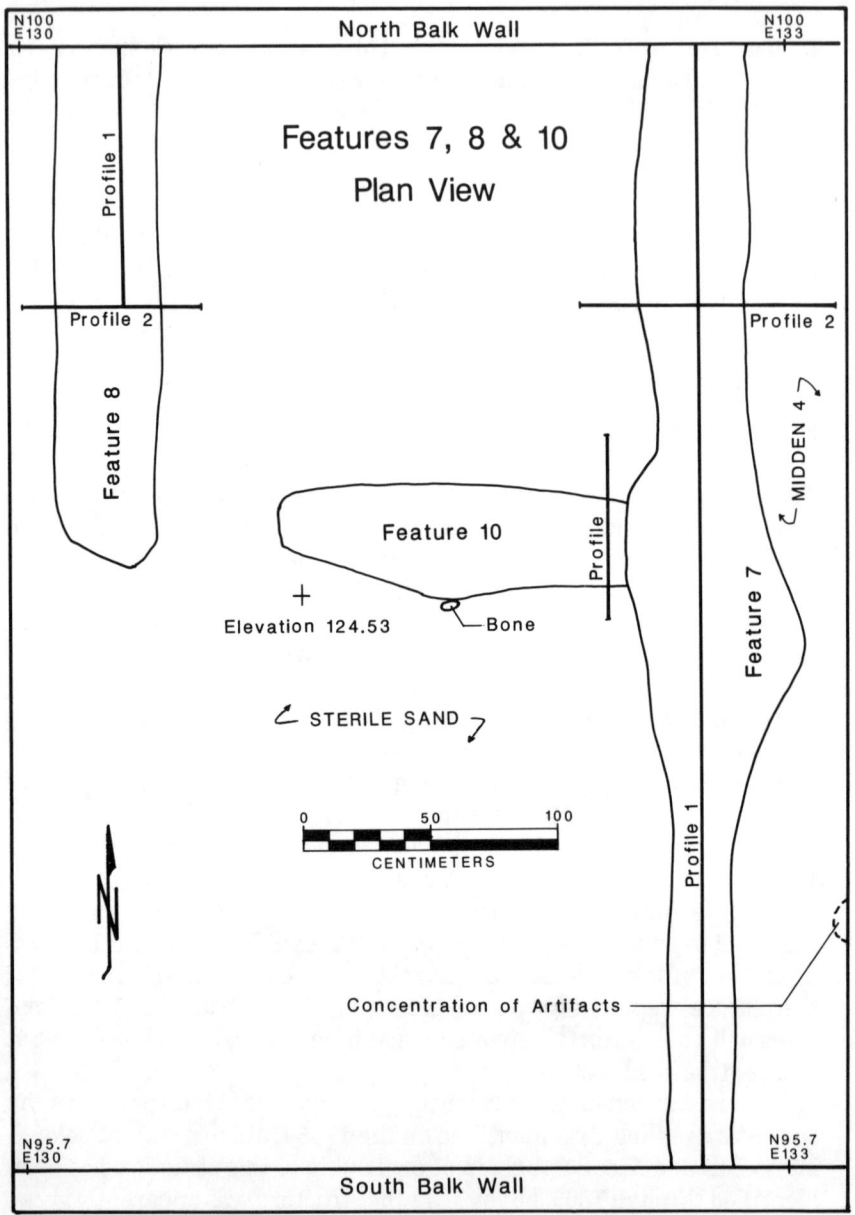

Fig. 34. Plan view map of Features 7, 8, and 10 wall trenches

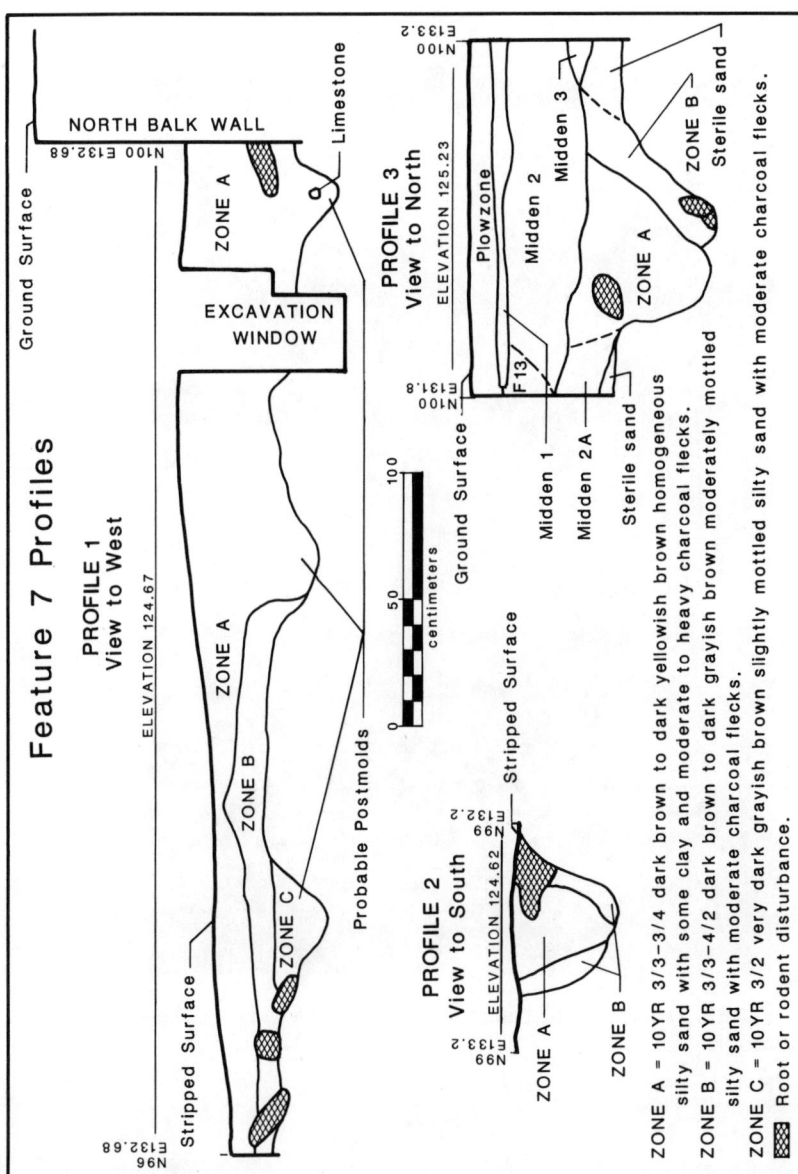

Fig. 35. Profile maps of Feature 7 wall trench

Plate 8. Feature 7 wall trench excavation shown in north balk profile

of the feature was indeterminate, and the north and south ends of the wall trench, indicating the probable corners of the structure, were not within the excavation trench.

In plan view, the width of Feature 7 varied from 44 cm at the north balk wall, to 60 cm in the midsection, which appeared to be disturbed, to 25 cm at the south balk wall. The southernmost portion of the wall trench was at a lower elevation due to an existing east-west drainage ditch, which runs parallel to First Street and probably removed the top 10–20 cm of Feature 7. The width of the wall trench at this area appeared thinner, because a lower level of the wall trench had been exposed; the top few centimeters of feature fill were inadvertently stripped away during machine excavation and shovel scraping in an attempt to define the feature.

In the lengthwise cross-section profile of Feature 7, the base of the wall trench was irregular (Figure 35; Profile 1). Three rounded protrusions, spaced at regular intervals, extended from the base of the wall trench into the sterile sand. These appeared to be postmolds indicating the positions of the main structural upright posts.

In a width cross-section profile (Figure 35; Profile 2) within the excavation trench, Feature 7 had inward sloping walls and a rounded base, with two soil zones. Zone A, located centrally within the profile, consisted of dark brown to dark yellowish brown (10YR 3/3–3/4) silty sand mottled with clay and abundant charcoal flecks. Zone B, located along the eastern and western edges of the wall trench, was dark grayish brown (10YR 4/2) silty sand. Rodent disturbances occurred along the western edge of the wall trench. Zone B may represent packing of the wall trench after the posts were emplaced. Maximum depth at this cross-section profile was 40 cm, and the maximum width was approximately 46 cm.

Another width cross-section profile view (Figure 35; Profile 3) was exposed in the north balk wall of the excavation trench after complete excavation of the feature fill. Feature 7 originated at 34 cm below the present ground surface at an elevation of 125.10 m. Feature 7 extended below Midden 2 and was intrusive into Midden 2A and extended into the sterile sand. This profile showed a poorly defined dispersed area of feature fill, with a maximum width of approximately 1.0 m, above the actual wall trench. The base of the wall trench appeared as a double rounded bottom; this may have been caused by heavy root disturbances from a large tree immediately north of the excavation trench. Zone A consisted of the western side of the wall trench, and Zone B was a 20 cm lens along the eastern edge of the feature. Maximum depth of Feature 7 was 46 cm.

Most of the diagnostic artifacts from Feature 7 fit into an eighteenth-century context. Artifacts collected were: three dark green bottle glass fragments, which include one kick-up; four blue-green bottle glass fragments; one kaolin pipe stem with a hole measuring 5/64 inch; catlinite; galena; and animal bone, including one fragment stained green by metal salts. The ceramic assemblage is comprised of 16 faience sherds, six coarse earthenware sherds, 10 creamware sherds, and four whiteware sherds. Metal artifacts include one triangular iron padlock with brass plating, 12 pieces of cut sheet copper, and one square iron ring. Building materials include rosehead and square nails, flat glass, and limestone rocks.

Feature 8 (Figure 36; Plate 9) was a portion of a linear wall trench, defined in plan view in the bottom of the excavation trench at an elevation of 124.51 m. The wall trench was oriented north-south and extended into the north balk wall. The exposed portion of Feature 8 measured 2 m in length from the north balk wall to the south end of the wall trench. The maximum east-west width of Feature 8, as seen in plan view, was 43 cm. After excavation of the feature fill, the Feature 8 profile in the north balk wall appeared to be wider, including a dispersed area of fill above the actual wall trench. In this profile (Figure 36; Profile 3), Feature 8 appeared to originate at 43 cm below the present ground surface at an elevation of 124.63 m. It was excavated into sterile sand, like Feature 7, and was overlain by Midden 2A. In this profile, the feature appeared to separate into two wall trenches, which was not noted in the original profile cut. These separate trenches may indicate rebuilding. The maximum depth of Feature 8 was 40 cm. In a cross-section length profile of Feature 8 (Figure 36; Profile 1), the fill consisted of three soil zones, Zones A, B, and C, which were interspersed within the wall trench. Zone A was a dark grayish brown to olive brown fine sandy loam (2.5Y 4/2–4/4) mottled with light brownish gray sand (2.5Y 6/2). Zone B was a very dark grayish brown to dark grayish brown mottled with a more compact sandy loam (2.5Y 3/2-4/2). Charcoal flecks were sparsely distributed throughout the feature fill and artifact density was higher within Zone A. Zone C was an olive brown and light grayish mottled sand (2.5Y 4/4–6/2) and appeared to be sterile fill. Zone C was located predominantly at the base of the wall trench, and it was difficult to distinguish between the Zone C fill and the sterile sand.

Feature 8 artifacts include one dark green bottle glass fragment, one iron clasp knife blade, four creamware sherds, and three decorated whiteware sherds, including blue shell edge and handpainted sherds.

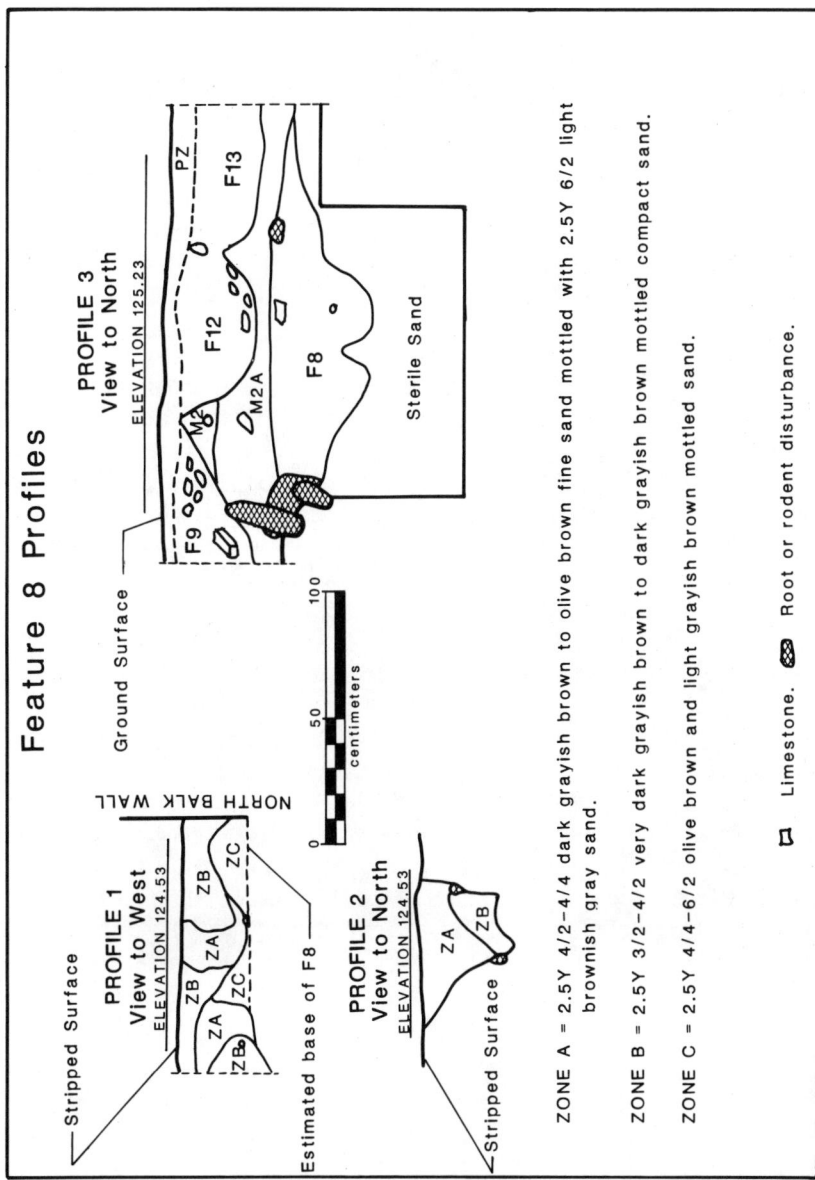

Fig. 36. Profile maps of Feature 8 wall trench

Plate 9. Feature 8 wall trench lengthwise profile

Building materials include one square nail, limestone rock, mortar, and brick.

Feature 10. The Feature 10 wall trench (Figure 37) was defined at the base of the excavation trench within sterile sand at an elevation of 124.51 m. Feature 10 appeared to be a short wall trench, measuring 1.38 m in length. Feature 10 was oriented east-west and at right angles to both Features 7 and 8. The eastern edge of Feature 10 was superimposed by Feature 7, which had slightly darker fill. The west end of Feature 10 was at a right angle to the south end of Feature 8, creating a corner of one structural element, possibly a gallery or addition to the main structure. There was a sterile gap of 50 cm between the ends of Features 8 and 10.

Feature 10 was not excavated; however, after the removal of Feature 7 fill, a profile cut was made into Feature 10, approximately 10 cm west of the overlapping junction of the two features. In cross-section, Feature 10 appeared to have fairly vertical to slightly sloping walls, with an irregular but rounded base. Feature 10 fill consisted of one zone of fairly homogeneous, brown (10YR 4/3) silty sand with a few pieces of limestone rock, sparse charcoal flecks, and several rodent disturbances. No diagnostic artifacts were noted within the profile cut or on the surface of Feature 10.

Discussion of Features 7, 8, and 10. Features 7, 8, and 10 are interpreted as wall trenches of an eighteenth-century French colonial structure of *poteaux-en-terre* construction. The structure was presumably occupied by Etienne Nicolle as early as 1766. In 1809, the house was occupied by Jean Meunier. Feature 7 is interpreted as the main wall for the structure because of its greater depth and relationship to Features 8 and 10, which constitute an adjoining structural element, such as a lean-to or gallery. This structural addition extended 1.9 m from the main wall. Features 8 and 10 were shallower than Feature 7, which supports the interpretation of these wall trenches as less substantial structural elements. If the interpretation of these features is correct, the structure should be rectangular in shape (like other French colonial domestic structures) with the long axis oriented east-west facing First Street.

Structural additions such as galleries or lean-tos were common for French colonial style domestic dwellings. For example, a similar lean-to was identified during the excavation of a mid- to late-eighteenth-century *poteaux-en-terre* structure at the Krelich site near the Saline Creek, south of St. Genevieve, Missouri (Michael Trimble, personal communication, 1987). The WPA excavation of the foundation of the Cahokia Courthouse revealed the original structure to have been

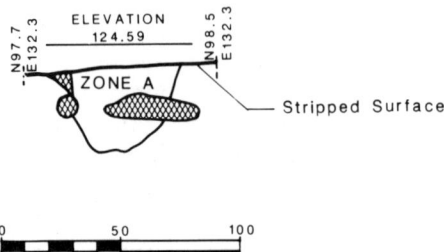

Fig. 37. Profile map of Feature 10 wall trench

constructed of a combination of *poteaux-en-terre* and *poteaux-sur-solle* (posts on sill) (Report on file at Cahokia Courthouse State Historic Site). A smaller rectangular wall trench structural element, 16 feet (4.87 m) in length, extended off the main foundation. This extension is a similar construction form to that defined by Features 8 and 10 in relation to Feature 7.

No other wall trench features were defined within the excavation trench that would indicate the opposite north-south wall of the Nicolle structure. The opposite wall for Feature 7 should be located to the east, based on the interpretation of Features 8 and 10 as an addition attached to the exterior of the main wall, Feature 7. French colonial domestic structures at other sites in the area are quite variable in size, measuring from 10 to 66 feet (3.0 m to 20.1 m) length or width, with an average of 22 by 35 feet (6.7 m by 10.8 m) (Peterson 1941, 1965; Porterfield 1969). Assuming that the long axis runs east-west, and in size this was an average French colonial house, the opposite wall trench should be located near Features 1 and 2. As discussed below, Feature 2 may represent the limestone chimney/fireplace for this structure and might therefore delimit the opposite side of this structure. It is possible that the wall trench is preserved underneath Midden 4, since this area to the east was not stripped to sterile sand due to the presence of features.

If this interpretation of the structure orientation is correct, then Feature 4, possibly Features 1 and 2, and Middens 3 and 4, may predate the construction of the house; these features and middens would have been located under the dwelling. Although considered unlikely, Middens 3 and 4 could be the result of construction activities.

Early descriptions of other French colonial style houses within Cahokia give a general idea of the appearance of the Nicolle/Meunier structure. John Reynolds (1852:50–51), who lived at Cahokia in the early 1800s, wrote that the French houses;

> ... were generally one story high, and made of wood.... These houses were formed of large posts or timbers; the posts being three or four feet apart in many of them. In others the posts were closer together, and the intervals filled up with mortar, made of common clay and cut straw ... Over the whole wall, outside and inside, it was generally white washed with fine white lime, so that these houses presented a clean, neat appearance ...
> Some dwelling houses and the stables and barns were made of longer posts set in the ground, instead of a sill as used in other houses. These posts were of cedar or other

durable wood. The small houses attached to the residences were generally set with posts in the ground. The covering of the houses, stables &c.,was generally of straw or long grass cut in the prairie. These thatched roofs looked well, and lasted longer than shingles. They were made steep and neat. All the houses, almost, had galleries all around them. The posts of the gallery were generally of cedar or mulberry. The floors of the galleries, as well as the floors of the houses, were made of puncheons, as sawed boards were scarce . . . .

The Nicolle/Meunier Structure. The *poteaux-en-terre* structural remains are interpreted as the house of Etienne Nicolle (Nicolt) identified on the 1766 map of Cahokia (Norris 1984). The structure, if originally constructed by Etienne Nicolle, would have to date after 1758 and before 1766, since marriage records show he was a resident of Kaskaskia in 1758 (Belting 1948:84). Ownership of this structure has been traced up to at least 1809 when it was owned by Jean Meunier. Based on the interpretation of the J. C. Wild lithograph of Cahokia, this structure was no longer present in 1841. The succession of identified owners is as follows:

ca. 1766 to 1779	Etienne and Angelique Nicolle (Nicolt); moved from the village of Kaskaskia to Cahokia some time after 1758 (Belting 1948:84). The Nicolles were murdered by their black servants in 1779 and the property was sold at auction (Alvord 1907:12–21).
1782 to 1786–87	Antoine Harmand (Sansfacon); property sold at auction (Alvord 1907:243).
1783 (?)	Greater Comsal (?) American State Papers, Public Lands (Lowrie and Franklin, eds., 1834:195). 1787 Francois Lefevre (Courier); died 1787 (Donnelly 1949:260).
1787? to 1793	Frederick Grater; property sold at auction.
1794 to 1809+	Jean Baptiste Meunier (Munier); a records search in the Illinois State Archives and the St. Clair County Archives failed to locate any notice of sale by Meunier after 1809.
ca. 1841	Structure no longer exists, based on J. C. Wild lithograph.

Documentation of the personal history of the inhabitants of Cahokia is uncommon. However, at least two events are documented in historical records to have occurred in the house during the Nicolle and Meunier occupations. In the winter of 1778–1779, several murders by poisoning of black slaves and "several of the good subjects of this Republic and soldiers of the garrison" were recorded, including the deaths of Etienne and Angelique Nicolle, presumably in their home (Alvord 1907:12–21). Two black slaves, Manuel and Moreau, were identified as the murderers. Their first victim was a Negro belonging to Marie Laurent of St. Louis, reportedly murdered because of jealousy over a Negro named Janette belonging to Mr. Martin of Cahokia. One witness, a Negro named Sasa, reported that Manuel had given the same Janette "a horn in which there was boiling blood . . . to put her master and mistress to death" (Alvord 1907:15). This murder attempt was interrupted when a Negro named Guanga, belonging to the Martins, found out about the plot and forced Manuel and Moreau "to dig up a poison which they had buried under the threshold of the door" (Alvord 1907:15). Etienne and Angelique Nicolle were not so fortunate. Moreau was accused of giving "medicine" to Angelique's female servant to make her mistress more gentle; poison was also given to the servant's husband for his master. After the murder of the Nicolles, the slaves denied knowing that it was poison and the female servant refused to grant Moreau the favor she had promised him, stating that "he was too old and she did not want to" (Alvord 1907:19). Soon after, she and her husband were also poisoned; their deaths may also have occurred in the Nicolle house. Manuel and Moreau were tried at Kaskaskia and sentenced to be hanged in June of 1779, ending a bizarre episode in Cahokia's history.

The second event, of a less sensational nature, took place during the Meunier occupation. On January 20, 1808, a meeting was held at the Meunier house to set up fencing regulations for the common fields (Boylan 1949:178-181). The resulting document appears to have been signed by 53 individuals, which probably represents most of the men of the village.

Features 1 and 2 are possibly associated features, which were identified within Midden 4 and date to the eighteenth century. Feature 1 was a pit feature composed of two zones and Feature 2 was a concentration of limestone rocks. Dense charcoal fragments were noted within and around both features.

Feature 2 (Figure 38; Plate 10), a cluster of limestone rocks, formed an irregular, rectangular feature measuring 2.5 m east-west by 1.8 m north-south. Feature 2 was defined by the presence of approximately

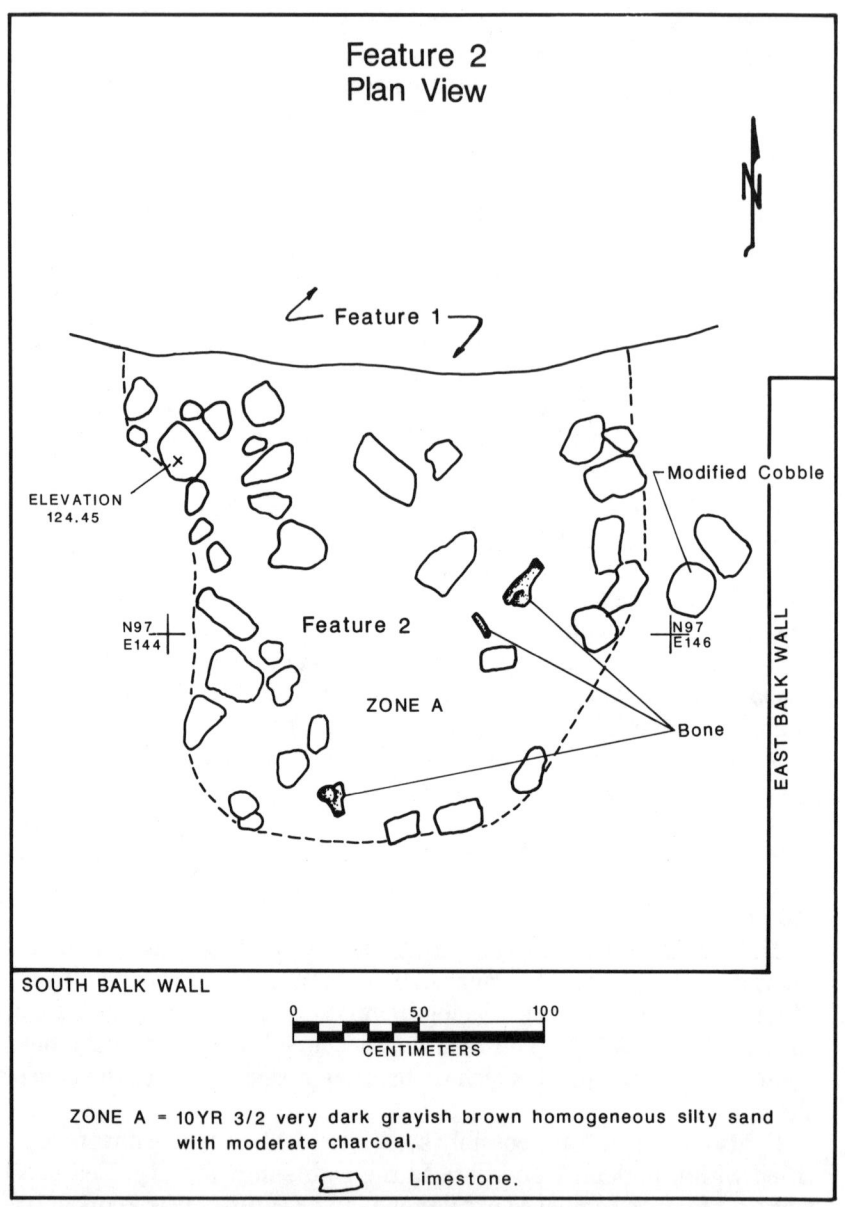

Fig. 38. Plan view map of Feature 2 limestone concentration

Plate 10. Mapping of Feature 2 limestone concentration

30 pieces of limestone of various sizes ranging from 5 cm to 20 cm. The limestone rocks were distributed in a rough configuration suggesting a foundation. Feature 2 extended off the south edge of Feature 1, at an elevation of 124.45 m. The profile shape is unknown, because it was not excavated; a soil probe in the center of the limestone concentration indicated approximately 5 cm of fill remaining before sterile sand was encountered.

No distinct soil differences were noted between Feature 2 and the surrounding Midden 4. Feature 2 fill consisted of a homogeneous, very dark gray (10YR 3/2) silty sand with a thin lens (1–2 cm) of wood charcoal located underneath the limestone. The lens of charcoal appeared to have been scattered to the west and northwest of Feature 2. The amount and size of the charcoal fragments were similar to the wood charcoal within Zone A of Feature 1.

Approximately 10 cm from the east edge of Feature 2 was a large, modified, glacial cobble and a piece of limestone, which were probably displaced from the main concentration during machine excavation. Other artifacts collected from the surface of Feature 2 include one coarse earthenware rim sherd, one dark green bottle glass fragment, one kaolin pipe stem fragment with a stem hole measuring 5/64 inch, one rectangular piece of worked catlinite, and 21 faunal remains. Metal artifacts include one iron (clasp?) knife blade fragment, one square iron spike, two rosehead nails, and one round nail. With the exception of the round nail, which is probably intrusive, diagnostic artifacts appear to date to the early- to mid-eighteenth century.

Feature 1 (Figure 39; Plate 11) was a shallow oblong pit with three distinct fill zones. Zone A overlapped a smaller oval pit containing fills designated Zones B and C. The feature first appeared as a large, dispersed area of dense wood charcoal intermixed with very dark gray (10YR 3/1) silty sand. Zone A was oblong, measuring 3.7 m east-west by 1.68 m north-south. The south edge of Feature 1 appeared to be adjoined to the Feature 2 limestone cluster. Feature 1 was one of the three features located entirely within the excavation trench; however Feature 1 was the only feature to be completely excavated.

The removal of Zone A fill, with a maximum depth of 8 cm, revealed the smaller oval pit, Zone B, located slightly off-center under Zone A. Zone B measured 1.6 m east-west by .95 m north-south. In profile, Zone A appeared as a shallow, irregular basin with very dark gray (10YR 3/1) silty sand and an abundance of wood charcoal. Zone B had inward sloping walls and a relatively flat bottom. The maximum depth was 32 cm. Zone B fill consisted of dark grayish brown (10YR 4/2) silty sand. Wood charcoal was less common within Zone B. At the base of Zone B along

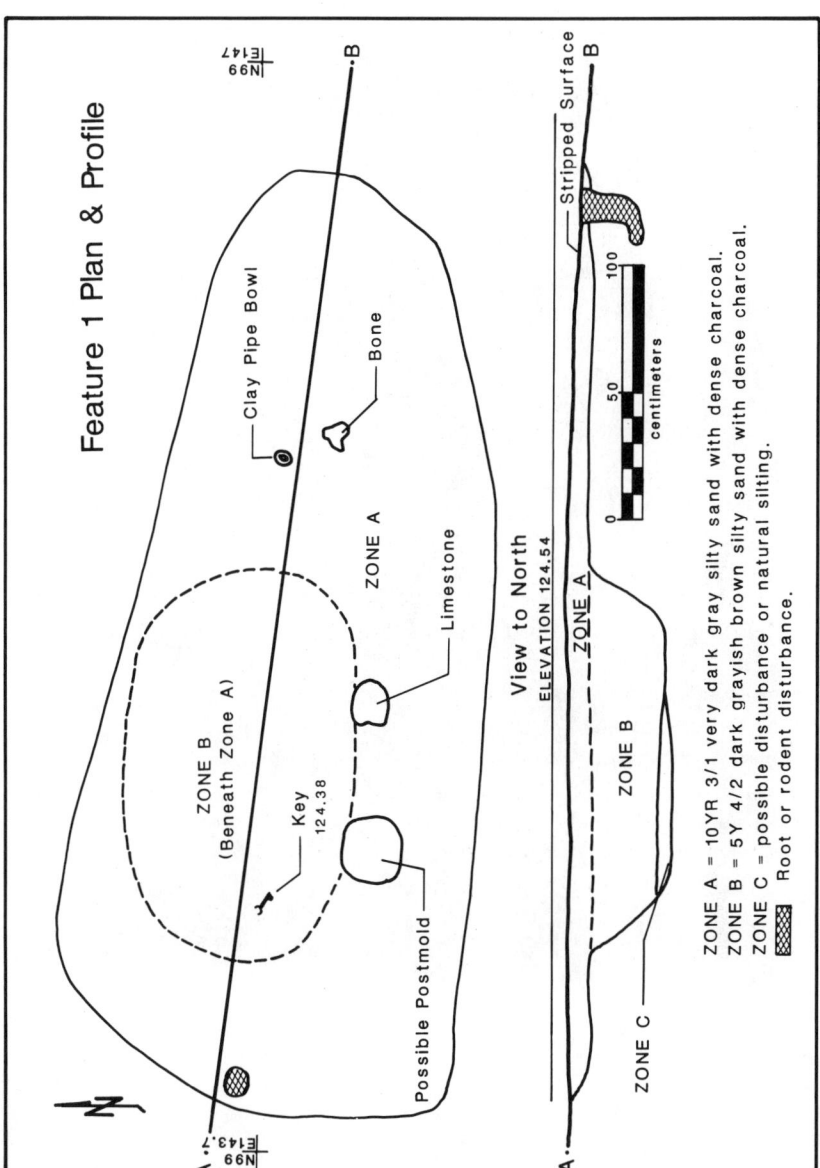

Fig. 39. Plan view and profile maps of Feature 1 pit

Plate 11. Feature 1 pit profile

the western edge of the pit was a 6 cm lens, Zone C, which contained less charcoal than Zones A and B. Zone C may have been a natural zone or disturbance.

Artifacts collected from Zone A include one triangular point, one complete incised earthenware pipe bowl, one dark green glass bottle kick-up fragment, one whiteware sherd, and one molded-edged and green-banded rim sherd with gold luster. Metal artifacts include one iron (clasp?) knife blade, one thumb lock catch, one leg from a cast iron kettle, lead mold waste with sprue attachments, and one barrel hoop. The presence of the nineteenth-century whiteware sherds is problematical because other diagnostic artifacts appear to date to the early- to mid-eighteenth century. There were a few rodent/root disturbances within the feature, which may account for the presence of these two sherds.

Artifacts from Zones B and C include one white glass seed bead, one clasp knife blade, one square brass buckle, two iron buttons, one scissors fragment, one iron key, one complete file, one iron punch or spike, one frizzen and one upper jaw of the cock from a Type D flintlock gun, and a cut and perforated scrap of sheet copper. Materials recovered from all zones are rosehead and square nails, wood charcoal, faunal remains, and limestone. There is a notable absence of eighteenth-century ceramics in Feature 1. The most abundant material from both zones were faunal remains with a total of 181 fragments (including the remains of a toad which is probably intrusive). Also abundant are metal artifacts, particularly iron tools and hardware, most of which were found within Zone B. It is noteworthy that several artifacts, such as the clay pipe bowl and the file, are not broken, even though they were apparently discarded in Feature 1.

Discussion of Features 1 and 2. Given the continuous distribution of charcoal within and around Features 1 and 2, they may have been contemporaneous with possible associated functions. The zones (A and B) of Feature 1 may represent the cleaning out of the waste products of Feature 2, which is interpreted as a limestone cooking/fire facility. Zone B was an intentionally dug out pit and Zone A represents the overflow or scattered residue after Zone B was filled-in. The dispersed charcoal lens extended from the defined and excavated limits of Zone A of Feature 1 to the north and west, although the charcoal lens appeared at a lower level outside of Feature 1. Additionally, the westernmost edge of the charcoal lens intruded into the eastern half of Feature 4, which appeared to be a discrete midden area, possibly associated with Features 1 and 2.

The identification of these facilities as relating to the on-going occupation of the Nicolle/Meunier structure is problematical. The features originate within Midden 4, which appeared to be below the structure; the elevations of Features 1 and 2 are approximately 30 cm deeper than the origin of the structural wall trenches, Features 7 and 8. If the opposite wall trench of the structure is to the east of Features 1 and 2, these features would probably pre-date the structure, being located underneath the structure.

An external cooking facility is a possible interpretation of Feature 2. It may have been a small enclosed oven-type feature constructed of limestone. A relative absence of limestone on the northern edge of Feature 2 may indicate the front or opening. The location of Feature 1, refuse pit, at this possible opening suggests a close and convenient area of disposal for the waste products from Feature 2. The large size of the charcoal fragments and the absence of ashy fill suggests that high temperatures or a long-lasting fire did not characterize the burning activity. Thus, some kind of low temperature or short term burning took place in the vicinity of these features, probably within Feature 2. This tends to support a cooking or smoking function. As further confirmation, an abundance of animal bone was recovered from within Feature 1 and on the surface of Feature 2.

More speculative interpretations of Features 1 and 2 are possible. The rectangular shape and small size of the feature and the presence of large pieces of limestone may also suggest that Feature 2 is the remains of a fireplace/chimney. If this proposed chimney were attached to the side of the Feature 7 structure, it would result in this structure having a length of ca. 12 m or 36 feet, which is within the size range expected for an early French colonial home. Since a corresponding north-south wall trench for Feature 7 was not identified in the vicinity of Feature 2, a fireplace function seems unlikely. However, it should be underscored that the sterile subsurface was not reached in this location and thus the remains of this wall trench could be buried underneath Midden 4, which surrounded Feature 2.

In summary, Feature 1 appeared to be a refuse pit for the waste products of Feature 2, as well as a disposal area for other artifactual materials. Feature 2 is interpreted as a cooking/fire-related facility constructed of limestone rocks. Artifact types and their estimated time span (early to mid-eighteenth century) from both features are similar, suggesting contemporaneity and probable association. The limited view exposed in the trench excavations leaves open to speculation that larger structural remains, which could assist in interpreting these features, may not have been identified.

Feature 4 (Figures 40 and 41) was a fairly large, yet poorly defined feature located partially within the excavation trench at an elevation of 124.29 m. No discernible stain was noted, and the feature was originally defined by the presence of abundant limestone rocks and artifacts, particularly large faunal remains. Three clusters of limestone were located in a roughly northeast-southwest orientation, suggesting the northern edge of the feature. A dense charcoal area was located along the eastern edge of Feature 4. This charcoal lens, which ends within Feature 4, is the continuation of the dispersed charcoal area within and associated with Features 1 and 2. Although the edges of Feature 4 were indistinct, the feature fill was noted as being slightly darker than the surrounding Midden 4.

A 50 cm wide east-west trench was excavated along the south balk wall of the excavation trench through Feature 4, to obtain a complete soil profile including topsoil, middens, feature fill, and sterile sand. In this profile (Figure 41; Profile 1), Feature 4 appeared to originate at the bottom of Midden 2, approximately 35 cm below the present ground surface, at an elevation of 124.66 m. Midden 2, above Feature 4, appeared to be slightly darker than elsewhere. The maximum depth of Feature 4 was 60 cm.

Three distinct zones, Zones A, B, C, and possibly a fourth zone, Zone D, were defined for Feature 4. Zone A consisted of a homogeneous, black to very dark brown (10YR 2/1–2/2) silty sand with moderate charcoal chunks and flecks, and a maximum depth of 30 cm. Zone B, charcoal lens, was a homogeneous, very dark grayish brown (10YR 3/2) silty sand. This zone, with a maximum depth of 28 cm, tapered to a thinner lens ending near the center of Feature 4. Zone B contained an abundance of wood charcoal, including several fairly large pieces of intact twigs. Zone C, defining the bottom of the eastern half of Feature 4, consisted of a mottled, dark brown (10YR 3/3) sand with sparse charcoal flecks. Maximum depth of Zone C was 32 cm, which was measured at a possible disturbed area. Zone D, a mottled, brown to dark brown (10YR 4/3) sand, was possibly the result of natural siltation and was relatively void of charcoal or artifacts. Zone D appeared along the western base of Feature 4 and extended beyond the poorly defined western edge of the feature and below Midden 4.

In comparing the profile of Feature 4 in the south balk wall and the corresponding soil profile in the north balk wall (a distance of 2 m), the Feature 4 zones appear very similar in soil color, texture, and thickness to the midden levels defined in the north balk wall. One difference is the presence of the charcoal lens, Zone B, in Feature 4. Zones A and C of Feature 4 correspond to Middens 3 and 4, respectively, in the north balk

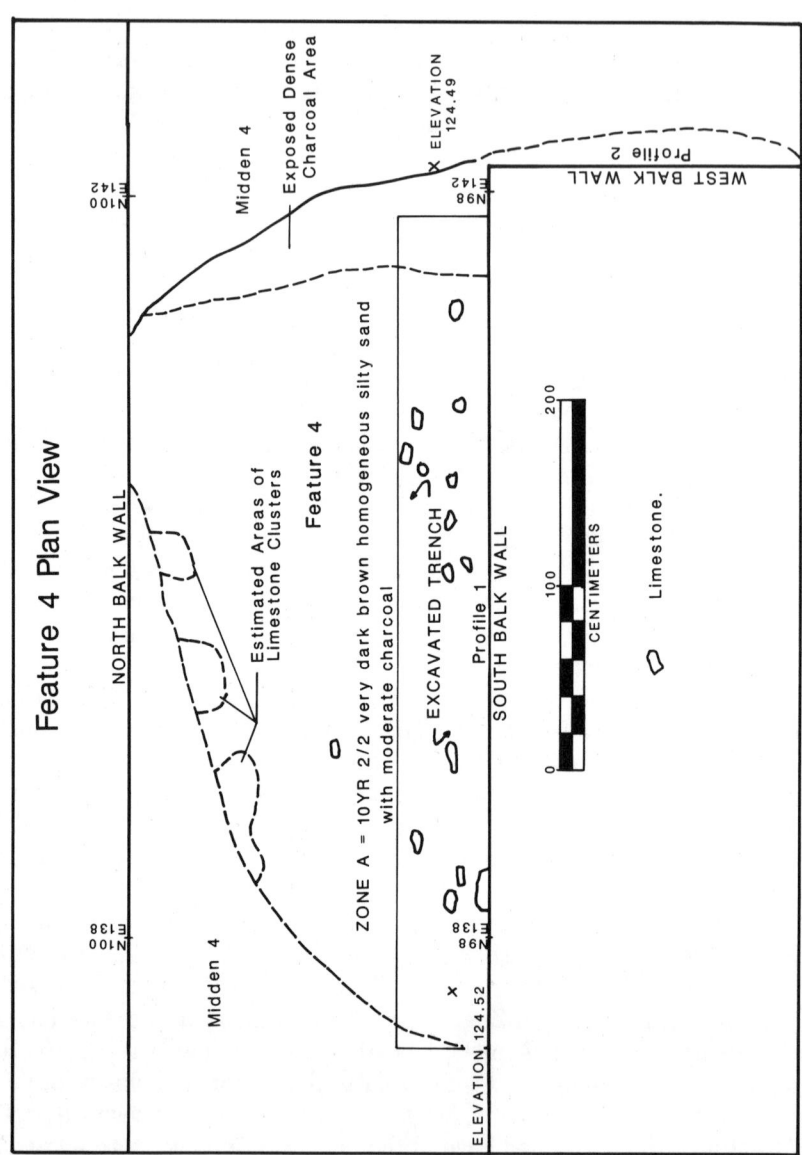

Fig. 40. Plan view map of Feature 4 midden area

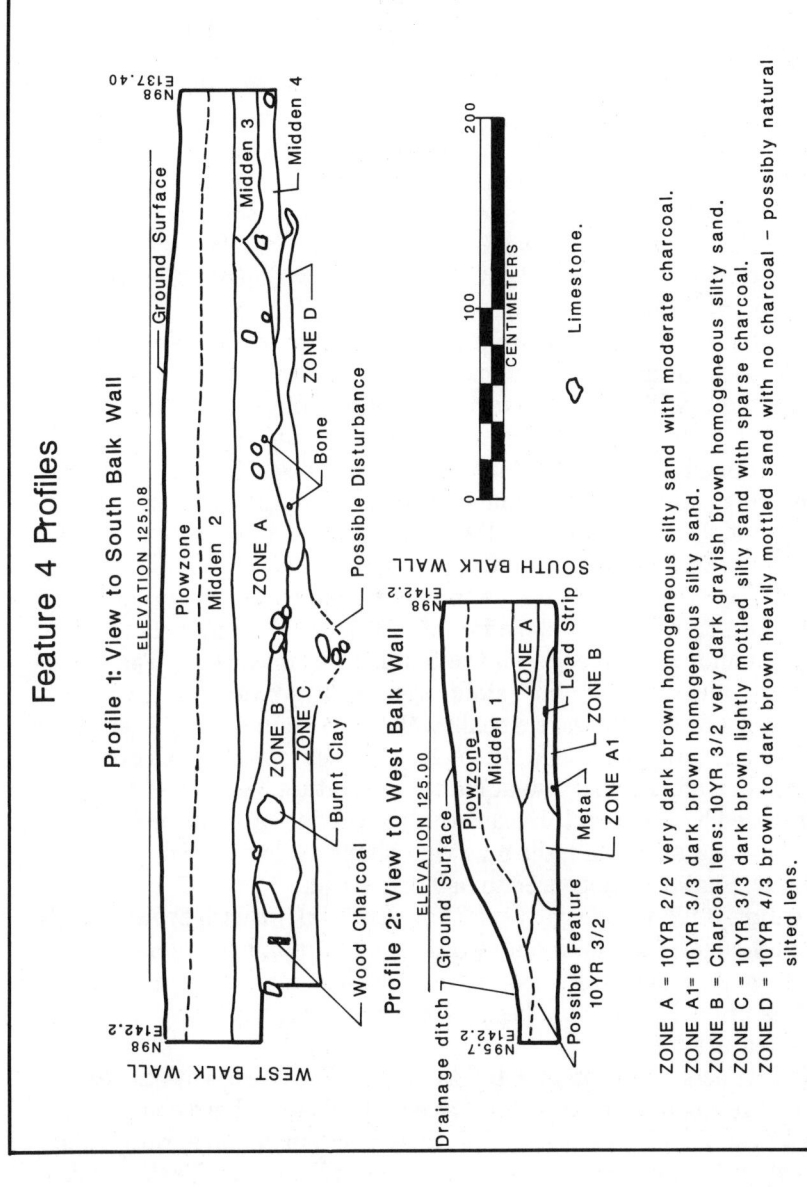

Fig. 41. Profile maps of Feature 4 midden area

wall. However, Feature 4 did contain considerably more artifacts than the midden levels.

Feature 4 artifacts include the following: one triangular point, one utilized flake, one whetstone fragment, two blue-green round-sectioned bottle kick-up fragments, two blue-green square-sectioned case bottle basal fragments, and faunal remains including one worked trumpeter swan humerus. Ceramics include one faience sherd, seven coarse earthenware sherds, two Westerwald sherds, and one porcelain sherd. Metal artifacts include three iron clasp knife blades, two kettle bail ears made of sheet copper, and rosehead, L-head, and other square nail fragments.

The diagnostic artifacts from Feature 4 date to the early- to mid-eighteenth century. Artifact types are similar to those found in Features 1 and 2, with a notable variety of eighteenth-century ceramics in Feature 4. With the abundance of artifacts and the apparent large, yet poorly defined size, Feature 4 may represent a discrete midden area related to the activities in the immediate vicinity and associated with Features 1 and 2. The intrusion of the charcoal lens from Features 1 and 2 into Feature 4 supports this interpretation.

Feature 3 (Figure 42) was defined in the easternmost corner of the excavation trench at an elevation of 124.37 m. Only a portion of the northern and western edges of the feature was uncovered. The northern edge, an irregular, dark stain oriented approximately east-west, measured 3.68 m from the east balk wall to the defined west edge of the feature. Feature 3 extended .78 m into the excavation trench off of the south balk wall. The northwest corner of Feature 3 appeared to be superimposed by Feature 1. Because only a portion of Feature 3 was exposed and not excavated, the plan view shape could not be determined, however, Feature 3 appeared to be fairly large.

Feature 3 fill was a lightly mottled, very dark grayish brown (10YR 3/2) silty sand. The depth and profile shape are unknown; several attempts were made with a soil probe to achieve a depth measurement, but this proved impossible because the probe merely compressed the sandy feature fill.

No artifacts were noted on the surface of Feature 3, with the exception of a few small pieces of limestone rock. The northern edge of Feature 3 described a roughly square or rectangular feature, rather than an oval or circular plan. This could possibly indicate that Feature 3 represents structural remains. Based on the probable superposition of Feature 1, which appeared to date to the early- to mid-eighteenth century, Feature 3 probably predates or is contemporaneous with Feature 1. The limited view of this feature and the absence of morphological data do not permit even a speculative interpretation.

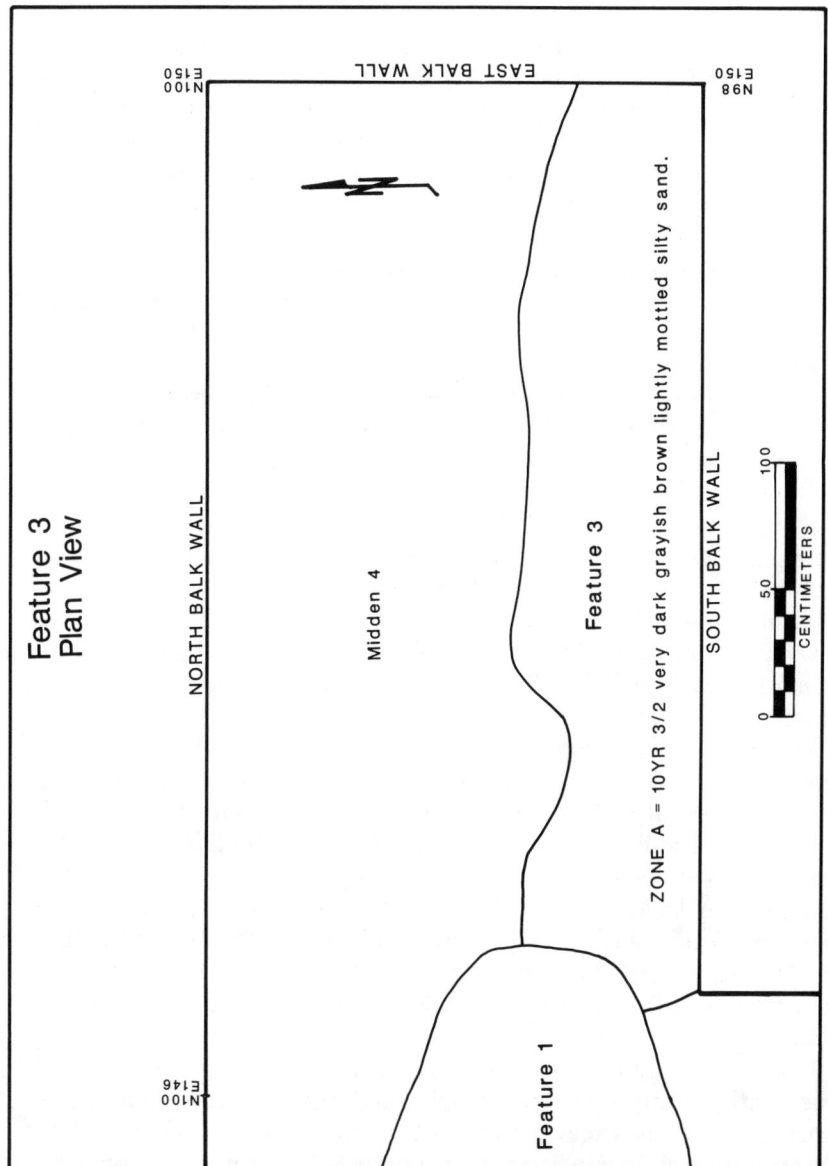

Fig. 42. Plan view map of Feature 3 (unexcavated)

Feature 11, a limestone concentration (Figure 43), was defined in the profile of the north balk wall (N100) and extended from E133.92 to E134.91 for a maximum east-west measurement of 99 cm. Feature 11 originated at 40 cm below the present ground surface and was completely within Midden 4. The maximum depth of the limestone concentration was 26 cm. Feature 11 consisted of approximately 10 pieces of limestone, averaging 10 cm in size, with a few smaller pieces. The limestone seemed to be arbitrarily piled together with no intentional stacking or arrangement. A few pieces of limestone were noted within the excavation trench, approximately 15 cm from the north balk wall at 63 cm below surface.

No definable stain was noted, although the midden underneath the limestone did dip into a basin shape, approximately 15 cm deeper into the sterile sand. Midden fill around the limestone was a moderately mottled, dark brown (10YR 3/3) silty sand with sparse charcoal flecks. Feature 11 was not excavated, and therefore the actual size and plan view shape were not determined. Artifacts collected from the profile wall include one small ceramic sherd (possibly pearlware) with an indeterminate blue decoration, one square nail, one animal bone, and two fairly large pieces of a highly vitrified material, which are dark greenish-grey in color and have a surface appearance of cinder-like material.

There is a lack of diagnostic artifacts from Feature 11. The possible pearlware sherd would indicate a temporal range from the late eighteenth century into the early to mid-nineteenth century. The depth of Feature 11 and its complete containment within Midden 4 (not intrusive from above) suggest that it probably does date to this time span. Feature 11 is located at the same elevations as Features 7 and 8 (see Figure 33), wall trenches which were located 4 m to the west of Feature 11. Feature 11 could be a structural remnant, possibly relating to the construction or dismantling of the structure represented by Features 7, 8, and 10.

Features 5 and 6 (Figures 44 and 45; Plates 12 and 13) represent nineteenth-century structural remains and were the westernmost features located in the excavation trench. Feature 6 was the main portion of a structural stain and basin, probably rectangular in plan view. Feature 5 was a smaller feature defined by a concentration of limestone mortar extending off the northeast edge of Feature 6. Feature 6 was defined at an elevation of 124.46 m within sterile sand, as a dark stain with an abundance of limestone, brick rubble, and artifacts. Large limestone slabs and rubble were concentrated in the northeast and northwest corners of the structural stain. The exposed northern edge

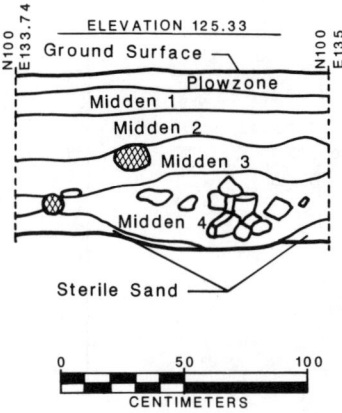

Fig. 43. Profile map of Feature 11 limestone concentration

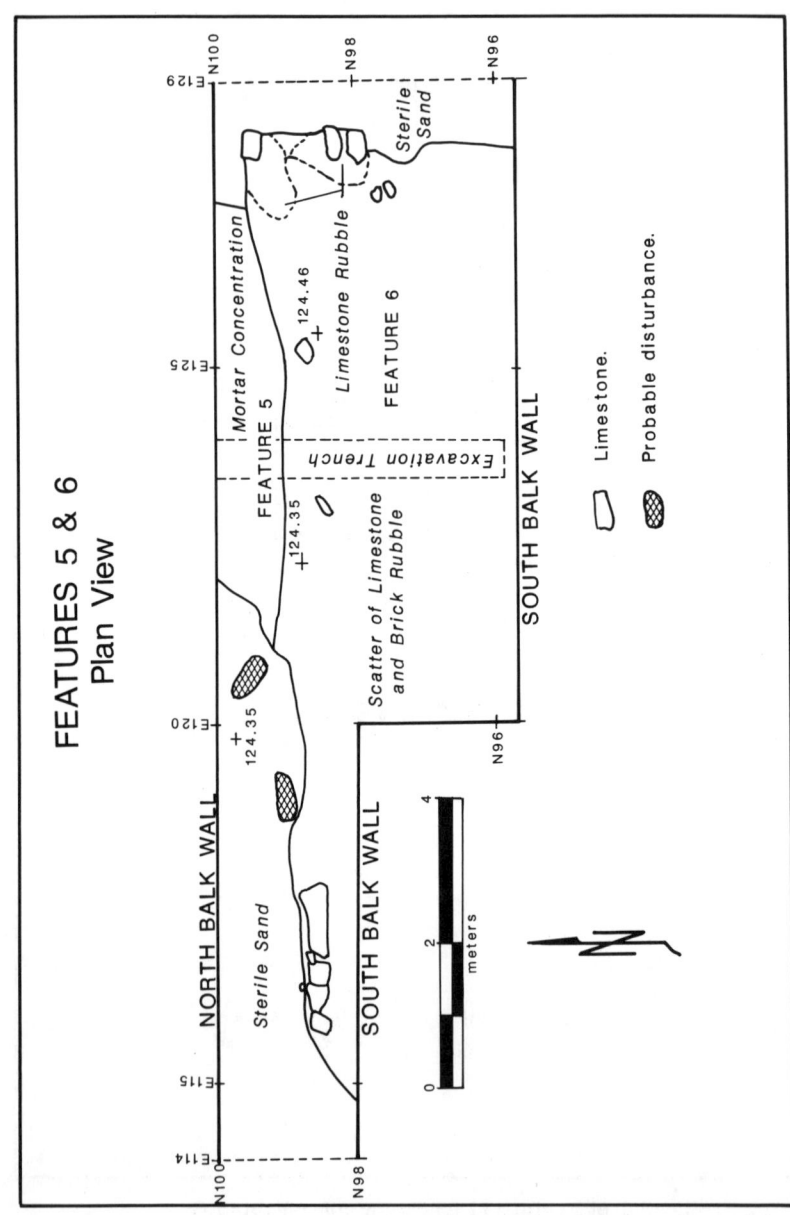

Fig. 44. Plan view map of Features 5 and 6 structural remains

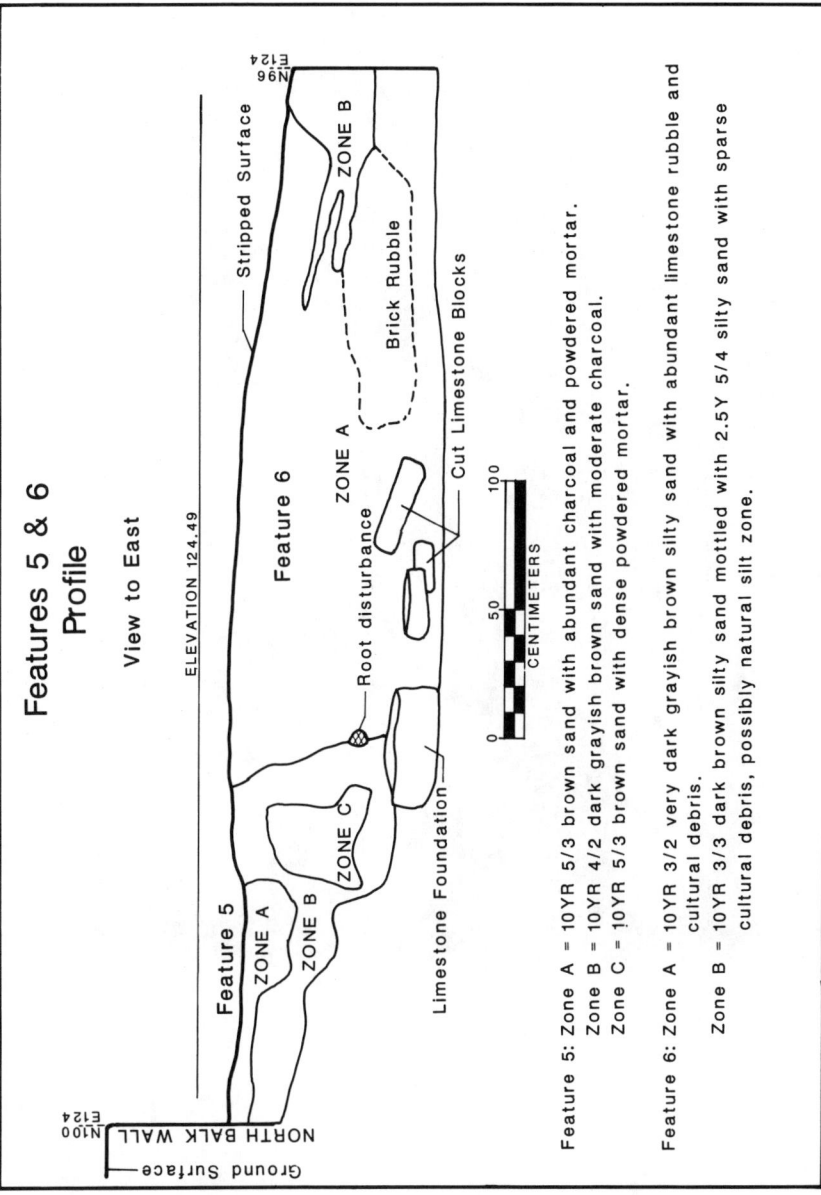

Fig. 45. Profile map of Features 5 and 6 structural remains

Plate 12. Plan view of Features 5 and 6 structural remains

Plate 13. View to south of test trench through Features 5 and 6 structural remains. Limestone block foundation seen in the bottom of the test trench

of Feature 6, oriented roughly east-west, extended from E114.8 to E128.34 for a maximum measurement of 13.54 m. The north-south measurement of Feature 6 was indeterminate because the feature continued into the south balk wall. Feature 5, as seen in profile in the north balk wall, extended from E121.32 to E127.26 for a maximum east-west measurement of 6.44 m. The north-south measurement for Feature 5 was also indeterminate because it continued into the north balk wall.

Features 5 and 6 were sampled with a north-south test trench. The 50 cm wide trench (E123.5 to E124.0) extended between the north and south balk walls from N95.9 to N100 for a maximum length of 4.1 m. In profile, Feature 5 was 18 cm in depth at the north balk wall and irregularly dipped down to a maximum depth of 66 cm at the area where it connected with Feature 6. Feature 5 consisted of three soil/mortar zones. Zone A was a brown sand (10YR 5/3) with moderate charcoal flecks and a moderate quantity of small pieces of limestone mortar. Zone B was an irregularly shaped pocket of fill located near the edge of Feature 6. Zone B was similar to Zone A, but contained more limestone mortar. Zone C, the more predominate fill defining the base of Feature 5, consisted of dark grayish brown sand (10YR 4/2) with charcoal flecks and sparse limestone mortar. In comparison with the fill of Feature 6, Feature 5 contained fewer artifacts and relatively little limestone or brick rubble.

One hundred ninety-eight artifacts were recovered from Feature 5, not including over one thousand pieces of limestone mortar. Ceramics include a few creamware and pearlware sherds, and an abundance of decorated whiteware sherds, including molded- and edge-decorated, monochrome and polychrome handpainted, annular-banded, and transfer prints. Other artifacts include bone and brass buttons, one bone-handled utensil, one slate pencil, faunal remains, and two kaolin pipe stems with stem holes measuring 4/64 inch and 5/64 inch. Building materials include rosehead and other square nails, flat glass, limestone mortar, and a few pieces of brick.

Feature 6 measured a maximum depth of 86 cm at the junction of Features 5 and 6. In this area, at the base of Feature 6, were several large cut limestone blocks defining the north wall of the structure. At the southern end of the test trench, the depth of Feature 6 was 61 cm. Feature 6 consisted of two soil zones. Zone A was a very dark grayish brown (10YR 3/2) silty sand with an abundance of limestone, brick rubble, and artifacts. Zone B was an isolated irregularly shaped area with a maximum depth of 35 cm along the southern end of the test trench. Zone B consisted of a dark brown (10YR 5/4) silty sand and appeared to be the result of natural siltation. Zone B contained very few artifacts and did not have limestone or brick rubble. Below and to the north of Zone B was an area of brick rubble measuring 1.11 m in length with a depth of 38 cm. This area of brick rubble was located approximately 10 cm above the base of Feature 6 and may represent the collapsed remains of a chimney or fireplace.

Three hundred seventy artifacts were collected from the Feature 6 test excavation. This total does not include brick and limestone, of which only a sample was collected. Ceramics in Feature 6 include a small number of faience sherds, coarse earthernwares, creamware, and pearlware. The ceramic assemblage consists primarily of nineteenth-century ceramic types, including edge-decorated, annular-banded, handpainted, sponge/spatterware, and transfer prints. Glass artifacts include a few pieces of dark green and brown bottle glass and an abundance of blue-green and clear bottle glass. Two kaolin pipe stems with stem holes measuring 4/64 inch were also recovered. Metal artifacts include one wood gouge, one triangular file, one knife blade, and one iron spring. Building materials are rosehead nails, other square nails, unidentifiable nail fragments, flat glass, limestone, and brick rubble.

Discussion of Features 5 and 6. Feature 5 appears to have been used for multiple purposes in the construction of the Feature 6 house basin. Initially, Feature 5 was probably a builder's trench, dug into the sterile sand as a rampway to the main structural basin, Feature 6. In profile, Feature 5 has three irregular steps leading down into Feature 6. Feature 5 was probably utilized for the removal of the soils from the structural basin and as an accessway to carry and set in the large limestone foundation slabs. The predominance of limestone mortar recovered from the fill of Feature 5 suggests that it may also have been used to prepare mortar for the construction of the house. The mortar may equally represent the filling-in of Feature 5 with construction debris after completion of the foundation.

Feature 6 was a structural cellar/basement excavated into the sterile sand. The basin foundation was constructed of large cut limestone blocks. The abundance of brick rubble within the basin fill suggests it was probably a brick structure resting on the limestone foundation.

Based on available documentary evidence, Features 5 and 6 represent a structure, which was probably constructed sometime after 1841 but well before 1927. It is not depicted in the 1841 lithograph nor is it present in the 1927 aerial photograph of the Wedge. As noted in the discussion of the Nicolle/Meunier structure, a records search failed to identify the ownership of this property, Lot 13, after 1809, making it impossible to determine the chain of owners for most of the nineteenth century. It is not until the 1872 Hilgard plat map that the lot owner was recorded as Henry Labuxier (Labusier). However, the plat map does not show what existed on the property at this time. In 1874, Lots 13 and 14 were sold by Melanie, Angelica, and Louis Labusier to John B. DeLorme. By 1927, all structures were gone and the lot was within cultivation. WPA researchers recorded in 1938 that the lot had been deeded to St. Clair County for use as an historical park, but the date of this transaction is unknown.

The artifact assemblages of Features 5 and 6 substantiate the suggested period of occupation, post-1841. Although eighteenth-century materials were scattered throughout the structural fill, this is to be expected because of the presence of the Nicolle/Meunier structural remains a few meters to the east. The majority of the artifacts within Features 5 and 6 date from the mid-nineteenth to the early twentieth century.

Feature 9, a basin-shaped pit (Figure 46), was defined in profile in the north balk wall (N100) of the excavation trench. It extended from E129.08 to E130.10 for a maximum east-west measurement of 1.02 m. In profile, Feature 9 appeared to originate 5–8 cm below the present ground surface and extended underneath the plowzone/soil level into Middens 1A and 2A. The feature had inward sloping walls with a rounded to pointed base and a maximum depth of 32 cm. Feature fill consisted of a single zone (A) of homogeneous, very dark brown (10YR 2/2) silty sand with moderate charcoal flecks. Feature 9 fill was darker in color and contained more wood charcoal, limestone, and artifacts than the surrounding middens. Several medium to large pieces of limestone were concentrated near the top of the eastern edge of the feature. The eastern edge of Feature 9 extended above Feature 8 (wall trench), which originated approximately 22 cm deeper than Feature 9.

Feature 9 was not excavated, and therefore the size and shape were not determined. Artifacts collected from the profile of Feature 9 include three whiteware sherds, one blue-stamped whiteware sherd, one saltglazed stoneware/crockery fragment with a brown paste and glaze, three square nails, one animal bone, and one brick fragment. The presence of whiteware ceramics and the stamp-decorated whiteware, which was introduced in the late 1840s (Price 1979:20), and the origin of Feature 9 immediately below the sod/plowzone level suggests that Feature 9 dates to the mid to late nineteenth century. The abundance of materials within the profile and the rich organic fill do suggest that Feature 9 was utilized as a refuse pit, possibly associated with Features 5 and 6 structural remains.

Feature 12, a moderately deep, basin-shaped pit (Figure 46), was defined in profile in the north balk wall (N100) of the excavation trench.

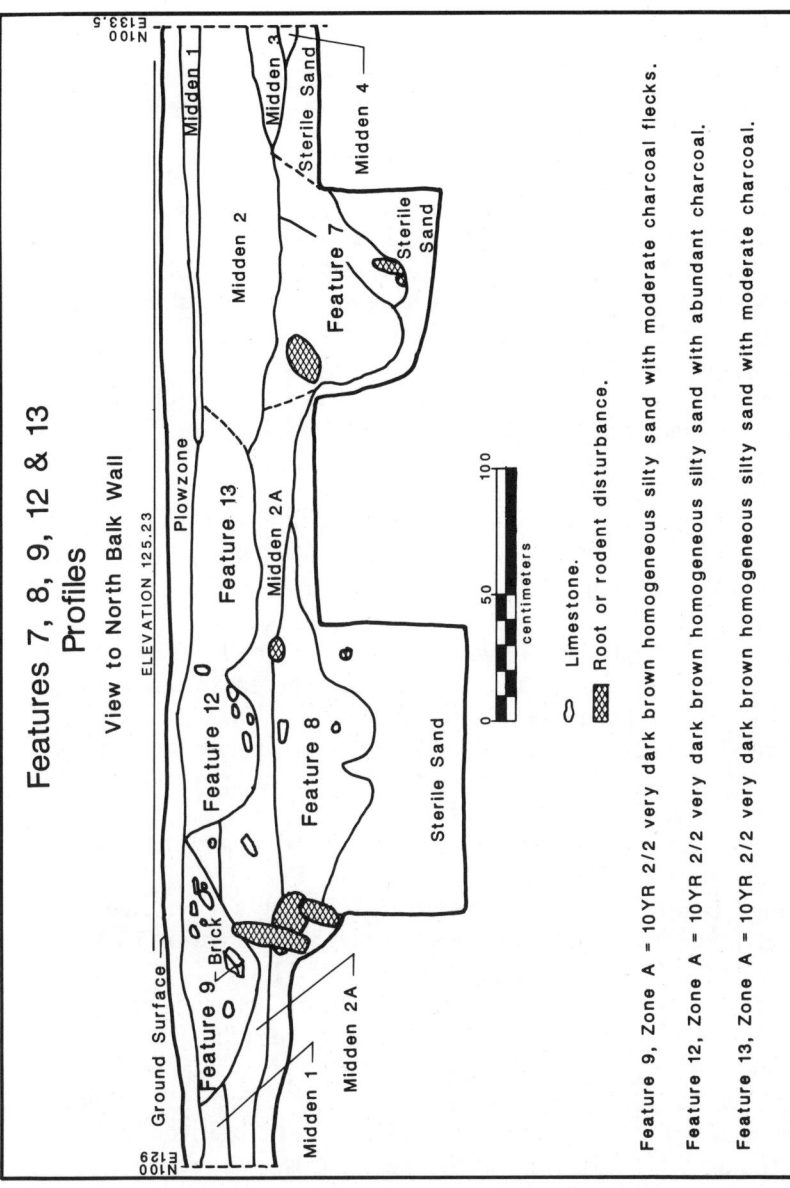

Fig. 46. Profile map of portion of north balk wall showing Features 7, 8, 9, 12, and 13

It extended from E130.24 to E130.85 for a maximum east-west measurement of 61 cm. The feature originated 5–7 cm below the present ground surface and extended below the plowzone/sod layer. Feature 12 intruded into Middens 1A and 2A and had darker fill and more charcoal than these middens. Feature 12 was not excavated, and therefore the plan view shape and size were not determined. In profile, Feature 12 had a maximum depth of 58 cm. Feature fill consisted of a single zone of homogeneous, very dark brown (10YR 2/2) silty sand, with abundant wood charcoal as well as several root disturbances. Only one artifact, a fragment of a clear glass rim probably from a drinking vessel, was collected. Based on the origin of Feature 12 at approximately 5 cm below the present ground surface, this feature probably dates to the late nineteenth or early twentieth century. Feature 12 appeared to be a basin-shaped refuse pit, possibly associated with Features 5 and 6 structural remains.

Feature 13, a shallow basin-shaped feature (Figure 46), was defined in the north balk wall (N100), extending from E130.80 to E131.95 for a maximum east-west measurement of 1.15 m. In profile, Feature 13 extended underneath the plowzone/sod level, approximately 10 cm below the present ground surface, with a maximum depth of 30 cm. The western edge of the feature was very distinct, whereas the eastern edge was poorly defined and intermixed with Midden 2. The western edge of Feature 13 connected with Feature 12, although superpositioning could not be determined. The base of Feature 13 was at approximately the same level as the base of Midden 2.

The remainder of Feature 13 was not excavated, and therefore the plan view shape and size were not determined. Feature 13 fill consisted of a single zone of very dark brown (10YR 2/2) sandy silt, with moderate wood charcoal flecks and several root disturbances. Feature 13 fill was slightly darker than surrounding Middens 2 and 2A.

Artifacts collected from the profile of Feature 13 include one creamware sherd, one square nail, one piece of blue-green flat glass, and one fragment of blue-green bottle glass. The bottle glass fragment is from a quart size flask and has a figure shown in relief. It is a crude depiction of a man using a staff or walking stick. This type of flask, commemorating Zebulon Pike's discovery in the early 1800s, was produced in the 1850s and 1860s in the United States when it was popular to climb and explore Pike's Peak (Lindsey 1967:385–386).

Feature 13 is somewhat questionable as a pit feature because of the indistinct eastern edge and the base of the feature appearing to correspond to the base of Midden 2. Feature 13 may represent a darker midden area within Midden 2. It is similar to Features 11 and 12 in terms of depth, size, and shape, but not as clearly defined as a cultural feature. Based primarily on the Pike's Peak flask fragment, Feature 13 probably dates to the second half of the nineteenth century and may also be associated with Features 5 and 6 structural remains.

SUMMARY AND CONCLUSIONS

The test excavations in Area A, as defined by the controlled surface collection, uncovered 12 cultural features, including two structural remains; a portion of an eighteenth-century French colonial *poteaux-en-terre* structure (Features 7, 8, and 10) and a structural basin postulated to date to the nineteenth century (Features 5 and 6). Other eighteenth-century features included a limestone cooking/fire facility (Feature 2), an associated refuse pit (Feature 1), a discrete midden area (Feature 4), and two features of unknown function (Features 3 and 11). Other nineteenth-century features included three refuse pits (Features 9, 12, and 13).

Features 7, 8, and 10 have been interpreted as the remains of a domestic dwelling owned by Etienne Nicolle and illustrated on the 1766 map of Cahokia. This structure, if built by Nicolle, would have been constructed sometime between 1758 and 1766, since records show that in 1758 Nicolle was residing at the village of Kaskaskia. Correlating the archaeological remains with available documents, the sequence of occupancy of this house has been identified to at least 1809 when it was owned by Jean Meunier, and by 1841 the structure was no longer present, based on the 1841 J. C. Wild lithograph. The subsurface remains of this structure had been predicted by the controlled surface collection. Eighteenth-century artifacts, particularly French faience and coarse earthenwares, were concentrated within Area A.

The second structure represented by Features 5 and 6, although not illustrated on nineteenth-century maps or referenced in the available documents, appears to have been built sometime after 1841 and was no longer present in 1927. The postulated nineteenth-century date can be correlated with the concentration of nineteenth-century materials recovered by the controlled surface collection within Area A. The artifact assemblages from Features 5 and 6 also indicate a mid to late nineteenth century date.

Soil stratigraphy within the eastern one-third of the test excavation trench was defined as four distinct midden levels lying upon sterile sand. These were identified as Middens 1–4, with a total maximum thickness of approximately 60 cm. Midden 4, the earliest deposit, appears to date to the eighteenth century, based on its depositional association with Features 1, 2, and 4. A second midden area, located within the central portion of the test excavation trench, consisted of Middens 1A and 2A, with a maximum depth of approximately 40 cm. These middens appear to date to the later occupation and may be associated with the postulated nineteenth-century structural remains, Features 5 and 6.

CHAPTER 4:
ARTIFACT DESCRIPTIONS

The archaeological investigations at the Cahokia Wedge site resulted in the recovery of 26,764 artifacts (controlled surface collection: n=15,986; excavations units: n=7,856; and features: n=2,922). A general analysis was conducted on all materials, with a detailed analysis focusing on artifacts that are associated with the following temporal/cultural groupings: prehistoric, protohistoric/historic Indian, eighteenth-century French and British colonial, and early nineteenth-century American.

Artifacts collected from the surface and the screened soil of the excavation units represent problematical contexts, reflecting the continuous Euro-American occupation of Cahokia since the 1700s. Further complications arise because of the abundance of several artifact types, such as dark green bottle glass, kaolin clay pipes, and various ceramic types, that range in time from the eighteenth century into the nineteenth century. Consequently, a detailed analysis of artifacts from feature fill contexts was conducted to obtain a better understanding of the chronological occupation.

When possible, artifact comparisons will be made primarily with materials from historic Indian villages and French colonial sites within the American Bottom. References will also be made to historic Indian village sites in the Illinois River Valley, Missouri, Wisconsin, and the lower Mississippi River Valley. Most of these sites were linked economically and culturally with Cahokia in the Indian and fur trade. Extensive archaeological work at French forts in western Indiana and Michigan provides comparative data for colonial military outposts representing the political outreaches of the eighteenth-century French Regime.

The surface proveniences of artifact types will be referenced to Areas A-F, when noteworthy. All artifacts from excavation units and features are from within Area A. The artifact descriptions will be presented under the following headings: Aboriginal Ceramics, Stone Artifacts, Smoking Pipes, Historic Ceramics, Glass Artifacts, Metal Artifacts, Weapons, and Miscellaneous Artifacts.

ABORIGINAL CERAMICS

by George R. Holley
Laboratory Director
Contract Archaeology Program—SIUE

A total of 15 sherds of aboriginal manufacture were recovered from the surface (n=4) and from excavation units (n=11) at the Cahokia Wedge site. Although some of these sherds can be definitively identified as prehistoric, a substantial number of shell-tempered sherds may conceivably date to the protohistoric time span. The fragmentary nature of the material, coupled with the poor understanding of late Mississippian culture in the American Bottom, preclude any definitive statements.

Four paste/surface groupings have been established for the sample: Red-slipped, Limestone-tempered; Red-slipped, Shell-tempered; Plain, Compact Paste; and Plain, Shell-tempered. These are discussed below.

Red-slipped, Limestone-tempered (n=1). This category is represented by only one sherd recovered from the surface near the concentration of human bone in the central area of the site. The sherd has a leached paste and slipping on the exterior. This type, and limestone tempering in general, had a prolonged popularity in the southern section of the American Bottom (Kelly et al. 1984) beginning in the Emergent Mississippian period and lasting well into the Mississippian period, at least until the Stirling phase. A dating anywhere from Emergent Mississippian into Stirling is possible for this sherd.

Red-slipped, Shell-tempered (n=1). This category is represented by only one sherd recovered from the surface near the southwestern corner of the site. The sherd is thick-walled with a red slip on the interior and exterior. The paste is tempered with relatively small, leached particles of shell, unlike the other shell-tempered specimens recovered from the Wedge. Red slipping and shell tempering are most often associated with Early Mississippian (Lohmann-Stirling phases, ca. A.D. 1000 to 1150) but could be present earlier as well as later. However, a late prehistoric (Sand Prairie or Vulcan phase, ca. A.D. 1300 to 1600?) association appears unlikely.

Plain, Compact Paste (n=1). One sherd is characterized by a very compact gray paste and surface. This fragment was recovered from an excavation unit. Temper particles may include small fragments of leached shell or limestone. This sherd probably derives from a handle or an appendage of unknown shape. The compact paste is usually associated with Mississippian period ceramics.

ARTIFACT DESCRIPTIONS

Plain, Shell-tempered (n = 12). The majority of the sherds recovered from the Wedge are of this category. In most specimens the shell temper is preserved and the surfaces, when intact, are plain and roughly smoothed or covered with a black pitch (?) but not a slip substance. The paste is dark gray with thin oxidized margins, which is typical of shell-tempered pastes in the American Bottom. The sherds are thick-walled (7–9 mm) and probably derive from jars; one neck sherd is present. Many of the sherds have an exfoliated surface and one specimen is vitrified. Ten of these sherds were from excavation units and the two sherds from the site surface were recovered from Area A.

It is impossible to precisely date non-diagnostic, shell-tempered sherds to any established phase in the American Bottom sequence. However, the presence of non-weathered temper is suggestive of a more recent association that may possibly date to protohistoric or historic period. Unfortunately, material culture for this time period is poorly documented in the American Bottom. As a result these small sherds cannot be reliably added to the study of Indian artifacts utilized slightly before or after French contact. Further study of reliable contexts for this material is needed.

STONE ARTIFACTS

LITHICS

A total of 150 lithic tools and debitage was recovered from the surface (n = 121), from excavation units (n = 24), and from feature fills (n = 5). Tool and debitage types were divided into eight categories based on various attributes. Identified chert types include Burlington, glacial till, Kincaid, Mill Creek, Cobden-Dongola, and unknown/local variety (Table 1). The predominance of Burlington chert from eastern Missouri and locally available glacial till indicates a reliance on easily obtainable raw materials. The few non-local chert types have source areas primarily to the south of the American Bottom region (Spielbauer 1976).

Lithic Tools

Triangular Points (n = 7; Figure 47 A-G). These small triangular points range in length from 2.0 cm to 2.9 cm (Table 2). The specimens have either a straight or concave base. Six of these points were manufactured of Burlington chert and one was made of glacial till. Five points were recovered from the surface and one specimen each from Features 1 and 4.

TABLE 1

CHERT TYPES

Chert Type	Counts	Percentages %
Burlington	53	35.0
Local glacial till	45	30.0
Blue/gray local variety	35	23.0
Kincaid	4	3.0
Mill Creek	1	.5
Cobden	2	1.5
Unknown	10	7.0
	150	100.0

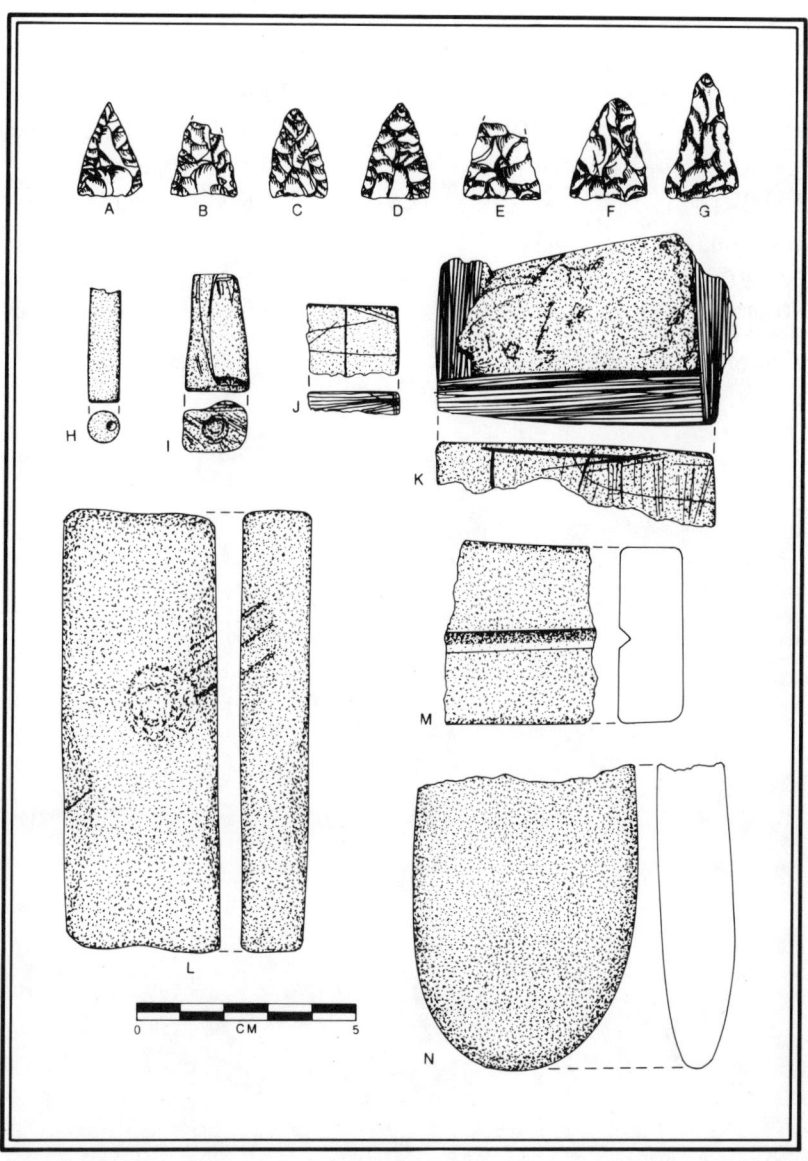

Fig. 47. Stone Artifacts. A-G, triangular points; H and I, catlinite beads; J, modified catlinite; K, modified catlinite (possible mold); L and M, whetstones; N, modified glacial cobble (possible grinding stone)

TABLE 2

Triangular Point Measurements

Provenience	Length (cm)	Width (cm)	Weight (g)	Chert Type
CSC*	2.0	1.4	1.0	Burlington
CSC	2.1 (est.)	1.2	.5	Unknown/local
CSC	2.9	1.8	2.7	Burlington
CSC	---	1.5	.5	Burlington
CSC	2.3 (est.)	1.7	2.5	Burlington
Feature 1	2.1	1.5	.5	Burlington
Feature 4	---	1.8	1.0	Unknown/local

*Controlled surface collection

Miscellaneous Bifaces (n = 2). Other bifacial tools include one small, oddly shaped biface, possibly a reworked triangular or notched point, and one distal end of a biface. One specimen was recovered from the surface and the other was from an excavation unit.

Utilized Flakes and Chert Chunks (n = 32). These are tools with one or more unifacial edges produced by utilization or retouch flaking. Most of these tools appeared to have been utilized as scrapers. The only formalized unifacial tool, which was recovered from an excavation unit, is a thumbnail scraper made of heat-treated Burlington chert. These artifacts were recovered from the surface (n = 27), from excavation units (n = 4), and from Feature 4 (n = 1).

Lithic Debitage

Cores (n = 7). Angular or blocky chert chunks are identified by the presence of one or more flake scars. These specimens were recovered from the surface (n = 5) and excavation units (n = 2).

Flakes (n = 13). These specimens are defined by the presence of a bulb of percussion and a striking platform. These artifacts were obtained from the surface (n = 10) and excavation units (n = 3).

Bifacial Thinning Flakes (n = 14). These artifacts are identified as small, thin flakes with an acute angle between the striking platform and the dorsal surface. This type of flake is generally produced by the resharpening of bifacial tools. These flakes were found on the surface (n = 12), in excavation units (n = 1), and in Feature 5 (n = 1).

Flake Shatter (n = 33). Broken fragments of flakes, lacking a striking platform and bulb of percussion and therefore unidentifiable as to flake type, are identified as flake shatter. These artifacts were recovered from the surface (n = 30), from excavation units (n = 2), and from Feature 7 (n = 1).

Angular Shatter (n = 42). Blocky, angular chunks, which may be in primary form, are identified as angular shatter. These were recovered from the surface (n = 32) and from excavation units (n = 10).

The lithic debitage cannot be securely placed in either the prehistoric, protohistoric, or historic Indian periods. However, the abundance of lithics is noteworthy when compared with the relative paucity of evidence for other prehistoric artifacts, such as ceramics. The prehistoric occupation, identified by a few limestone- and shell-tempered sherds, appears to be minimal. Thus, it is possible that the bulk of the chipped stone artifacts may date to the protohistoric/historic Indian occupation.

The triangular points may also date to either the prehistoric Mississippian occupation or the protohistoric/historic Indian use of the site prior to or contemporaneous with the French occupation. Two triangular points from the surface of the Area C concentration were associated with two glass beads dating to the Middle Historic period (Quimby 1966a) and lithic debitage. Two other points were recovered from features that date to the early- to mid-eighteenth-century occupation; however, these points may have been intrusive.

Triangular points are commonly found on historic Indian sites, such as the Kaskaskia village known as the Guebert site (Good 1972:67), the Missouri Indian villages known as the Little Osage site and the Late Missouri site, (Chapman 1959:50), and at a Fox village, the Bell site, in Wisconsin (Wittry 1963:29). In the Illinois River Valley, triangular points were reported from the Zimmerman site in both prehistoric Mississippian and historic Indian contexts (Brown 1961:51). These types of points have also been recovered from French colonial sites including Fort de Chartres I, the Laurens site (Jelks and Ekberg 1984:41) and Fort Ouiatenon (Noble 1983:276).

STONE ORNAMENTS

Catlinite Beads (n = 2; Figure 47 H, I). One tubular piece of worked catlinite, probably representing a bead, is present in the surface collection. The artifact is round in cross-section, with a diameter of 0.7 cm. The longitudinal perforation, located off-center, measures 0.2 cm. Although fragmentary, with only one end finished into a flat surface, it measures 2.55 cm in length. The very symmetrical shape of this bead and the very finely drilled perforation suggest that it may have been manufactured with iron tools, possibly by the French for use in the Indian trade. Tubular catlinite beads, mostly square or rectangular in cross-section, have been found at the Lasanen site in Michigan and were interpreted as being manufactured with iron tools by the historic Indians and Europeans (How 1971:48).

One piece of worked catlinite, recovered from an excavation unit, forms a slightly expanding triangle with all four sides and the two ends having been ground. It measures 2.55 cm in length and 1.45 cm in width, with a maximum thickness of 1.1 cm. The beginning of a drilled hole is apparent on the larger end. Although unfinished, the relatively small size and shape of this artifact suggest that it may represent the initial stage of a bead or ornament. The piece is very rough and shows no clear evidence of manufacture with iron tools, suggesting that it may be of aboriginal manufacture. This artifact is similar to trapezoidal catlinite ornaments from the Lasanen site (How 1971:46). Catlinite ornaments of the historic Indians were commonly formed into triangular or trapezoidal pendant shapes (Wittry 1963:33-34; Good 1972:86; Walthall and Benchley 1987:74).

MISCELLANEOUS MODIFIED ROCK

Whetstones (n = 7; Figure 47 L, M). Seven whetstones and whetstone fragments were recovered from the controlled surface collection (n = 4), from excavation units (n = 2), and from Feature 4 (n = 1). One complete whetstone, manufactured from a micaceous sandstone, measures 9.8 cm in length and 3.5 cm in width, with a maximum thickness of 1.6 cm. The whetstone has a small, circular, iron stain on one surface and several worked grooves on the longitudinal edges. The other whetstone fragments are made of igneous rock or sandstone. One igneous fragment has a V-shaped groove down the longitudinal center of one flat plane. Whetstones, utilized as sharpening implements, are commonly found on eighteenth- and nineteenth-century historic sites. Similar sandstone whetstones have also been recovered from historic Indian sites, the Little Osage Village (Chapman 1959:14), the Gros Cap Cemetery site (Nern and Cleland 1974:48), and the Bell site (Wittry 1963:33).

Other Modified Rocks and Minerals

These artifacts include hematite (n = 6), red ochre (n = 1), catlinite (n = 3), siltstone (n = 1), glacial cobbles (n = 2), limestone (n = 7), sandstone (n = 8), and igneous rock (n = 2).

Hematite (n = 6). Fragments of ground hematite were recovered from the surface (n = 4) and from excavation units (n = 2). The specimens are amorphous in shape and exhibit one or more ground surfaces. Hematite residue is often found ground into sandstone, suggesting its use as a pigment. Commonly found on prehistoric sites, ground hematite has also been associated with historic Kaskaskia Indians at the Guebert site (Good 1972:78) and with the historic Missouri Indians at the Gumbo Point site (Chapman 1959:48). The specimens at the Cahokia Wedge may date to the prehistoric and/or protohistoric/historic Indian occupations. Two pieces in the surface collection were found in association with a copper tinkler, three glass trade beads, a catlinite bead, and lithic debitage in Area E.

Red Ochre (n = 1). A piece of soft red ochre was found on the surface. It is a rough and pitted sphere with a maximum diameter of 2.1 cm and appears to have been roughly shaped or ground. This soft material was probably also used as a pigment. This piece was found in association with two triangular points, a copper tinkler, and lithic debitage in Area F.

Catlinite (n=3; Figure 47 J, K). Three pieces of modified catlinite were recovered from the surface (n=1), from an excavation unit (n=1), and from Feature 2 (n=1). One rectangular piece has three worked edges and a worked border or frame, with numerous striations on the one roughly flat surface. This piece was found on the surface of Feature 2. The length measures 6.8 cm. Although unfinished, the rectangular, slab-like shape of this artifact suggests that the intention may have been to produce a catlinite mold. Such molds are commonly found on historic Indian sites for use in making molten lead ornaments or crosses (Chapman 1959:30–31; Good 1972:87). A second small piece of modified catlinite, recovered from screened unit fill above Feature 2, appears to be a fragment of the same artifact, although the pieces do not fit together. These specimens may indicate French use in the Indian trade. The third piece of worked catlinite is a thin tabular piece with one ground, flat surface that has several irregularly-placed incised lines.

Siltstone (n=1). A small, worked siltstone fragment was recovered from an excavation unit. It is grayish/tan in color and has an irregular rectangular shape with three sides exhibiting longitudinal striations. Its length is 2.4 cm and maximum width is 1.15 cm. The form and function of this piece is indeterminate.

Modified Glacial Cobbles (n=2; Figure 47 N). One oblong and flat fragment of igneous rock with rounded edges was excavated from Feature 1. It measures 4.9 cm in maximum width, with a thickness of 1.7 cm. This artifact has been heavily ground, with visible striations on several surfaces, and may have been used as a grinding stone or whetstone.

A large modified glacial cobble was recovered from the area around Feature 2. This artifact has one ground, concave surface with one battered or pecked edge and may have been used as a metate and/or hammerstone. The modified cobbles are from features that are interpreted as contemporaneous and date to the early- to mid-eighteenth century.

Sandstone (n=1). One piece of worked sandstone is an irregular sphere with a drilled perforation completely through the center, and the beginning of another drilled perforation off to the side, of the complete perforation. This piece is fragmentary and its original shape and function are indeterminate.

ARTIFACT DESCRIPTIONS

Other Worked Rock (n = 18). Most of the other worked sandstone, limestone, and igneous fragments have one or more ground, flat or slightly concave surfaces. One sandstone fragment has a pinkish-red residue, which is probably hematite or red ochre.

The presence of modified rock at the Cahokia Wedge site may be associated with the prehistoric occupation of the site. It is more probable, particularly when modified rocks were found in eighteenth-century feature contexts, that some these artifacts relate to the historic Indian occupation or possibly represent a French adaptation to utilize raw materials.

SMOKING PIPES

MICMAC PIPES

Nine Micmac pipe fragments were recovered from the surface (n = 7) and from excavation units (n = 2). Eight of the fragments were made of local limestone and one fragment was made of catlinite imported from Pipestone County, Minnesota.

Catlinite Micmac Pipe (n = 1; Figure 48 A). The catlinite fragment consists of the keel and a portion of an octagonal stem leading to the missing pipe bowl. The keel portion is fairly small in size compared to the limestone keel fragments in the Cahokia Wedge collection. The keel has faint, horizontally incised lines located at the top and bottom on two sides. At the base of the keel is a small protrusion, which expands slightly to the pipe base. Within this protrusion is a drilled hole measuring 0.2 cm, through which a thong would have been threaded for suspension. The elaboration of the keel base is dissimilar to the more typical simple, triangular or rounded keels. However, one complete catlinite Micmac pipe from the Guebert site has a similar protrusion extending off of the keel (Good 1972:73).

Decorated Micmac Pipes (n = 2; Figure 48 B, C). One specimen made of a mottled tan and light gray limestone is a fragment of the keel and the rounded section leading to the missing pipe bowl. An incised line runs horizontally around and just below the top of the keel. Immediately below this incised line are two incised concentric circles with a maximum diameter of 0.4 cm. This design element is similar to that noted on Micmac pipes from the Guebert site (Good 1972:74).

One pipe bowl fragment made of dark grey limestone measures 2.4 cm in length from the rim to the bowl base. A single, circumferentially-incised line is located just above the bowl base.

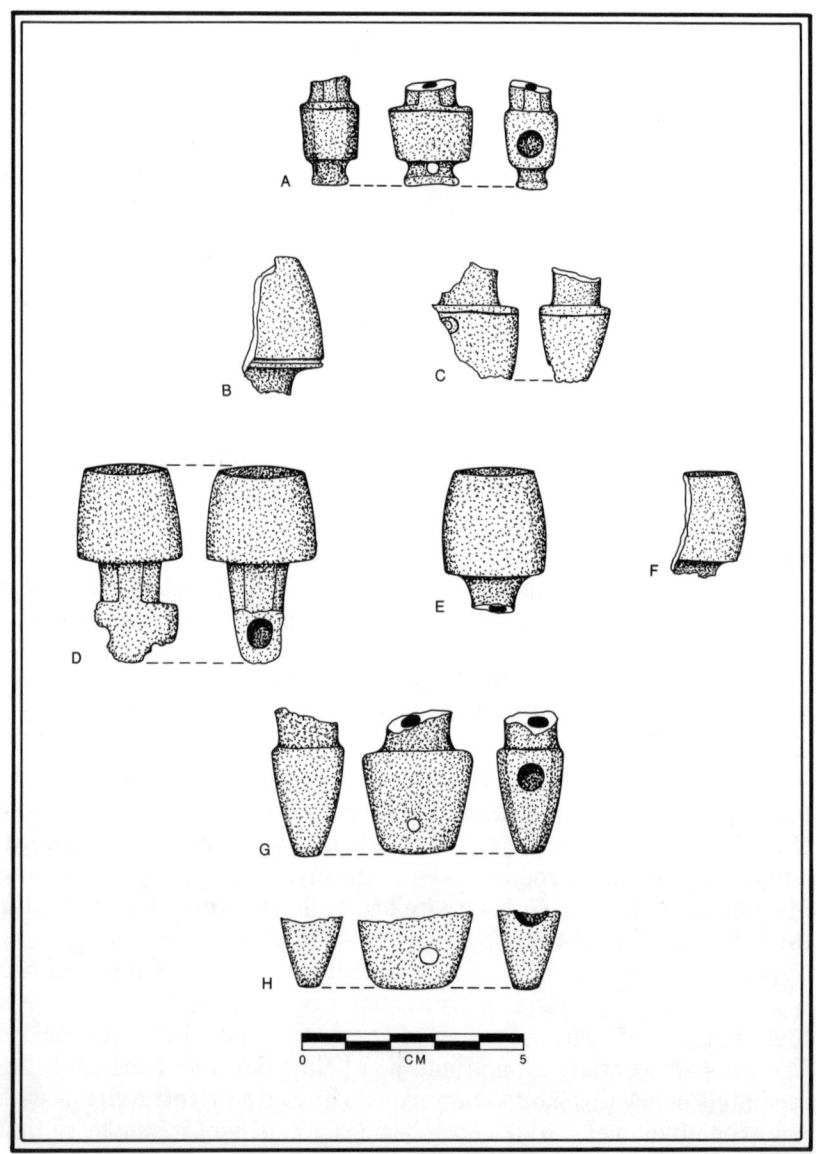

Fig. 48. Micmac pipes. A, decorated catlinite Micmac pipe; B and C, decorated limestone Micmac pipes; D-H, limestone Micmac pipes

Undecorated Micmac Pipes (n = 6; Figure 48 D-H). The most complete Micmac pipe is made of a tan/gray limestone. Although portions of the incurving-lipped bowl have been broken, the diameter measures 2.05 cm. The bowl measures 2.0 cm in length with a maximum diameter of 2.55 cm. The segment extending from the base of the bowl to the keel is seven-sided with a diameter of 1.4 cm. This pipe is similar in bowl base treatment to the catlinite pipe from the Cahokia Wedge collection, as well as pipes collected from the Guebert site (Good 1972:73). The keel is fragmentary, broken at both the stem and the thong holes, and the exact shape of the keel could not be determined.

One fragment, which consists of a complete bowl with a portion of a rounded bowl base, is made of a medium gray limestone. The bowl rim diameter is 1.75 cm and the length of the bowl from the flattened lip to the bowl base is 2.2 cm.

The remaining four Micmac pipes consist of small, undecorated bowl or keel fragments manufactured of limestone.

Micmac pipes are commonly found on seventeenth- and eighteenth-century historic Indian sites, such as the Guebert site in Illinois (Good 1972:73–75) and the Krelich site at the Saline Springs in Missouri (Keslin 1964:61). Micmac pipes found at French and British forts suggest that the pipes were also used by the colonists (Stone 1974; Hanson and Hsu 1975; Hulse 1981; Noble 1983; Jelks and Ekberg 1984). At Fort Michilimackinac, Micmac pipes were reported in contexts that indicated the pipes were of French rather than Indian manufacture (Armour 1966:2).

Five of the Micmac pipes at the Cahokia Wedge were found within Area A, which has been identified as the eighteenth-century French habitational area. The pipes do not exhibit clear evidence of manufacture with metal tools, suggesting that they may have been of aboriginal manufacture. The abundance of Micmac pipes from the Cahokia Wedge may indicate Indian influence and interaction through trade with the French.

KAOLIN CLAY PIPES

A total of 239 kaolin pipe fragments was recovered from the surface (n = 119), from excavation units (n = 114), and from features (n = 6). Twenty-eight specimens are fragments of decorated bowls, heels, and stems (Figure 49). Undecorated fragments include 18 pipe bowls, 192 pipe stems, and one spur heel.

Decorated Kaolin Pipe Bowls

'TD' Pipes (n = 8; Figure 49 A-H). The most elaborate 'TD' pipe in the Cahokia Wedge collection is a fragment of the bowl back face. The raised letters 'TD', one on each side of a very apparent mold seam, are encircled within a raised, double-lined element, possibly of a chevron or heart shape. Inside this element are two curved lines above the letters, and above this a fragmentary raised design. Floral or leaf designs extend off the chevron or heart shape. Below this is a seven-pointed star or floral design.

Another bowl fragment has the initials 'TD' within a stamped or impressed circular design on the bowl back. A smaller impressed circle is located between the initials, and below this is a single floral and double leaf design. On the left side of the flattened heel is a raised circle or 'O'. The right side of the heel is fragmentary. The stem hole measures 5/64 inch. Similar pipes have been found at Fort Michilimackinac (Stone 1974:149).

One fragmentary bowl has the impressed linear designs above the letter 'D'. These decorations are encircled with a dashed line or rope design. Another small bowl fragment also has the impressed rope design encircling an impressed letter 'T'. Several examples of the dashed or rope circle decorations were recovered from Fort Michilimackinac (Stone 1974:149) and the British colonial site of Fort Stanwix (Hanson and Hsu 1975:142).

One stem and flattened heel fragment has raised letters 'T' and 'D' placed vertically, one on each side of the heel. Although the bowl of this pipe is missing, comparative examples from Fort Michilimackinac have this type of heel decoration on pipes that also have 'TD' design elements on the bowl back (Stone 1974:149).

The most complete pipe in the Cahokia Wedge collection has a portion of a raised letter, probably the base of the letter 'T', located on the left side of the mold seam. The pipe bowl is perpendicular to the stem and the heel has been broken off. The stem hole measures 6/64 inch. Another small bowl fragment has a raised letter 'T' without any other apparent decoration.

A small bowl fragment has an impressed design encircling the letter 'D' and curved linear designs above and below the letter.

The 'TD' pipes, which can date as early as 1730, are primarily of English manufacture (Walker 1967). Several individuals with these initials, including Thomas Dean, Thomas Darkes, and Thomas Dormer, were producing 'TD' pipes in the eighteenth century (Omwake 1955).

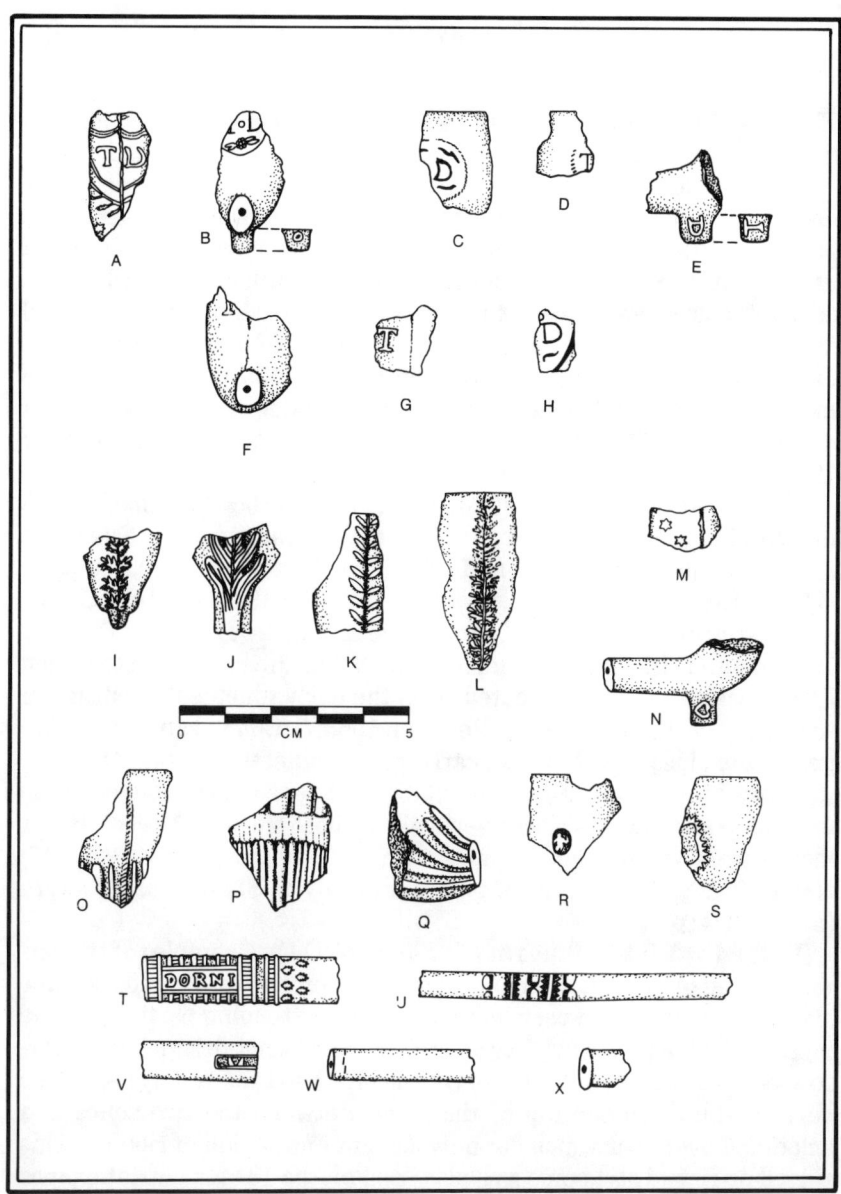

Fig. 49. Kaolin clay pipes. A-H, 'TD' pipes; I-L, leaf or floral motifs; M, star motif; N, heart motif; O-Q, ridged or ribbed pipes; R, cartouche; S, unknown decoration; T, 'Peter Dorni' pipe stem; U and V, impressed pipe stems; W, incised and reworked mouthpiece; X, original mouthpiece

The styles became very popular and these pipes were produced into the mid-nineteenth century, well after the original pipemakers had died.

Leaf or Floral Motif (n = 4; Figure 49 I-L). Four pipe fragments are decorated with raised leaf or floral motifs on the bowl face. These pipes have a vertical line of leaves or floral designs symmetrically placed on each side of the mold seam. This decorative treatment was used to conceal the mold seam by incorporating it into the design. One small bowl fragment has a spur heel, which is characteristic of late eighteenth- and early nineteenth-century pipes (Peterson 1963:5). The stem hole measures 6/64 inch. The leaf or floral motif along the mold seam was often used on 'TD' pipes and the 13-star patriotic pipes (Humphrey 1969:26).

Star Motif (n = 1; Figure 49 M). One small pipe bowl fragment, lacking the rim, has three raised and diagonally arranged stars. The three stars may represent a portion of a circle of stars to enclose the initials 'TD' or 'LF'. This specimen is possibly from the 13-star patriotic pipe, a common motif often used in conjunction with 'TD' pipes (Walker 1967:89) and 'LF' pipes (Humphrey 1969:25). Pipes of this type from Fort Mackinac have been dated from the early nineteenth century to the period of the War of 1812 (Peterson 1963:7). Comparative data suggest these pipes date from the early- to mid-nineteenth century.

Heart Motif (n = 1; Figure 49 N). One flattened heel and stem fragment has raised hearts placed vertically on both sides of the heel. Heart motifs were often used on pipes with 'RT' initials (Stone 1974:146; Noble 1983:313). This type of pipe is probably of English manufacture (Stone 1974:147).

Ridged or Ribbed Pipes (n = 6; Figure 49 O-Q). Examples of the vertical ridged or ribbed kaolin pipes include four pipe bowls and two pipe stem fragments. Two specimens have ridges extending partially up the pipe bowl. One pipe bowl fragment has two distinct design zones; narrow vertical ridges on the bottom of the pipe bowl and widely separated vertical ridges on the top of the bowl. Between the two zones is a smoothed-over area which has only a slight impression of ribbing. This ridged or ribbed style pipe was also used on the 13-star patriotic pipes of the early nineteenth century (Noel Hume 1970:307) and have been interpreted to be of English manufacture (Hanson 1971:94). The ribbed pipes in the Cahokia Wedge collection probably date to the late eighteenth or early nineteenth centuries.

Cartouche (n = 1; Figure 49 R). One bowl fragment has a small, impressed cartouche located 1.1 cm below the bowl rim. The cartouche measures approximately 0.6 cm in length and 0.4 cm in width. Although difficult to distinguish, it appears to be a human figure. Other figural cartouches, such as a mermaid and a milkmaid, have been attributed to Dutch pipemakers of the mid-eighteenth century (Walker 1967:192).

Unknown Decoration (n=1; Figure 49 S). One bowl fragment has an unidentified decorative motif located 0.7 cm below the rim on the bowl front. It is a raised, rounded, or rectangular design that has pointed appendages extending off the exterior. Inside of this is a portion of an indeterminate raised design element. The design gives an appearance of a cartouche or an element which possibly enclosed initials. Comparative examples have not been identified.

Undecorated Pipe Bowls (n=18). Undecorated pipe bowl fragments in the Cahokia Wedge collection numbered 18 specimens.

Decorated Kaolin Pipe Stems

Three decorated kaolin pipe stem fragments have relief and/or impressed design elements. Several stem fragments appear to have the original tapered mouthpieces and other stem fragments have ends that have been reworked, whittled, or ground to produce functional mouthpieces.

'Peter Dorni' Pipe (n=1; Figure 49 T). One pipe stem has an intricate raised design of lines or ribs, tobacco leaves, and the inscription 'PETER DORNI'. The stem hole diameter measures 4/64 inch. Peter Dorni was a pipemaker in northern France around 1850. This style of pipe became so popular that it was imitated by pipemakers in Gouda, Holland, for export (Omwake 1965:130). An identical pipe stem fragment was recovered from the Alorton site, a mid-nineteenth century farmstead located several miles east of Cahokia (Anderson 1981:66). 'Peter Dorni' pipes were common at Fort Stanwix in New York (Hanson 1971:94) and at Old Sacramento in California (Humphrey 1969:94).

Impressed Designs (n=2; Figure 49 U, V). One stem fragment has a circumferentially-impressed alternating design of circles or dots with saw-tooth or triangular elements. The saw-tooth design is typical of Dutch pipes manufactured in Gouda in the early- to mid-eighteenth century (Walker 1967:193). Pipes of this type have been found at the Fortress of Louisbourg in Canada (Walker 1967:193), Fort Michilimackinac (Stone 1974:150), Fort Ouiatenon (Noble 1983:319), and Old Sacramento (Humphrey 1967:70). However, the specimen in the Cahokia Wedge collection may be of English manufacture, based on the combined use of circles or dots with the saw-tooth triangular motifs (Walker 1967:193).

One decorated pipe stem has a raised design element consisting of triangular forms within a rectangular border or frame horizontally placed on the pipe stem.

Mouthpieces (n = 2; Figure 49 W, X). One pipe stem fragment has an unevenly applied, mustard-colored glaze. This type of treatment usually appeared near the mouthpiece. The use of glaze, although uncommon, dates to the eighteenth century (Noel Hume 1970:302).

One reworked pipe stem end has been ground to create the mouthpiece and has a series of seven incised lines around the circumference, .1 cm from the mouthpiece.

Miscellaneous Pipe Fragments (n = 2). Two flattened heel fragments have indeterminate raised designs that probably represent initials.

Undecorated stem fragments numbered 192. Of the 199 measurable pipe stem fragments, 21 (10.5%) had stem holes that measured 6/64 inch, 112 (56.3%) measured 5/64 inch, and 66 (33.2%) measured 4/64 inch. Comparing the stem hole measurements with the suggested time periods set forth by J. C. Harrington (1954), the Cahokia Wedge collection compares favorably with the 1710–1750 period, with a tendency toward the later period of 1750–1800. However, the inherent problems of this comparison, such as sample size, population fluctuations, and the influx of American-made pipes after 1780, as examined in other studies (Stone 1974; Hanson and Hsu 1975), also applies to the Cahokia Wedge collection.

OTHER CLAY PIPES

Earthenware Pipe (n = 1; Figure 50 A). A complete and undamaged fired clay pipe bowl was found in Zone A of Feature 1. The pipe, weighing 83.9 grams, is light yellowish brown (10YR 6/4) in color and appears to be untempered. The shape is round to bulbous, with a slight shoulder facet located centrally at the maximum circumference diameter of 3.9 cm. The height of the pipe from rim to base is 4.4 cm. The rim diameter measures 2.6 cm. The interior of the bowl tapers dramatically inward to the base, creating a relatively small bowl. The bowl lip is flattened, with several areas having the appearance of being cut. The flat pipe base has a diameter of approximately 2.5 cm. The inward tapering stem hole, located below the shoulder facet, is fairly large at the pipe exterior, measuring 1.2 cm in diameter. Around the bowl circumference and above the shoulder facet is a single, very irregular, interrupted or dashed, incised line. This decoration ranges from 1.2 cm to 2.2 cm below the bowl rim. Underneath this line is a series of verti-

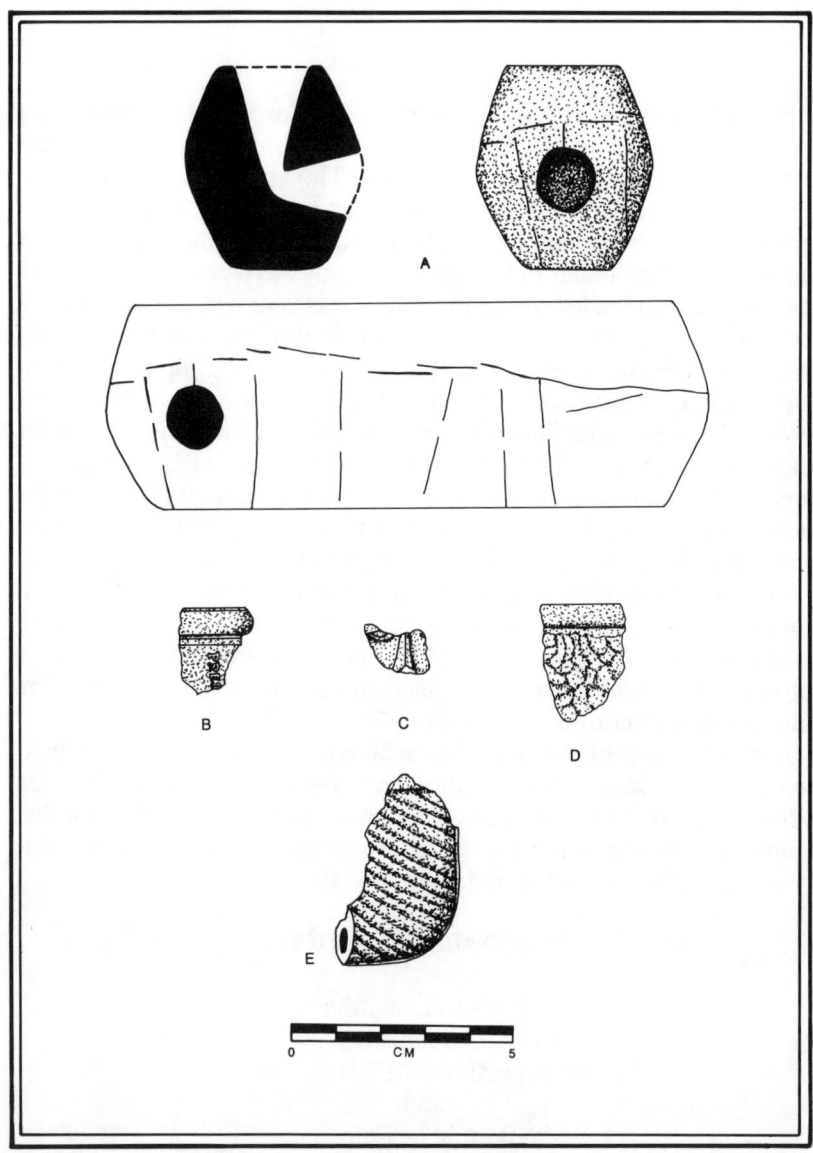

Fig. 50. Other clay pipes. A, incised earthenware pipe bowl; B, glazed commemorative presidential pipe; C and D, glazed figural pipes; E, glazed ribbed pipe

cal, dashed incisions, arranged at slightly regular intervals around the pipe and extending to the pipe base. These scratched lines are very faint and the design is crudely executed. The style of the pipe is dissimilar to typical historic Indian pipes, such as Micmac, elbow, and effigy pipes. However, there is an Indian ceramic tradition, including the manufacture of smoking pipes. This pipe may have been of aboriginal manufacture and traded to the French; it was recovered from Feature 1, which is interpreted as an early to mid-eighteenth-century pit.

Glazed Figural Pipes (n = 3; Figure 50 B-D). Two pipe fragments have a similar orange paste with a clear glaze. These fragments were recovered from excavation units. One specimen has a human face with molded eyes and nose. The other is a bowl fragment with a lipped rim above an incised line. Underneath the lip are the raised letters 'PRES', placed vertically on the bowl body. This fragment probably represents a commemorative presidential pipe dating to the nineteenth century.

Another figural pipe with orange paste and dark brown glaze has a lipped rim and human hair shown in relief. A similar pipe was found at the Alorton Site (Anderson 1981:31). Figural pipes, generally with a stub end for a detachable stem, probably date to the nineteenth century and were manufactured in the United States.

Glazed Ribbed Pipe (n = 1; Figure 50 E). One nearly complete pipe bowl with grey paste and a tan glaze has raised diagonal ridges or ribs on the bowl and stem. This pipe would have had a stub end. It is similar to pipes manufactured in Ohio, which was a major area of pipe production in the 1850s (Hamilton and Hamilton 1972).

HISTORIC CERAMICS

by John A. Walthall
Chief Archaeologist
Illinois Department of Transportation
and
Bonnie L. Gums
Project Director
Contract Archaeology Program—SIUE

The archaeological investigations, both the surface collection and excavations, at the Cahokia Wedge site yielded nearly 4,000 historic ceramic sherds. Approximately 75% of this total are fragments from vessels used and/or disposed of at the site during the nineteenth century. Of the remaining 975 sherds, approximately half (504) may be confidently associated with the pre-Revolutionary War French occupation.

The association of the 471 English creamware and pearlware sherds recovered from the site is less certain. It is likely that the majority of these fragments are from vessels dating to the early nineteenth century. Since the research effort in the Wedge locality focused on the French component, only the specimens attributable to this period are described in detail. Data on the nineteenth-century ceramics are summarized in this volume. This latter sample does, however, constitute an important source of information for the later successive occupations of the village of Cahokia, and should be subjected to more intensive study in the future.

The eighteenth-century French-related ceramics are composed of tin-glazed earthenwares, coarse lead-glazed earthenwares, and salt-glazed stoneware. Two sherds identified as Chinese porcelain may also be associated with the colonial occupation, since such porcelain sherds have been recovered from nearby contemporaneous sites. The bulk of the tin-glazed earthenwares from the Cahokia Wedge is composed of several types of plain and underglaze-decorated faience. Fragments of a few vessels of English delftware and Spanish majolica are also present. This ceramic sample is similar to assemblages recovered at other contemporaneous French colonial sites in North America (Miller and Stone 1970; Brain 1979; Parker 1982; Waselkov et al. 1982).

Eighteenth-century French earthenwares, particularly faience, have only recently been the subject of more than a passing interest to archaeologists (Brain 1979; Barton 1981). As part of a current, comprehensive study of ceramics from French colonial components at settlements in the Illinois Country, Walthall (in press) has recently recognized seven faience and four coarse earthenware types. A number of faience rim border styles have also been delineated. Six rim border styles were identified in the Cahokia Wedge collection (Figure 51). Formal definition and supporting documentation for these types are provided in that volume. Brief descriptions and illustrations of each formal ceramic type found at the Cahokia Wedge are provided below. In addition, sherds which cannot, at present, be placed into an established type are described informally according to glaze and paste characteristics.

Descriptions of the ceramic sample recovered during the archaeological investigations are contained in the following pages. Sherd counts and provenience are provided in Table 3. These data reveal that a minimum of 50 vessels of earthenware and stoneware was used by the successive occupants of the excavated structure. Counts of these vessels by ware, form, and presumed function are provided in Table 4. Tin-glazed earthenware plates and platters are by far the most common

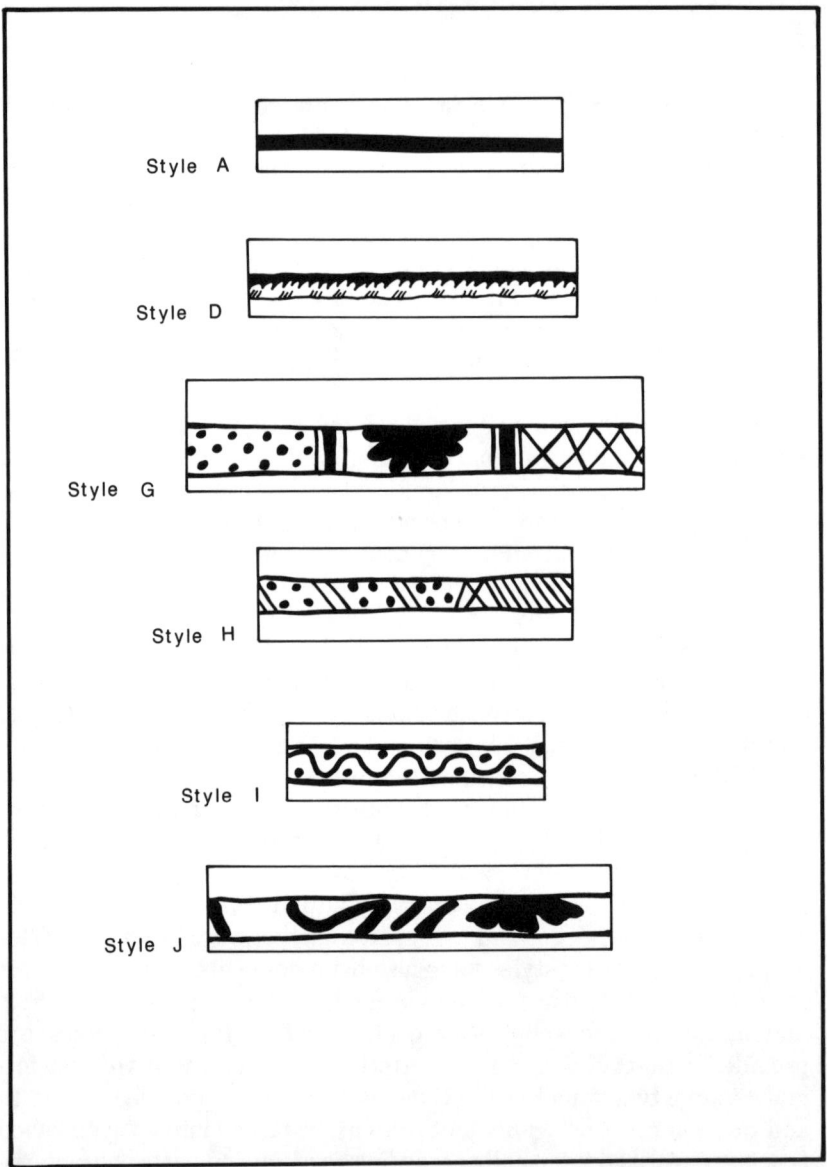

Fig. 51. Faience rim border styles represented at the Cahokia Wedge site (Adapted from Walthall in press)

TABLE 3

EIGHTEENTH- AND EARLY NINETEENTH-CENTURY CERAMICS COUNTS AND PROVENIENCE

Ceramic Type	CSC*	Excavation Units	Features		Totals
Faience	55	172	Feature 4	1	246
			Feature 6	3	
			Feature 7	15	
Delftware	8		Feature 7	1	9
Majolica	3	6			9
Westerwald Stoneware		2	Feature 4	2	4
English White Saltglazed Stoneware		1			1
Coarse Earthenwares	96	124	Feature 2	1	235
			Feature 4	7	
			Feature 6	2	
			Feature 7	5	
Miscellaneous Earthenwares	23	22	Feature 6	1	47
			Feature 7	1	
Creamware	104	278	Feature 5	5	406
			Feature 6	4	
			Feature 7	10	
			Feature 8	4	
			Feature 13	1	
Pearlware	30	31	Feature 5	2	65
			Feature 6	1	
			Feature 11	1	
Porcelain	55	4	Feature 4	1	60
			Grand total		1082

*Controlled surface collection

TABLE 4

Eighteenth Century Ceramic Vessel Form and Function

	Plates	Platters	Serving Vessels Bowls	Cups/Mugs	Tureens	Storage Vessels Jars	Jugs
Faience	18	3		4	1		
Delft/Majolica	2		2				
Stoneware	1			1			
Coarse earthenware			11	2		4	1
Subtotals	21	3	13	7	1	4	1
Subtotals	Serving Vessels – 45				Storage Vessels – 5		
Grand total	50 vessels						

vessel forms in the assemblage. Bowls dominate the coarse earthenware category. The data summarized in Table 4 suggest that ceramics in French colonial frontier contexts primarily functioned as serving vessels. Unlike contemporary British and Spanish colonists (Stone 1973; Smith 1965), French settlers do not appear to have utilized ceramic vessels in food preparation activities such as cooking or baking. Rather, vessels of other materials such as iron, brass, and copper were likely used in French frontier culinary practices.

FRENCH FAIENCE

A total of 246 faience sherds was recovered from the surface (n = 55), from excavation units (n = 172), and from features (n = 19). These specimens represent a minimum of 26 vessels and are described, by type, below.

Normandy Plain (n = 151; 14 rims; Figure 52; Plate 14). A total of 151 faience sherds are undecorated. These sherds represent fragments of plain faience vessels as well as fragments of the plain portions of vessels which may have been decorated. The sample includes 14 rims, two annular-footed basal sherds, and one handle. Thirteen sherds lack curvature and may represent fragments of flat bases. Glaze colors range from white to off-white to pinkish-white. Two Normandy Plain body sherds have evidence of drilled repair holes.

A minimum of four undecorated vessels is present in the sample. One small plate, approximately 22.0 cm in diameter, is represented by nine rim sherds, a basal fragment, and five body sherds. This plate has a simple rounded lip and an annular-footed base. Large sections of the pinkish-white enamel have spalled leaving, much of the vessel fabric exposed. It is noteworthy that the fabric of this simple vessel is of two distinct hues. From the vessel lip 3.0 cm to the edge of the marli, the fabric is salmon-colored. The interior of the plate and the footed base have a buff yellow paste. These differences in the paste color of this plate, of which there are large fragments, should serve as a caution to researchers reconstructing minimum vessel counts from small sherds. It is likely that the differences in paste color would lead to the identification of two vessels instead of the one present.

Five rim sherds from three vertical-sided cups are also present in the plainware sample. These cups, with simple rounded rims, range from 6.0 cm to 10.0 cm in diameter. One sherd has an annular-footed base, 4.0 cm in interior diameter. The foot is 1.0 cm high and 2.0 cm thick. A plain white handle fragment is straight and "D" shaped in cross-section. The fragment, 5.0 cm in length, is from an unidentified vessel, although

Fig. 52. Faience. Normandy Plain: A and B, plate with ring base; C, cup; D, ring base; E, handle

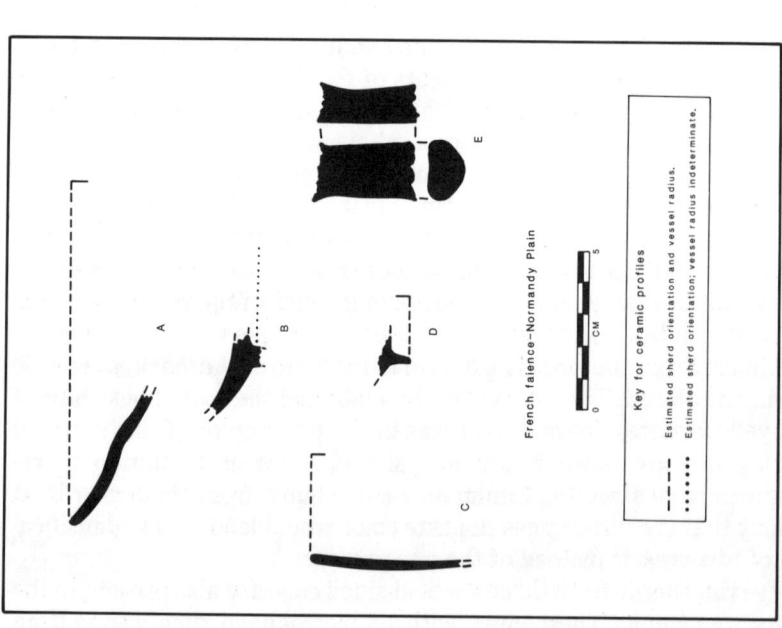

Plate 14. Faience. Normandy Plain: A and B, plate with ring base; C, cup; D, ring base; E, handle

the lack of curvature suggests that the handle may have been attached to a pipkin or similar vessel form.

Normandy Blue on White (n = 47; 27 rims). *variety Normandy* (Figure 53 A-D; Plate 15). There are 22 faience sherds in the collection which have unlined blue decorations. In this total are eleven rims representing a minimum of four vessels, all plates. Ten rim sherds are from three plates with Style J rim motifs (Figure 51). One of these plates has an estimated diameter of 24.0 cm. A small rim sherd from a plate exhibits an unidentifiable fragment of blue decoration 1.7 cm below the lip on the interior rim plane. This sherd has evidence of one drilled repair hole.

One body sherd has a broadly brushed blue floral design with tendril motifs in manganese on the exterior of the vessel. A red substance is adhered to the interior of the sherd. The relatively small curvature of this sherd suggests a globular vessel form, probably a pitcher. Similar designs are on a nearly complete pitcher from the Trudeau site in Louisiana (Brain 1979:43). The other sherds in this category are all fragments of decorated rim planes probably representing plates or platters.

variety St. Cloud (Figure 53 E-M; Plate 15). Twenty-five sherds including 16 rims and four base sherds have blue decorations outlined in dark blue, black, or manganese. Six plates, a platter, a cup, and a tureen are represented by rim sherds. Two rim sherds are from a plate with a Style D rim border, one is from a Style H plate, and one is from a Style I plate (Figure 51). Eleven rim sherds including one with a drilled repair hole are from three Style G (Figure 51) plates. A platter rim has a complex decorative rim band composed of three elements: a Style G motif with a scale design; a plain blue line or band; and a tendril motif (Figure 51). Most of these rim sherds exhibit scalloped edges.

One small rim sherd, probably from a cup, has a thin black line parallel to the lip on the vessel interior. It is not known if the remainder of this vessel was decorated. One rim and one body sherd are from a tureen. This vessel has a brilliant white enamel. The exterior walls are decorated with floral motifs composed of heavy black outlines filled with blue. On the interior of the rim sherd is a black curved line which may represent a floral or stem motif. The rim is rounded and ground to fit a lid. The vessel body is molded with raised vertical ridges.

Four flat basal sherds from plates or platters have floral decorations that are within the interior of the vessels. One of the bases has a estimated diameter of 18.0 cm.

Brittainy Blue on White (n = 10; 8 rims; Figure 54 A-C; Plate 16). Four plates with plain blue, unlined bands below the interior vessel lip

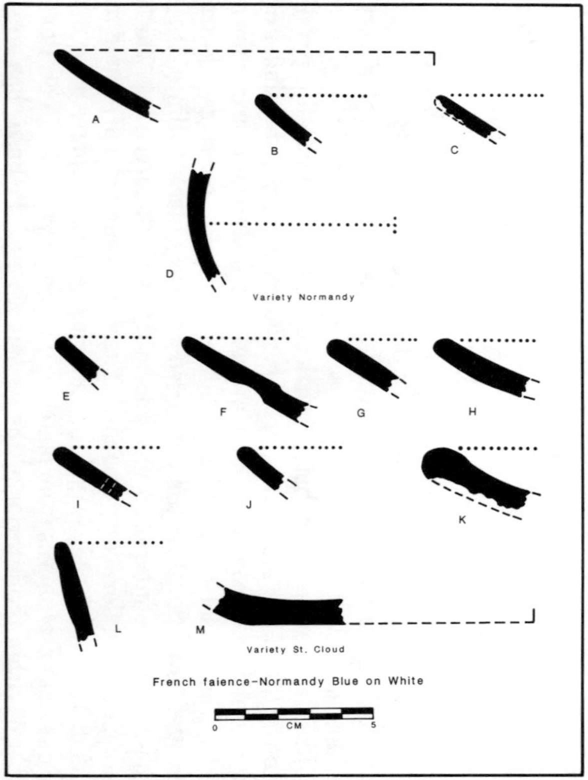

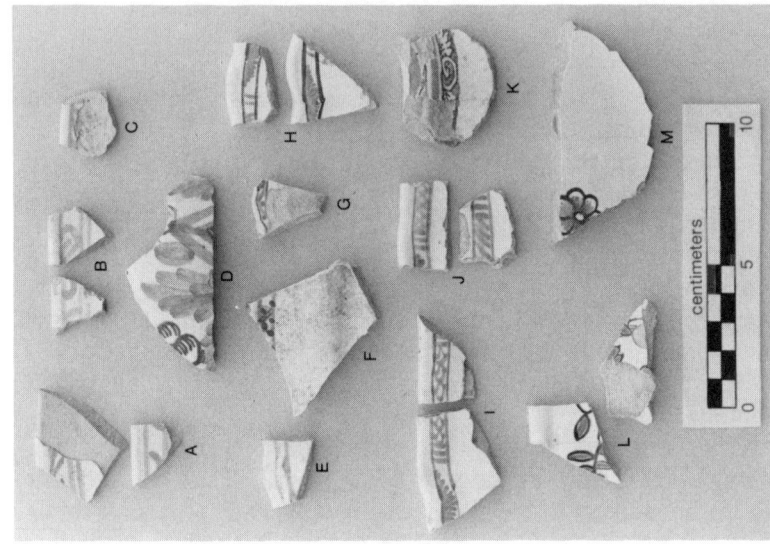

Fig. 53. Faience - Normandy Blue on White. Variety Normandy: A-C, plates; D, pitcher. Variety St. Cloud: E-K, plates/platters; L, tureen; M, base

Plate 15. Faience - Normandy Blue on White. Variety Normandy: A-C, plates; D, pitcher. Variety St. Cloud: E-K, plates/platters; L, tureen; M, base

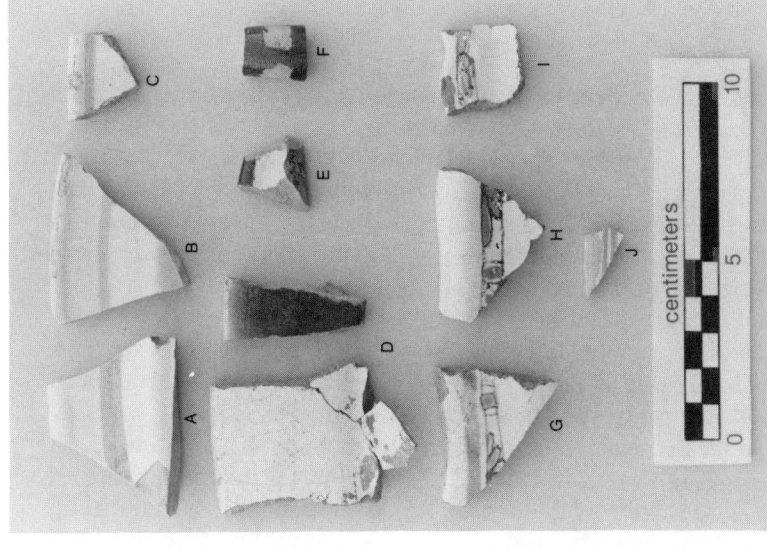

Fig. 54. Faience. Brittany Blue on White: A-C, plates. Rouen Plain: D, plate; E lid; F, handle. Rouen Blue on White: G-I, plates/platters. Provence Yellow on White: J, plate

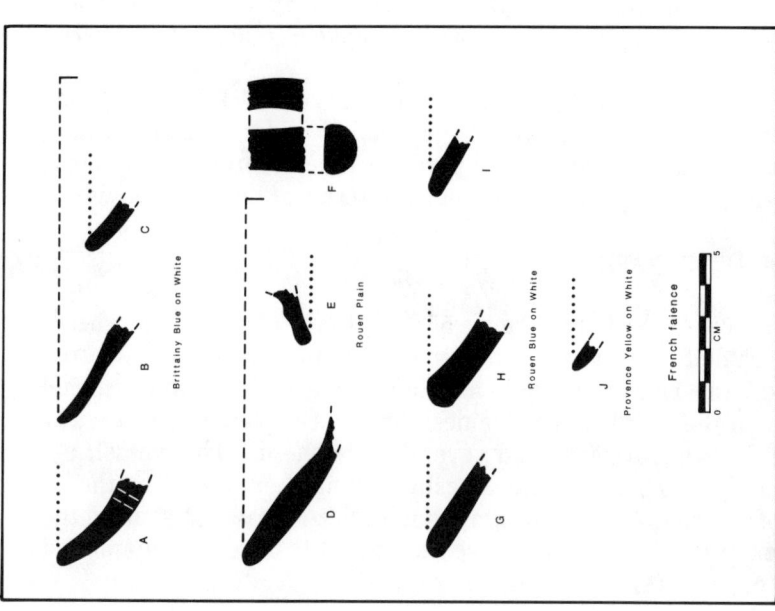

Plate 16. Faience. Brittany Blue on White: A-C, plates. Rouen Plain: D, plate; E, lid; F, handle. Rouen Blue on White: G-I, plates/platters. Provence Yellow on White: J, plate

are present in the collection. These single bands range in width from 0.3 cm to 0.6 cm. This simple rim decoration corresponds to Walthall's (in press) Style A border (Figure 51). One plate had been broken and repaired by drilling two holes for rivets (likely of lead) into the opposing edges of the breaks. These repair holes measure 0.5 cm in diameter. One plate has an estimated diameter of 22.0 cm and another rim sherd also has evidence of one drilled repair hole.

Rouen Plain (n = 31; 4 rims; Figure 54 D-F; Plate 16). One vessel, probably a plate, has an interior white enamel and an exterior dark brown lead glaze. It is represented by three rim sherds, three basal sherds, and several body sherds. The rim fragments exhibit a rounded lip and the plate measures approximately 23.0 cm in diameter. A red substance, perhaps vermillion, was found adhering to the interior of some of the fragments of this vessel. A lid fragment with a rounded lip and a curved handle midsection are also present in the collection.

Rouen Blue on White (n = 6; 4 rims; Figure 54 G-I; Plate 16). The six blue-decorated faience sherds with brown lead-glazed exteriors represent a minimum of three vessels, two platters and a plate. All three of these flatware pieces have Style G (Figure 51) rim border motifs and scalloped rims. The plate sherd exhibits a molded treatment on the rim plane.

Provence Yellow on White (n = 1; 1 rim; Figure 54 J; Plate 16). One rim sherd from a plate has an orangish-yellow underglaze decoration. The fragment is small and only a portion of the decorative treatment, represented by two parallel lines on the interior of the rim, remains.

ENGLISH DELFTWARE

Delftware (n = 9; 1 rim; Figure 55 A-D; Plate 17 A-D). Nine sherds of English delft were recovered from excavation units (n = 8) and from Feature 7 (n = 1). These sherds have a bluish-gray, tin-glazed enamel and five of the sherds have blue decorations. One vessel, a bowl, was identified by a rim sherd and several body sherds. This vessel, approximately 20.0 cm in diameter, exhibits a hatchered band on the interior of the rim. A floral design in underglaze blue is present on the vessel exterior. Vessels with these design motifs have been attributed to Bristol potteries (Garner 1949).

SPANISH MAJOLICA

A total of nine sherds of Spanish majolica were recovered from the surface (n = 3) and from excavation units (n = 6).

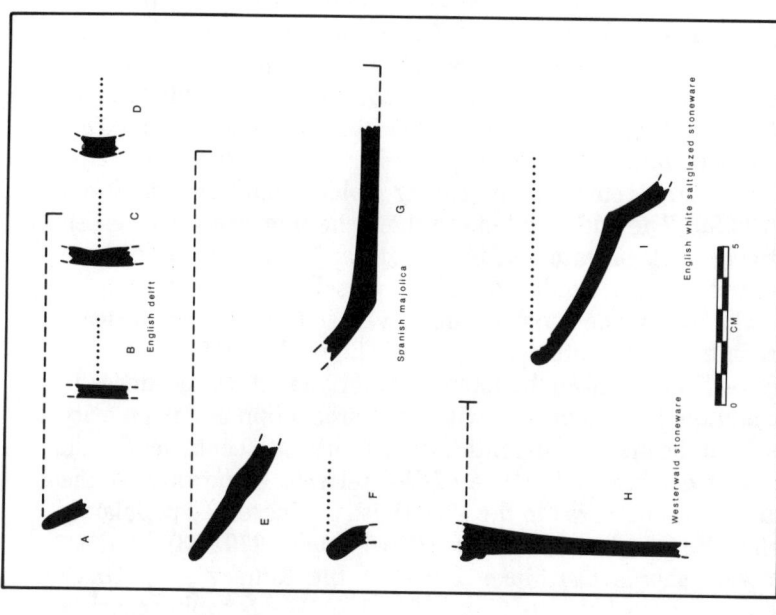

Fig. 55. English delftware: A-D, bowls. Spanish majolica: E, Puebla Blue on White plate; F and G, Plain majolica bowl and base. Westerwald stoneware: H, mug. English white saltglazed stoneware: I, plate/platter

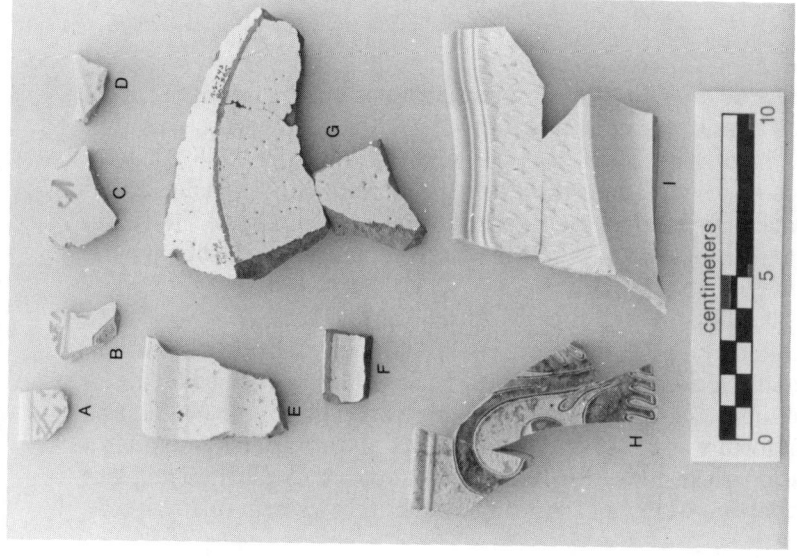

Plate 17. English delftware: A-D, bowls. Spanish majolica: E, Puelba Blue on White plate; F and G, Plain majolica bowl and base. Westerwald stoneware: H, mug. English white saltglazed stoneware: I, plate/platter

Puebla Blue on White (n = 2; 2 rims; Figure 55 E; Plate 17 E). Two rim sherds possibly from a single plate can be assigned to this previously defined Spanish colonial ceramic type (Goggin 1968; Deagan 1987). This plate, with an estimated diameter of 26.0 cm, is decorated with a broad blue band on the interior of the rim, parallel to the vessel lip. A second, thinner band runs the vessel circumference just below the upper band.

Plain Majolica (n = 7; 2 rims; Figure 55 F, G; Plate 17 F, G). Seven undecorated majolica sherds were recovered, representing a minimum of two vessels, a bowl and a plate. A rim sherd from a plain bowl has an estimated diameter of 20.0 cm. The other rim sherd is very small and the vessel form was indeterminate. The six plate fragments exhibit a white crackle glaze and a deep orange, slightly sandy fabric. The plate has a flat bottom which measures approximately 15.0 cm in diameter.

RHENISH STONEWARE

Westerwald Stoneware (n = 4; Figure 55 H; Plate 17 H). Four sherds of Westerwald stoneware were recovered from test excavations. Two sherds were located on the surface of Feature 4 and the other two sherds, which mend with one sherd from Feature 4, were recovered from the screened soil above the feature. The specimens have a gray paste and a clear salt glaze. The mended sherds have a molded flange above an incised floral or leaf motif decorated with cobalt blue. This type of incised design became popular in the first quarter of the eighteenth century, replacing the earlier molded relief designs (Noel Hume 1970:282). The undecorated sherd may be from the same vessel. The relatively small curvature of the sherds, approximately 10.0 cm in diameter, indicates a small cylindrical vessel, probably a mug or tankard, which was the most common vessel form of Westerwald stoneware in the eighteenth century (Noel Hume 1970:282).

Westerwald derives from the Rhenish tradition that was produced in Germany and the Low Countries with peak production and popularity occurring from the mid-seventeenth to mid-eighteenth centuries (Brain 1979:77). The decline in the use of Westerwald stoneware in the American colonies occurred in the 1760s with the increased popularity of English white saltglazed stoneware (Noel Hume 1970:283).

Westerwald sherds have been found at the Kolmer site, (Orser 1975:158) and the Guebert site (Good 1972:175). Westerwald ceramics from Fort Michilimackinac were dated from 1725 to 1775 (Miller and Stone 1970:74). A complete Westerwald mug, with a design very similar to that on the sherds in the Cahokia Wedge collection, was found at Fort Louisbourg, in Nova Scotia, dating from 1720 to 1755 (Lunn 1972:182). Similar mugs are also in the collection from the Trudeau site and date predominantly to the second half of the eighteenth century (Brain 1979:77).

Westerwald sherds are notably absent from the surface collection at the Cahokia Wedge site. The recovery of the sherds in and around Feature 4 supports the identification of the feature as dating to the early to mid-eighteenth century.

ENGLISH WHITE SALTGLAZED STONEWARE

English White Saltglazed Stoneware (n = 1; Figure 55 I; Plate 17 I). One sherd of English white saltglazed stoneware was recovered from an excavation unit. It is probably from a plate or platter and has a scalloped rim. The sherd has an off-white paste with a clear saltglaze and is decorated with intricate molded relief designs on the rim plane. The relief design consists of a barley or grain motif encircled with wavy lines within panels separated by ribbing. This decorative motif corresponds to Gusset's (1980:97–99) type MII-3.2, dating to ca. 1755.

White saltglazed stoneware was manufactured predominantly in Staffordshire between 1750 and 1770, with the most common vessel forms being dinner plates and dinner services (Miller and Stone 1970:68; Noel Hume 1970:115–118). By 1760, this ware was the most common regimental tableware found at British Canadian military sites; however, by 1780, with the appearance of English creamware, the use of white saltglazed stoneware declined (Sussman 1978:96). The paucity of this ceramic type at the Cahokia Wedge is noteworthy and may represent the brief British influence at Cahokia in the mid-1760s.

COARSE EARTHENWARES

A total of 235 sherds of coarse earthenware ceramics was recovered from the surface (n = 96), from excavation units (n = 124), and from features (n = 15). Six types have been identified based on glaze and paste differences.

Saintonge Plain (n = 4; 2 rims; Figure 56 A, B; Plate 18 A, B). Four sherds with a white fabric and a green lead glaze may be assigned to this type. Two bowls are represented. One vessel is a vertical-sided bowl with a narrow flange, 5.0 cm in width, on the interior of the rim for fitting a lid. The rim is comma-shaped in cross-section. This bowl measures approximately 22.0 cm in diameter. The second bowl has a mottled green and yellow-green glaze. The rim has a wide flange and a

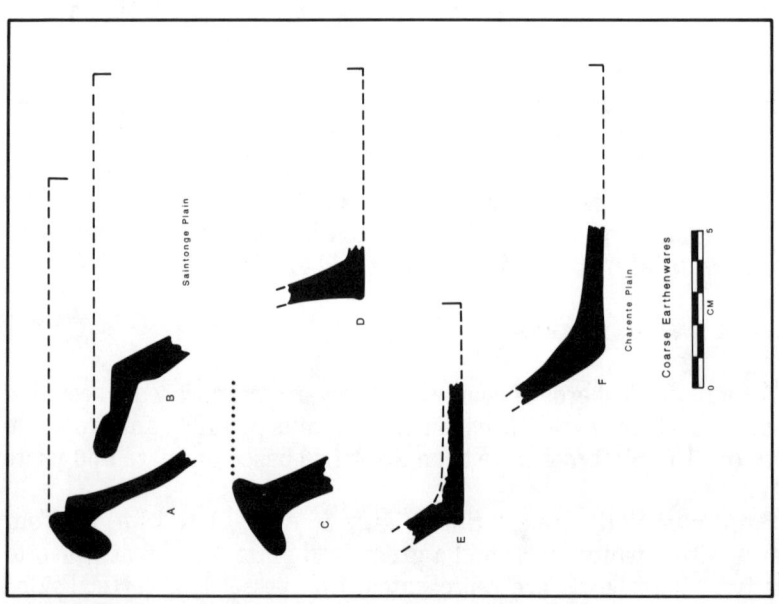

Fig. 56. Coarse earthenwares. Saintonge Plain: A and B, bowls. Charente Plain: C-F, bowls

Plate 18. Coarse earthenwares. Saintonge Plain: A and B, bowls. Charente Plain: C-F, bowls

rolled lip, with a diameter of approximately 24.0 cm. Both bowls are glazed only on the interiors.

Saintonge Slip Plain (n = 15). These sherds have a salmon-colored fabric and a white slip covered with a deep green lead glaze. Although no rims were recovered, one basal fragment probably represents a bowl with a flat base.

Charente Plain (n = 62; 4 rims; Figure 56 C-F; Plate 18 C-F). Charente Plain vessels are characterized by a dull orange to deep red paste containing a small amount of iron, which has bled into the glaze, creating minute brown flecks. The glaze, which is clear and lustrous, takes on a caramel to honey hue when applied to the red fabric. Rims from three bowls and a lid are present in this sample. The bowls are glazed only on the interiors. One large bowl has a broad, flattened T-shaped rim that is 2.8 cm in width. The two other bowls have straight rim profiles with simple rolled lips. The lid fragment has a flat, unglazed lip. A body sherd from a shallow bowl is decorated with lightly scattered, green splotches. Six basal sherds appear to be from flat-bottomed bowls. Diameters of these bases range from 14.0 cm to 18.0 cm.

Two small body sherds, which exhibit Charente Plain paste and glaze characteristics, are decorated. One has large, closely spaced, dark brown splotches. The other has a portion of a slip decoration represented by a 0.4 cm wide line of dull yellow slip. Such slip-decorated wares were common at the Fortress of Louisbourg in Nova Scotia (Barton 1981), but are rare at French colonial sites in the Illinois Country.

Clear Glaze Coarse Earthenwares (n = 45; 5 rims; Figure 57 A-I; Plate 19 A-C). These sherds have a red body and a clear, lustrous glaze. The rims are from two jars, a jug, and two mugs. The two jars have inverted, flat to rounded rims and probably had flat bases. One of these vessels is 10.0 cm in diameter and appears to represent an ointment jar (Brain 1979:56). The second vessel is a globular-shaped jar or pot. A small fragment of a jug rim, glazed on both sides, measures approximately 7.0 cm in diameter. Both of the mug rims are from finely potted vessels of 8.0 cm to 10.0 cm in diameter. These mugs were glazed on both the interior and exterior.

Four basal sherds were identified; one from a flat- bottomed bowl and three are from mugs. The bowl base measures 16.0 cm in diameter. The three mug bases measure approximately 12.0 cm in diameter. These sherds are glazed on both the interior and exterior vessel walls and the bottoms are unglazed. One of the mug bases has deep incised lines running the circumference of the vessel, creating an upward-stepped profile.

Fig. 57. Coarse earthenwares. Clear glaze: A, ointment (?) jar; B, jug; C, jar; D and E, mugs; F, bowl base; G-I, mug bases. Brown glaze: J, jar; K, bowl; L, bowl base

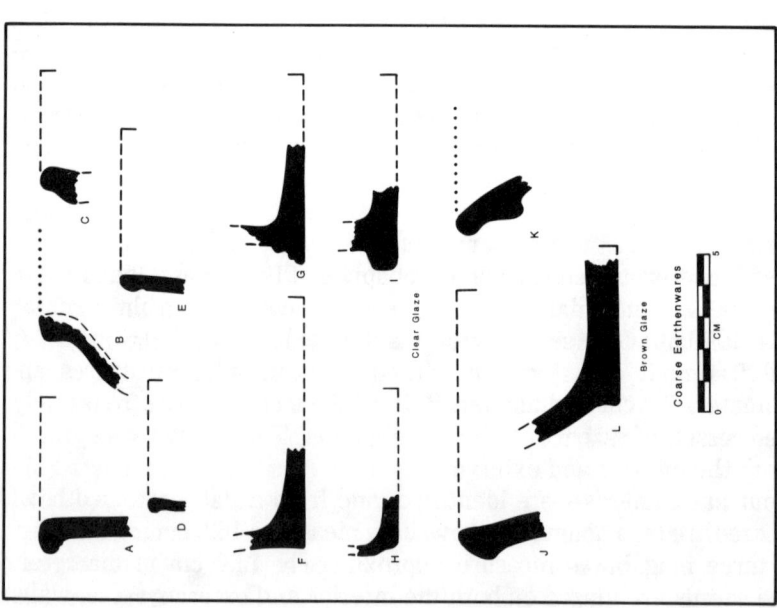

Plate 19. Coarse earthenwares. Clear glaze: A, ointment (?) jar; B, bowl base; C, mug base. Brown glaze: D, jar; E and F, bowls

Brown Glaze Coarse Earthenwares (n = 37; 4 rims; Figure 57 J-L; Plate 19 D-F). Vessels with a dull orange to red fabric and a translucent brown glaze have been placed into this category. Three of the rim sherds are from a vertical-sided jar with a flattened, outward-slanting rim. The exterior of the vessel is unglazed. The interior has a dark brown to almost black, heavy glaze. This jar measures approximately 16.0 cm in diameter. The remaining rim is from a bowl with heavy brown glaze containing dark brown streaks. The rim of this vessel is flared and the lip is rounded. Four base sherds appear to be from flat-bottomed bowls. Two of these bases have estimated diameters of 10.0 cm and 14.0 cm.

Green Glaze Coarse Earthenwares (n = 25; 4 rims; Figure 58 A-D; Plate 20 A-D). These earthenware fragments exhibit a range of green hues, from light brownish-green to deep olive. The glazes are translucent and lustrous. Pastes are most commonly orange, although reduced, gray pastes occur. Four vessels can be identified. Two bowls have flattened, flanged rims. One is glazed only on the interior; the other has glaze on both vessel walls. These bowls were approximately 22.0 cm in diameter. A third bowl has a straight rim profile and a simple round lip. Two base fragments were identified; one from a bowl and one from a jar. The basal sherd from a large, thick vertical-sided jar has a simple flat base and interior glaze. The unglazed exterior has incised parallel lines around the vessel circumference. The base of this jar measures approximately 16.0 cm in diameter.

OTHER EARTHENWARES

Unidentified Earthenware Vessel (n = 2; Figure 58 E; Plate 20 E). Two large earthenware rim sherds were recovered from the surface. These sherds have an orange paste with a clear, crackle glaze and are from the same vessel. The rim is everted measuring 2.3 cm in width. One of the sherds is a rounded to squared corner indicating that this vessel was rectangular or square in shape. The size of the sherds and the wall thickness (1.3 cm) suggest that this was a vessel of considerable dimensions.

Miscellaneous Earthenwares (n = 45). Forty-five unidentified earthenware sherds were recovered from the surface (n = 21), from excavation units (n = 22), and from features (n = 2). This category consists of earthenware sherds with an orange paste; however much of the glaze has flaked or spalled off and further type identification could not be determined. The majority of the specimens are very fragmentary and all appear to be body sherds.

Plate 20. Coarse earthenwares. Green glaze: A-D, bowls. Clear glaze: E, square or rectangular vessel

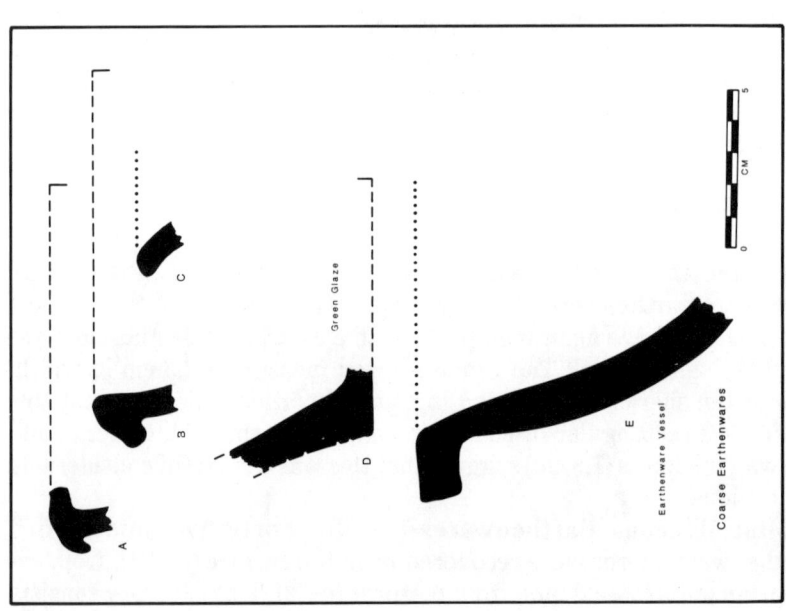

Fig. 58. Coarse earthenwares. Green glaze: A-D, bowls. Clear glaze: E, square or rectangular vessel

CREAMWARE

Creamware (n = 406; Figure 59). Four hundred six pieces of creamware were collected from the surface (n = 104), from excavation units (n = 278), and from features (n = 24). Most of the creamware sherds are very small and undecorated. The few decorated sherds have simple fluted or molded designs. Identified vessel forms include plates/platters, small bowls and/or cups. Several plate/platter rim sherds have scalloped edges and ridged rims. Most of the rim sherds from small bowls or cups are undecorated and have very thin vessel walls. The diameters of two of these vessels are estimated at 9.0 cm and 13.0 cm. One rim, possibly from a bowl, has a beaded and fluted decoration. One bowl fragment has a fluted design and a ring base with an interior diameter of approximately 15.0 cm.

English cream-colored earthenware, also known as Queen's Ware or Queen Anne's Ware, has a characteristic pale yellow or cream paste with a clear lead glaze (Noel Hume 1970:123). Creamware was perfected in the 1760s with the two major areas of production at Staffordshire and Yorkshire. The most common vessel forms were dinner plates/platters, soup plates, pitchers, and tea services. By the 1770s creamware had become the major ceramic export, replacing English delftware and white saltglazed stoneware (Miller and Stone 1970:42). Nearly all of the creamware found at Fort Michilimackinac derived from British contexts and probably dated post-1770 (Miller and Stone 1970:42). In the 1780s pearlware was introduced and by 1800, creamware and pearlware were the most common wares until the decline of both in the 1820s (Sussman 1978:99).

The creamware recovered from the Cahokia Wedge may date as early as the 1770s; however the majority probably date to the early nineteenth century. Most of the sherds from the surface were located in and around Area A. Ten sherds, including the two decorated bowl fragments, were recovered from Feature 7, the wall trench of the eighteenth- and early nineteenth-century structure identified as the Nicolle/Meunier house.

PEARLWARE

Pearlware (n = 65). Sixty-five pearlware sherds were conservatively identified in the controlled surface collection (n = 30), from excavation units (n = 31), and from feature fills (n = 4). The majority of the sherds are plain and probably represent the undecorated portions of vessels, since pearlware ceramics were rarely undecorated (Price 1979:11). The

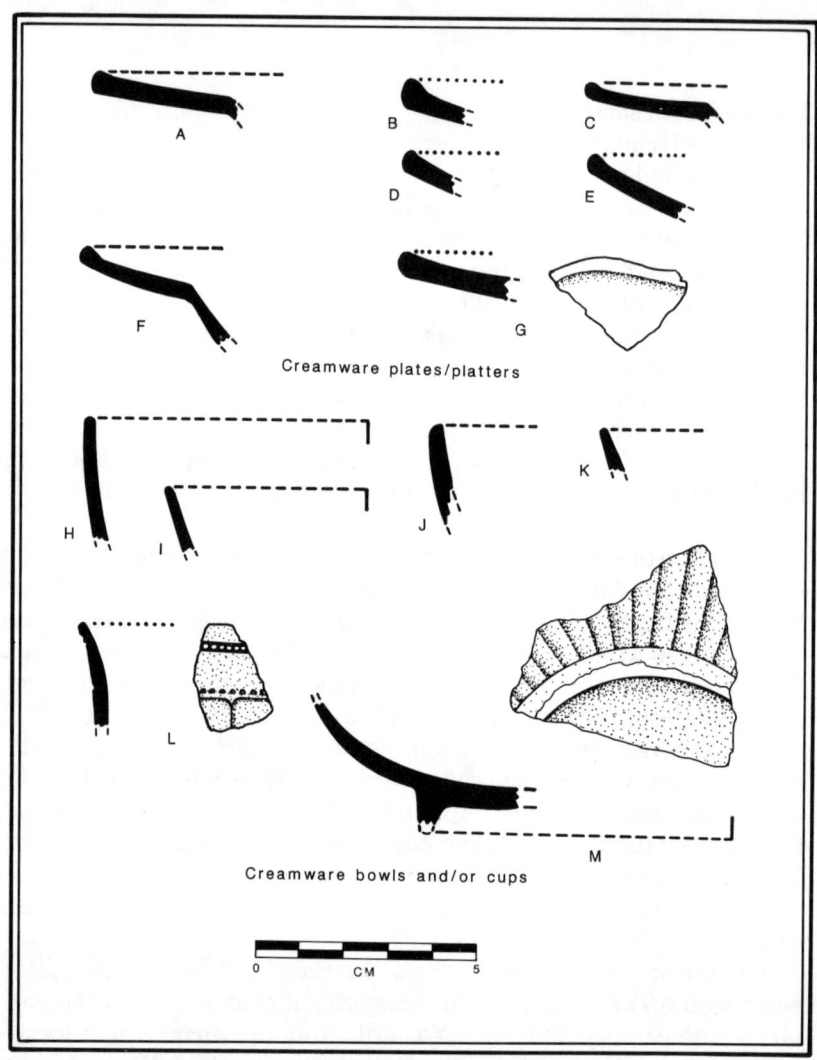

Fig. 59. Creamware. A-G, plates/platters; H-M, bowls and/or cups

ARTIFACT DESCRIPTIONS 155

few decorated sherds include molded blue herringbone, shell edge, and blue and polychrome transfer prints. The edge-decorated sherds represent plates and/or platters.

Pearlware has a white paste and a clear lead glaze to which cobalt was added, creating a bluish tint. The bluish tint is particularly evident in areas where the glaze collects, such as basal crevices. Pearlware was introduced in England by Josiah Wedgwood in the 1770s and became common in the early nineteenth century, with a decline in use in the 1820s (Noel Hume 1970:130–131). The types of pearlware decorations in the Cahokia Wedge collection did not appear until the later period of production (Noel Hume 1970:130–131; Price 1979:12).

Porcelain

Porcelain (n = 60). Sixty pieces of porcelain were recovered from the surface (n = 55), from excavation units (n = 4), and from Feature 4 (n = 1). Most of the fragments in the surface collection came from two porcelain figural pieces which do not appear to be very old. Other sherds are undecorated and are probably imitation porcelain dating to the nineteenth century.

Only two very fragmentary decorated sherds, from the site surface, appear to be Chinese export porcelain and probably date to the eighteenth century. One specimen has blue handpainted decorations on both sides of the sherd. The exterior design appears to be a scene with oriental style buildings. The opposite side suggests a floral motif. The other sherd has an indeterminate, blue handpainted decoration on one side.

Nineteenth- and Twentieth-Century Ceramics

Whiteware (n = 2,552). A total of 2,552 sherds of whiteware and decorated whiteware is from the site: whiteware (controlled surface collection: n = 930; excavation units: n = 777; and features: n = 24), decorated whiteware (controlled surface collection: n = 374; excavation units: n = 400; and features: n = 47). This ceramic assemblage is presented in Table 5. The predominant decorations are edge-decorated, monochrome and polychrome handpainted, and transfer prints. Identified vessel forms include all types of dinner services, however, plates/platters appear most common. The greatest density of these ceramic types were recovered from the surface in Area E.

Stoneware/Crockery (n = 367). A total of 367 sherds of saltglazed stoneware/crockery sherds was recovered from the controlled surface

TABLE 5

NINETEENTH- AND TWENTIETH-CENTURY CERAMICS COUNTS AND PROVENIENCE

Ceramic Type	CSC*	Excavation Units	Features	Totals
Whiteware	930	777	24	1731
Molded Edge-decorated	57	23	2	82
Edge-decorated				
Blue/green shell	9	48	3	60
Blue cord and herringbone	-	-	1	1
Hanging fern and cord	-	2	-	2
Hanging fern and tassel	1	-	-	1
Blue cord and hanging fern	-	-	3	3
Blue edge-plume and dot decorated	1	2	1	4
Indeterminate	7	3	-	10
Handpainted (floral and/or banded)				
Monochrome	9	42	4	55
Polychrome	17	29	7	53
Handpainted-banded				
Monochrome	26	11	-	37
Polychrome	3	6	2	11
Other	4	33	1	38
Sponge/spatterware				
Blue/green	17	32	4	53
Other	-	2	-	2
Transfer Prints				
Blue	36	47	5	88
Black	1	8	-	9
Brown	16	24	3	43
Green	3	-	-	3
Red	11	-	-	11
Purple	8	19	-	27
Orange	1	-	-	1
Polychrome	20	3	1	24
Flow blue	9	1	-	10
Other	1	-	-	1
Annular-banded	8	18	2	28
Dendritic	17	-	-	17
Mocha	3	-	-	3

TABLE 5 — *Continued*

Ceramic Type	CSC*	Excavation Units	Features	Totals
Yellowware	36	18	1	55
Bennington	6	2	-	8
Lusterware	1	2	1	4
Miscellaneous Unident./unknown	46	25	6	77
Totals	1304	1177	71	2552

*Controlled surface collection

collection (n = 242), from excavation units (n = 119), and from features (n = 6). This type of utilitarian ware temporally ranges throughout the nineteenth and early twentieth centuries. Represented vessel forms include bowls, jugs, bottles, and crocks.

Unglazed Earthenwares (n = 35). Thirty-five unglazed earthenware sherds were recovered from the surface (n = 33) and from excavation units (n = 2). In this total are 13 rim sherds and two flat basal sherds. Generally these sherds have a deep orange or red paste. Several of the rims are bolstered or folded over and may represent flowerpots probably dating to the nineteenth century.

GLASS ARTIFACTS

Glass Beads

Ten European-made glass trade beads are present in the surface collection (n = 7), and from Features 1 (n = 1) and 7 (n = 2). All of the glass beads were manufactured by the "drawn" bead technique, having been cut from a long, hollow tube of glass. Seven of these are large necklace beads and three are seed beads. Bead measurements are provided in Table 6. Comparisons have been made with the typologies developed for glass beads from the Guebert site in Illinois (Good 1972) and the Trudeau site in Louisiana (Brain 1979). Most of the bead types in the Cahokia Wedge collection are represented at these two sites, and extensive descriptions and comparative analyses have been reported in the respective publications. The bead types in the Cahokia Wedge collection are commonly found on Indian and colonial sites dating to the Middle Historic period, 1670 to 1760 (Quimby 1966a). The glass beads from the site probably date from the early to mid-eighteenth century.

Oblong White Opaque Glass Beads (n = 2; Plate 21 A, B). Two opaque white, oblong beads of simple construction have rounded ends and are slightly lopsided in shape. These beads correspond to Type 96 described by Good (1972:118) from the Guebert Site, and to Variety IIA1 described by Brain (1979:101) from the Trudeau site. Similar beads have been found in Illinois at the Hotel Plaza site (Schnell 1974:45) and the Kolmer site (Orser 1975:116). This bead type was also commonly found at the Bell site, an historic Fox village in Wisconsin dating from 1680–1730 (Wittry 1963:31–32) and at Fort Ouiatenon (Noble 1983:106–107). At Fort Michilimackinac, these beads were interpreted as used by the French between 1710–1750 (Stone 1974:109). Beads of this type were probably manufactured in Amsterdam (Karklins 1975:69).

TABLE 6

GLASS BEAD MEASUREMENTS (in millimeters)

	Provenience	Length	Diameter	Perforation
Oblong Beads				
Opaque white	CSC*	16.1	7.3	2.1
Opaque white	CSC	18.4	8.5	2.3
Opaque white and blue stripe	CSC	14.0	7.2	2.5
Translucent dark green	CSC	14.7	7.6	2.1

	Provenience	Diameter	Thickness	Perforation
Round Beads				
Opaque turquoise	CSC	8.8	6.0	3.5
Opaque turquoise	CSC	8.2	-	2.0
Opaque black	CSC	8.9	7.0	2.2
Seed Beads				
White	Feature 1	3.4	1.9	.8
Brown	Feature 7 (Flotation)	2.4	1.0	.8
Brown	Feature 7 (Flotation)	3.5 (est.)	2.3	.9

*Controlled surface collection

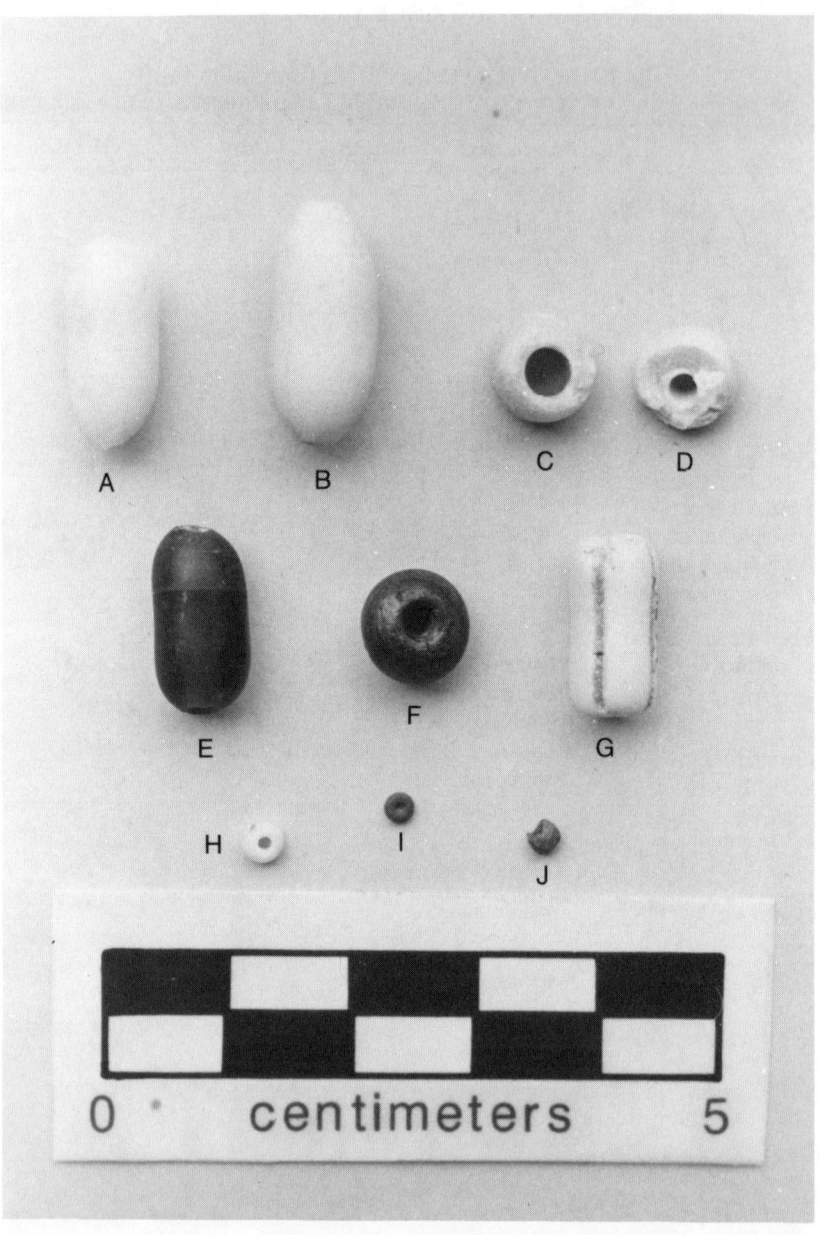

Plate 21. Glass beads. A and B, opaque white; C and D, opaque turquoise; E, translucent emerald green; F, opaque black; G, opaque white bead with blue stripes; H, opaque white seed bead; I and J, brown seed beads

Opaque Turquoise Glass Beads (n = 2; Plate 21 C, D). Two opaque turquoise beads are made of simple construction. One bead is barrel-shaped and the other, although fragmentary, appears to be a rounded bead. This type of bead is similar to Type 90 from the Guebert Site (Good 1972:117) and Variety IIA7 from the Trudeau site (Brain 1979:102). Similar beads were also found at the Kolmer site (Orser 1975:120), the Gros Cap Cemetery site (Nern and Cleland 1974:34), Fort Michilimackinac (Stone 1974:90), Fort St. Joseph (Hulse 1977:104), and Fort Ouiatenon (Noble 1983:105; Tordoff 1983:392).

Translucent Dark Emerald Green Glass Bead (n = 1; Plate 21 E). One translucent, dark emerald green bead is oblong in shape with rounded ends. It is made of simple construction. This bead corresponds to Type 36 found at the Guebert site (Good 1972:110) and Variety IIA15 from the Trudeau Site (Brain 1979:103).

Opaque Black Glass Bead (n = 1; Plate 21 F). One opaque bead made of a deep burgundy glass has a black appearance with a shiny iridescent patina. It is a drawn bead of simple construction. The bead is a rounded necklace bead and corresponds to Type 82 at the Guebert site (Good 1972:116) and Variety IIA5 at the Trudeau site (Brain 1979:102). Similar beads have been identified from the Kolmer site (Orser 1975:114), the Hotel Plaza site (Schnell 1974:45), Fort Michilimackinac (Stone 1974:90), and the Gros Cap Cemetery site (Nern and Cleland 1974:32). This type was also found with an historic Indian burial on the First Terrace of Monks Mound, dating to the 1735–1752 occupation by the Cahokia Illini (Walthall and Benchley 1987:35). This variety of glass bead is believed to have been manufactured in Amsterdam (Karklins 1975:71).

Opaque White and Blue Striped Glass Bead (n = 1; Plate 21 G). This bead is of simple construction with a complex structure, having blue glass inlays applied before the bead was drawn out. The bead is tubular, round in cross-section, and has slightly rounded ends. Four longitudinal, medium to light blue inlaid stripes are at evenly spaced intervals around the circumference.

This bead corresponds to Type 142 at the Guebert site (Good 1972:124) and Variety IIB2 at the Trudeau site (Brain 1979:104). Comparative analysis by Brain suggests a temporal range from 1699 to 1833. Beads of this type have been found in Illinois at the Kolmer site (Orser 1975:115), the Kaskaskia site (Perino 1967:128), and the Hotel Plaza site (Schnell 1974:45). This bead type was also found at the Bayou Goula site in Louisiana (Quimby 1957:135) and the Bell site (Wittry 1963:31–32).

Opaque White Seed Bead (n = 1; Plate 21 H). One opaque seed bead was recovered from Zone A of Feature 1. The donut-shaped bead is of compound construction with an opaque white core surrounded by translucent white glass. The seed bead corresponds to Type 107A from the Guebert Site (Good 1972:119) and Variety IVA1 from the Trudeau Site (Brain 1979:105–106). These types of beads were also found at Fort Michilimackinac (Stone 1974:113), Fort St. Joseph (Hulse 1977:106), and Fort Ouiatenon (Noble 1983:108–109; Tordoff 1983:397).

Dark Brown Seed Beads (n = 2; Plate 21 I, J). Two seed beads were recovered in flotation samples from Feature 7, a wall trench feature interpreted as a main wall of the Nicolle/Meunier house. These beads appear to be dull brown in color, however, they may have been burned.

DARK GREEN/OLIVE GREEN BOTTLE GLASS

A total of 352 fragments of dark green/olive green bottle glass was recovered from the surface (n = 199), from excavation units (n = 143), and from features (n = 10). Of this total, 17 are rim/lip fragments, 38 are basal and/or kick-up fragments, and one is a bottle seal fragment. Most of the specimens exhibit irregularities in vessel wall thicknesses, shape, and lip tooling, and contain imperfections in the glass that typify eighteenth-century handblown glass.

Eighteenth-century liquid storage containers generally had the volume capacity of the French *pinte* (31.7 ounces), or the British wine quart (32 ounces) (Brown 1971:101). The earliest form of the applied string rim is the V-sectioned string rim, with the flat string rim appearing as the latest form (Brown 1971:106–7). The irregularities in most of the V-sectioned and rounded string rims indicate French manufacture, while the flat string rims, often more carefully tooled, may be of English manufacture (Noel Hume 1970:70).

The base and kick-up fragments in the Cahokia Wedge collection represent a cylindrical, rounded form of storage container. Many of the base fragments have glass-tipped pontil marks or an inverted dome or bubble within the kick-up.

Rim/Neck Fragments

Thirteen of the dark green/olive green rim and neck fragments have applied string rims in various forms (Plate 22). Measurements of these rim/neck fragments include the following: orifice diameter or interior of rim, lip diameter or exterior of rim, vertical width of applied string rim, distance from lip to applied string rim, and maximum wall thick-

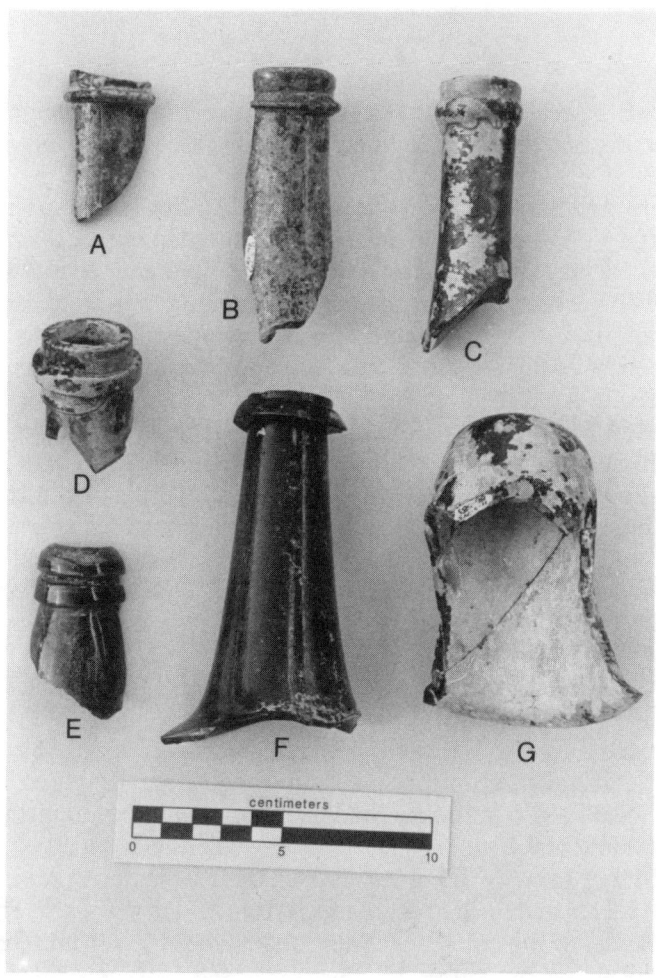

Plate 22. Dark green bottle glass. A and B, rounded string rim; C, wide, rounded string rim; D, flat string rim; E, everted lip with flat string rim; F, everted string rim; G, kick-up with inverted dome or bubble

ness of bottle neck (Brown 1971). Many of the rim/neck fragments that appear to date to the eighteenth century were recovered from excavation units.

V-sectioned String Rim (n = 1; Figure 60 A). The single specimen is fragmentary and irregular in shape. The estimated orifice diameter is 1.8 cm to 1.9 cm, and the estimated inverted lip diameter is 2.4 cm to 2.6 cm. The vertical width of the applied string ranges from 0.7 cm to 1.0 cm, and the string is located 0.35 cm from the lip. The maximum wall thickness of the neck is 0.7 cm. This specimen was recovered from the surface in Area A.

Rounded String Rim (n = 4; Figure 60 B-E). All specimens are irregular in thickness. The orifice diameters range from 1.7 cm to 2.2 cm, and the lip diameters are 3.0 cm. The vertical widths of the rounded string rims range from 0.3 cm to 0.7 cm in thickness. The string rims range from 0.4 cm to 0.8 cm below the lip. Maximum neck wall thicknesses range from 0.4 cm to 0.6 cm. Most of the complete bottles in the collection from the Trudeau site have similar rounded string rims (Brain 1979:88–91).

Wide, Rounded String Rim (n = 1; Figure 60 F). The rounded string rim appears to be tooled heavily into the neck body. The orifice diameter measures 1.7 cm and the lip diameter measures 2.75 cm. The irregular vertical width of the string rim ranges from 0.7 cm to 1.4 cm, and it is located 0.45 cm below the lip. The maximum wall thickness of the bottle neck is 0.4 cm.

Flat String Rim (n = 5; Figure 60 G-L). Orifice diameters range from 1.5 cm to 2.7 cm and lip diameters range from 2.5 cm to 4.1 cm. The vertical thickness of the flat strings range from 0.8 cm to 1.4 cm. The location of the string rim varies from 0.1 cm to 0.8 cm below the lip. The neck wall thicknesses range from 0.3 cm to 0.7 cm.

Everted String Rim (n = 1; Figure 60 M). This is the most complete bottle rim and neck fragment and includes the shoulder facet. The orifice diameter measures 2.1 cm and the lip diameter measures 2.8 cm. The vertical width of the string is 0.7 cm and it is located 0.2 cm below the lip. The maximum neck wall thickness is 0.4 cm and the length of the neck is 9.2 cm.

Everted Lip with Flat String Rim (n = 1; Figure 60 N). The orifice diameter measures 1.6 cm, and the lip diameter is 1.8 cm to 1.9 cm. The vertical everted lip width is 1.0 cm and the vertical flat string thickness is 0.8 cm. The string is located 1.3 cm below the lip. The maximum neck wall thickness measures 0.6 cm.

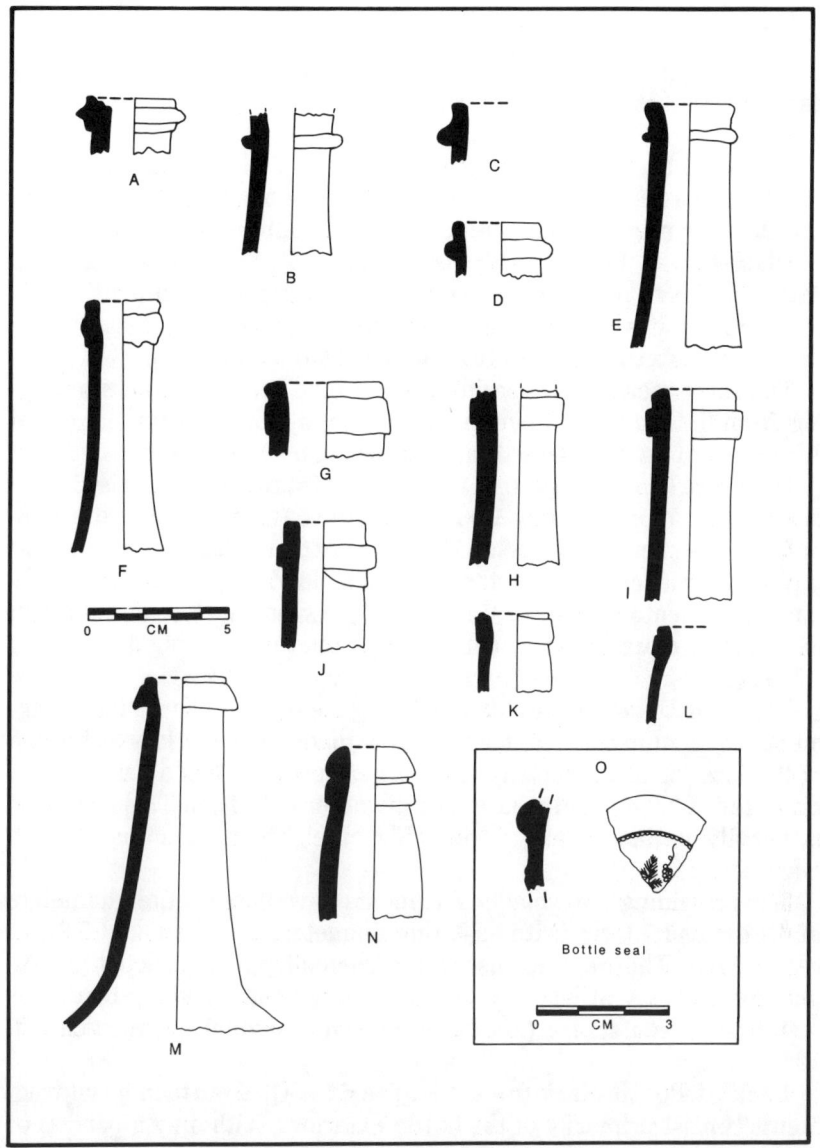

Fig. 60. Dark green bottle glass; rim/neck fragments. A, v-sectioned string rim; B-E, rounded string rim; F, wide, rounded string rim; G-L, flat string rim; M, everted string rim; N, everted lip with flat string rim; O, bottle seal

Base Fragments

Of the 35 basal and/or kick-up fragments, 24 have diameters that could be measured at the basal exterior of the bottle, or base section, and the base ring on which the container actually rests (Brown 1971).

Glass-tipped Pontil (n = 6; Figure 61 A-E). Six base and kick-up fragments have pontil marks produced by a glass-tipped pontil. This technique creates a rough scar of excess glass chips, which remained on the kick-up after removal of the pontil rod (Jones 1971:68).

The three measurable specimens have base section diameters ranging from 8.7 cm to 10.2 cm, and base ring diameters from 6.5 cm to 8.7 cm. All of these fragments appear to date to the eighteenth century.

Mold Mark (n = 1; Figure 61 F). One base fragment has a raised mold line located approximately 1.0 cm from the base ring within the kick-up, and a vertical mold line on the bottle exterior. This fragment was probably produced with a three-piece mold developed in the early nineteenth century (Jones 1971:66–67). The specimen has an estimated base section diameter of 9.5 cm and an estimated base ring diameter of 8.8 cm.

Inverted Dome or Bubble (n = 3; Figure 61 G-I). Three base fragments have an inverted dome or bubble made of solid glass at the top of the interior of the kick-up. The larger specimen has a base section diameter of 9.9 cm and a base ring diameter of 8.2 cm. This fragment is heavily patinated and is probably of eighteenth-century French manufacture.

The remaining two smaller fragments have base section diameters of 6.7 cm and 7.0 cm, with base ring diameters of 5.5 cm and 5.9 cm, respectively. These specimens are of high-quality glass, lack patination, and are probably of late eighteenth- or nineteenth-century British or American manufacture (Margaret Brown, personal communication, 1987).

Lack of Pontil Mark (n = 26; Figure 62 A-Q). Fourteen basal fragments consist primarily of the bottle exteriors, with only a portion of the kick-up present near the base ring; therefore pontil marks are lacking. The base section diameters range from 7.1 cm to 9.8 cm, and the base ring diameters range from 5.9 cm to 8.5 cm. Quality of the glass varies from heavy patination with imperfections, such as air bubbles, to the absence of patination and imperfections, indicating that these specimens probably represent both eighteenth- and nineteenth-century manufacture.

Twelve basal and/or kick-up fragments, without evidence of pontil marks, were very fragmentary and no measurements could be attained.

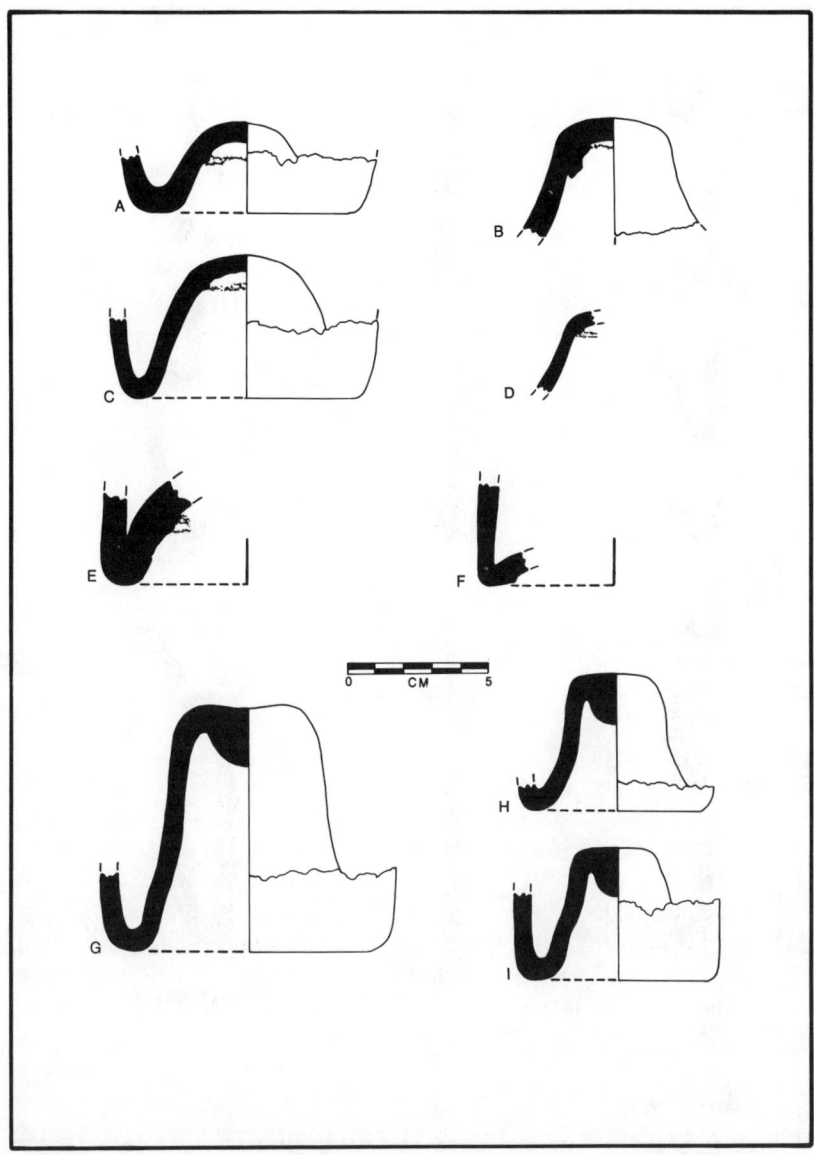

Fig. 61. Dark green bottle glass; kick-ups. A-E, glass-tipped pontil mark; F, mold mark; G-I, inverted dome or bubble

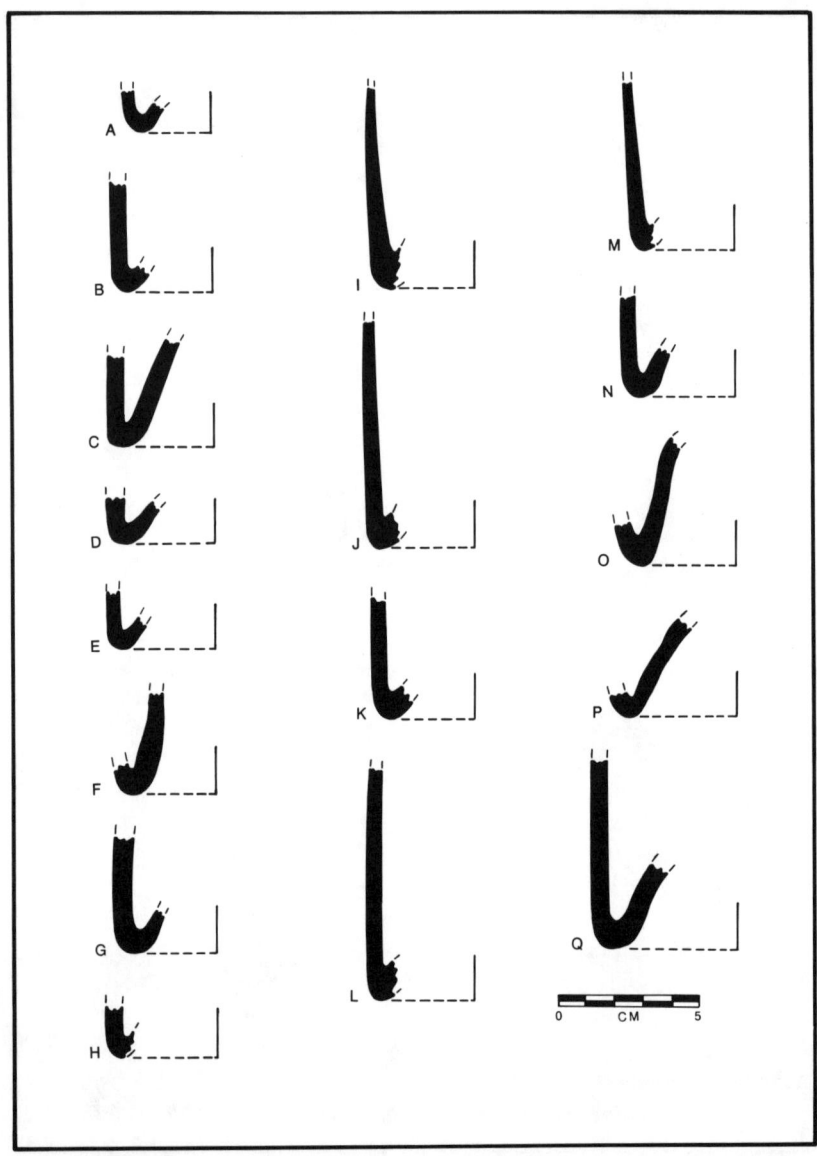

Fig. 62. Dark green bottle glass. A-Q, base fragments lacking pontil marks

Bottle Seal

Bottle Seal (n = 1; Figure 60 O). One medium green glass bottle seal fragment, from the surface collection, represents approximately one-fourth of a rounded seal. The piece has heavy, opaque patination. The circumference of the seal is slightly irregular and the estimated diameter is 3.0 cm to 3.5 cm. The maximum thickness is 0.6 cm. The interior plane on the back of the seal is concave and conforms to the bottle shape. Inside the raised border of the seal is a circular, beaded design, enclosing a relief representation of grapes and probably grape leaves. The use of bottle seals was introduced in the mid-seventeenth century and continued into the nineteenth century. Designs on bottle seals represented individual customers, taverns, government ownership, and names of growers, or else they indicated the bottled contents (Noel Hume 1970:61). The fragmentary design of grapes may indicate the bottle content (wine), or it may be a portion of a design surrounding other elements, such as a name. Generally, bottle seals on French wine bottles represented the name of the grower (Noel Hume 1970:62).

One complete bottle seal of olive green glass from Fort Michilimackinac has a relief design of an unidentified coat of arms (Brown 1971:177). This seal measured approximately 5.0 cm in diameter. An olive green seal from the Bayou Goula site in Louisiana (Quimby 1957:136) had the inscription "MEDOC" within the cartouche, which refers to a wine-producing region in western France on the Atlantic coast. In the collection from the Trudeau site are fourteen complete bottles, none of which have a bottle seal (Brain 1979:85–91).

BLUE-GREEN BOTTLE GLASS

A total of 1,422 fragments of blue-green bottle glass was collected from the surface (n = 1,206), from excavation units (n = 176), and from features (n = 40). Most of the pieces were non-diagnostic body fragments, and the assemblage appears to date primarily to the nineteenth and twentieth centuries.

Rim/Neck Fragments

Three lip to shoulder fragments of handblown blue-green storage containers probably date to the eighteenth century. The specimens are irregular in form with varying wall thicknesses and patination. These were recovered from excavation units.

Flat String Rim (n = 1; Figure 63 A). One specimen with an applied flat string rim has an orifice diameter of 2.0 cm to 2.1 cm and a lip diameter of 2.65 cm to 2.8 cm. The vertical width of the string rim is approximately 0.7 cm. The string is very poorly tooled, with excess glass extending off the bottom of the string. The string rim is located 0.5 cm to 0.6 cm below the lip. The length of the bottle neck from the lip to the shoulder facet is 3.8 cm, with a maximum wall thickness of 0.4 cm.

Tooled String Rim (n = 2; Figure 63 B, C). These two fragments have an applied string rim, which is heavily tooled to create a slightly thicker and rounded lip. One specimen has an orifice diameter of 1.6 cm to 1.7 cm, and a lip diameter of 2.3 cm. The length of the bottle neck from the lip to the shoulder is 6.8 cm, with a maximum wall thickness of 0.25 cm. The other fragment has an orifice diameter of 1.5 cm and a lip diameter of 2.0 cm. The bottle neck is relatively short, measuring 2.8 cm, with a maximum wall thickness of 0.2 cm.

Figural Flask (n = 2; Figure 63 D). Two fragments of Pike's Peak figural flasks were recovered, one from an excavation unit and one from Feature 13. The body fragment from Feature 13 shows a crude figure in relief, and the other piece is a base having a fragmentary relief cartouche with the letter 'O'. The two fragments may be from the same flask. This type of flask was produced in the 1850s and 1860s in the United States (Lindsey 1967:385–386).

Base Fragments

Glass-tipped Pontil (n = 5; Figure 63 E-I). Five base and kick-up fragments of blue-green glass have pontil marks produced by a glass-tipped pontil rod. These were recovered from the surface (n = 2), from an excavation unit (n = 1), and from Feature 4 (n = 2). One fragment is fairly large, with a base section diameter of 9.9 cm and a base ring diameter of 8.1 cm. The remaining four fragments have base section diameters ranging from 6.7 cm to 7.8 cm and base ring diameters ranging from 5.4 cm to 6.5 cm. Two of these latter specimens were found in Feature 4.

Bare Iron Pontil (n = 1; Figure 63 J). One kick-up fragment has a bare iron pontil mark. This type of pontil produced a circular scar that was covered with a reddish-black residue of iron oxide (Toulouse 1968:141).

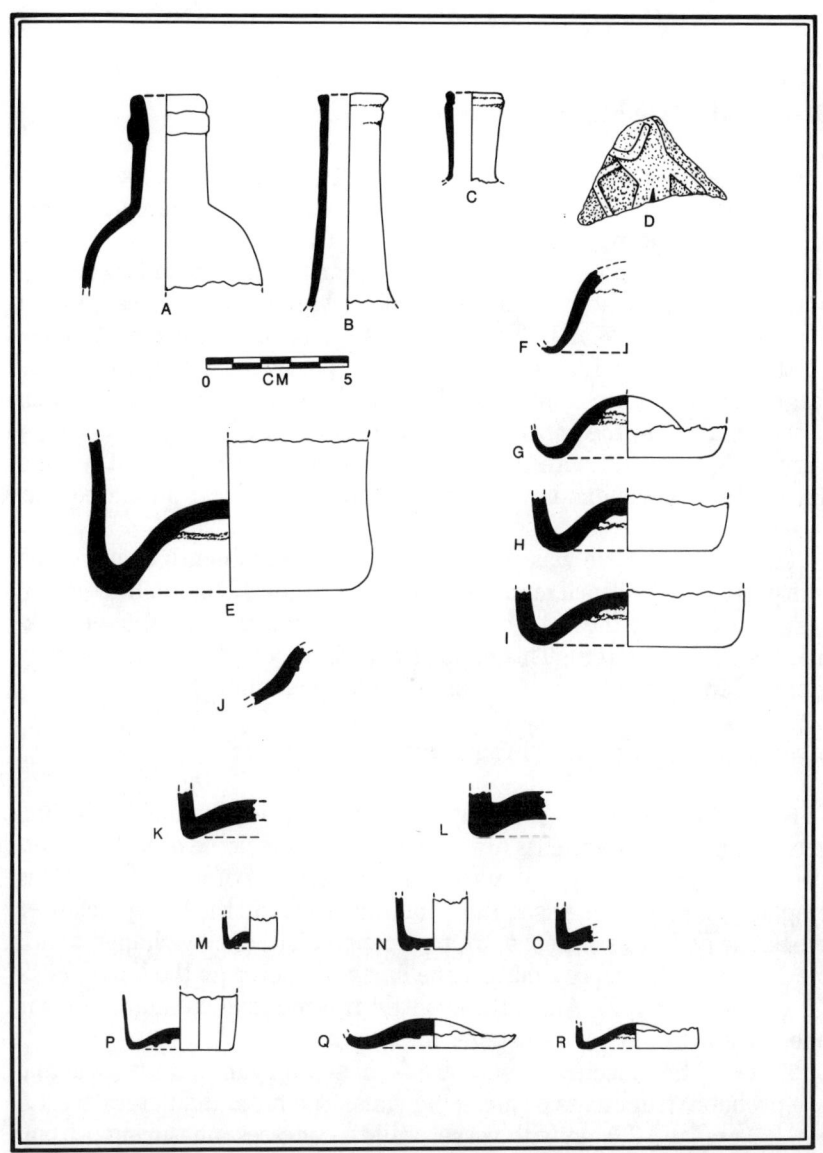

Fig. 63. Blue-green bottle glass. A, flat string rim; B and C, tooled string rim; D, figural flask; E-I, glass-tipped pontil mark; J, bare iron pontil mark; K and L, case bottle bases; M-R, medicinal/toiletry bottle bases

Case Bottle Base Fragments

Case Bottles (n = 2; Figure 63 K, L). Two base and kick-up fragments, recovered from Feature 4, are from blue-green square-sectioned case bottles. Although measurements for the size of the case bottles could not be attained, the specimens appear to come from larger case bottles with a capacity of a quart and a half in wine measurement (Brown 1971:101). Wall thicknesses are 0.9 cm and 0.5 cm, and the kick-up thicknesses are 1.0 cm and 0.8 cm, respectively. The thicker base fragment has a glass-tipped pontil mark. The other specimen is broken in the area where the pontil mark would have been; however, there is a slight ridge located within the kick-up, which may represent a mold mark. Both specimens have numerous air bubbles and patinated surfaces.

This type of bottle was common in the mid-eighteenth century and was probably of French manufacture (Noel Hume 1970:70). Blue-green case bottles were the most common bottle found at Fort Michilimackinac (Brown 1971:108). This contrasts with only two case bottle fragments identified from the Cahokia Wedge collection.

Medicinal/Toiletry Bottle Fragments

Blowpipe Pontil (n = 5; Figure 63 M-Q). Five small handblown blue-green glass base fragments are probably from medicine or toiletry bottles. Each exhibits a pontil mark made by the use of a blowpipe. This empontilling technique used the remaining glass on the blowpipe, after the bottle body was snapped off, to create a distinct ring-shaped pontil mark which was approximately the same diameter as the bottle neck (Toulouse 1968:139). All of these bottle fragments have numerous air bubbles and are at various stages of patination.

Three of the base fragments are from small cylindrical vessels and are probably fragments of medicine vials. The basal diameters are 1.8 cm, 2.0 cm, and 3.5 cm with vessel wall thicknesses measuring 0.2 cm, 0.25 cm, and 0.35 cm, respectively. Similar medicinal vials were found at Fort Independence in South Carolina, which dates from 1777 to 1779 (Bastian 1982:96). These types of medicine bottles with blowpipe pontils were also produced in the nineteenth century (Margaret Brown, personal communication, 1987).

One basal fragment with a diameter of 3.7 cm and a vessel wall thickness of 0.1 cm is from an eleven-sided vessel. The fragility of this bottle and the elaborate body form suggests that this may be a toiletry bottle.

ARTIFACT DESCRIPTIONS

The fifth base fragment has an estimated diameter of 5.5 cm. The fragment does not have any portion of the vessel wall present, and the actual bottle type and form could not be determined.

Glass-tipped Pontil (n = 1; Figure 63 R). One base and kick-up fragment from a small bottle, probably a medicinal bottle, has a glass-tipped pontil mark. The base ring measures 3.8 cm in diameter and the vessel wall thickness is 0.25 cm.

BROWN BOTTLE GLASS

Most of the brown glass comprises molded pieces of medicinal and liquor bottles dating to the mid to late nineteenth and twentieth centuries. Only two fragments of handblown brown bottle glass, one base and one rim/neck from the surface collection, appear to date to the eighteenth or early nineteenth centuries. Additionally, there are many non-diagnostic body fragments which have patination and imperfections within the glass, suggesting that these pieces may also date to the eighteenth or early nineteenth centuries.

Flat String Rim (n = 1; Figure 64 A). One rim/neck fragment of medium brown glass has an applied flat string rim. The orifice diameter is 1.9 cm to 2.0 cm, and the lip diameter is 2.75 cm to 2.85 cm. The vertical width of the string rim is 0.7 cm to 0.8 cm, and it is located 0.9 cm to 1.0 cm below the lip. The maximum wall thickness of the neck is 0.4 cm. The carefully tooled, flat string and the medium brown color of the glass suggest a late eighteenth- or early nineteenth-century date, possibly of English manufacture.

Base (n = 1; Figure 64 B). One base and kick-up fragment from a rounded cylindrical storage container is dark brown glass. The slight patination and numerous air bubbles within the glass suggest that it may have been manufactured in the eighteenth century. The base section measures 7.8 cm in diameter and the base ring measures 6.5 cm.

CLEAR GLASS

A total of 3,267 fragments of clear bottle glass was recovered from the surface (n = 2,697), from excavation units (n = 536), and from features (n = 34). Most of the fragments are non-diagnostic and probably date to the nineteenth and twentieth centuries. Five pieces of clear glass are illustrated and discussed here because of the possibility of dating to the eighteenth or early nineteenth centuries.

Medicinal Bottle (n = 1; Figure 64 C). A bottle neck, probably from a medicine bottle, appears to have a rectangular or square-sectioned

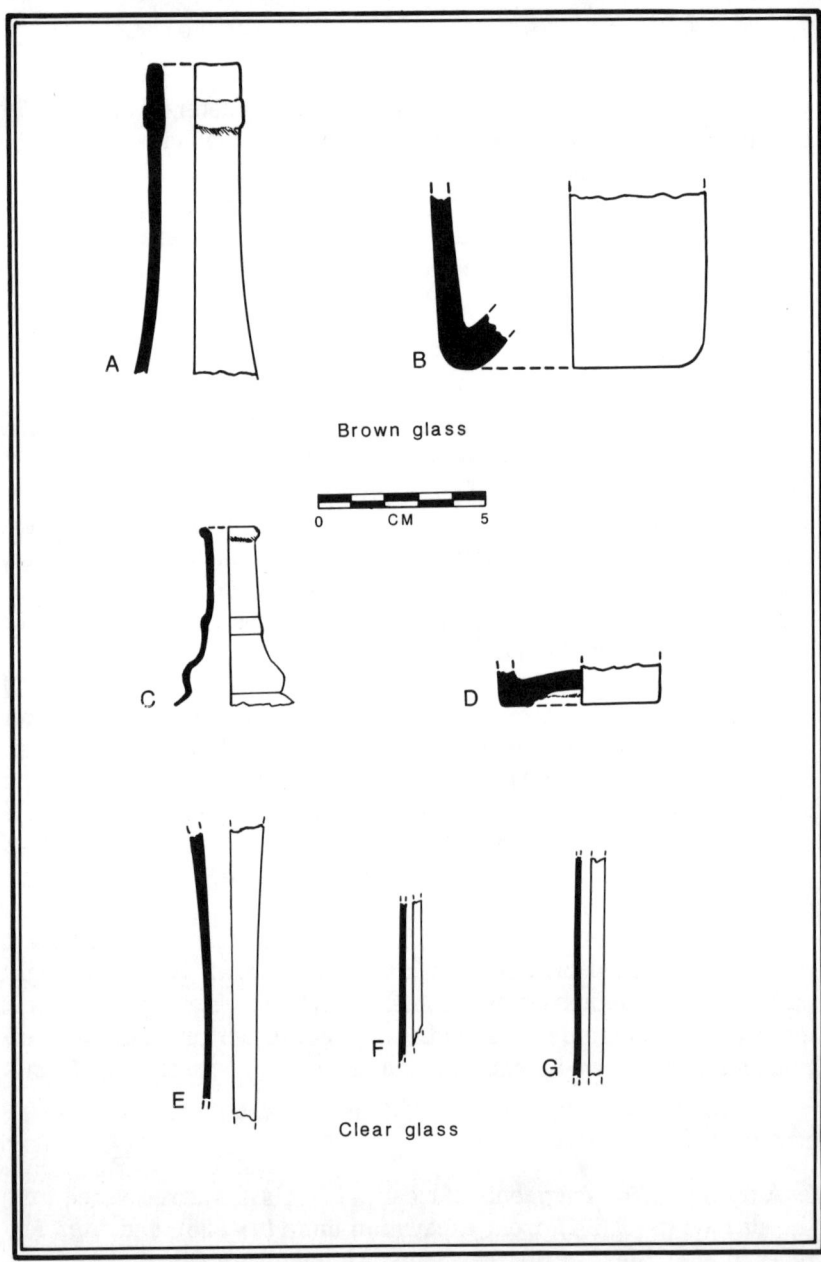

Fig. 64. Brown glass: A, flat string rim; B, base. Clear glass: C, medicinal bottle; D, tumbler base; E-G, unidentifed hollow tubes

body, which begins at the shoulder facet. Vertical mold marks indicate it was probably produced with a three-piece mold and could date to the early nineteenth century. The rim has a tooled string lip with a diameter of 1.75 cm. The bottle surface has an iridescent patination.

Tumbler (n = 1; Figure 64 D). One basal fragment, probably from a drinking vessel or tumbler, has a shallow kick-up and a glass-tipped pontil mark indicating it was handblown. The basal diameter measures 4.5 cm and the vessel wall thickness is 0.5 cm. This fragment is similar to the clear lead and soda glass tumblers found at Fort Michilimackinac, dating to the British occupation from 1771 to 1781 (Brown 1971:105), and at Fort Ouiatenon (Noble 1983:187–190; Tordoff 1983:285–267).

Miscellaneous (n = 3; Figure 64 E-G). Three unidentifiable clear glass fragments are sections of hollow tubes ranging in diameter from 0.5 cm to 2.1 cm. The specimens appear to be handblown and are at various stages of patination. The complete form of these fragments is indeterminate, and with a lack of comparative examples, the function also remains unknown.

Miscellaneous Glass Artifacts

Utilized Glass (n = 10). Ten bottle glass fragments appear to have one or more utilized edges, possibly the result of use as scraping tools. All of these specimens appear to be eighteenth-century glass. Of this total, eight fragments are dark green glass and one each of dark brown glass and blue-green glass. The specimens exhibit flake scars produced by utilization as a scraping edge and are similar in appearance to aboriginal chert tools. Other examples of utilized glass fragments were recovered from the excavation of the Cahokia Illini settlement on the First Terrace of Monks Mound (Walthall and Benchley 1987:46).

Flat Glass (n = 1,859). A total of 1,859 fragments of flat glass were recovered from the surface (n = 1,262), from excavation units (n = 576), and from features (n = 21). The fragments were primarily of a blue-green color with varying thicknesses and degrees of patination. Flat glass is assumed to represent window glass and the surface concentrations of flat glass were associated with structural remains in Areas A, D, E, and F. Although a detailed analysis of the flat glass was not conducted, it is likely that window pane glass from the eighteenth-century French colonial period was recovered.

METAL ARTIFACTS

ORNAMENTS

Copper Tinkling Cones and Preforms (n = 4; Figure 65 A-D). Two rolled tinklers made of sheet copper were identified in the controlled surface collection. Both have been slightly flattened and measure 2.5 cm and 2.2 cm in length. Two possible tinkler preforms were also recovered, one from the surface and one from an excavation unit. The preforms or blanks are small, cut pieces of sheet copper, which have one edge folded into a cone or bead; however, the excess sheet copper has not been removed. Tinklers are commonly found at historic Indian sites and have been interpreted as clothing adornment. The artifacts have openings at both ends through which hair, a cord, or a leather thong would have been threaded for attachment to a garment. Copper tinklers and beads were probably produced from the scrap copper of fragments or mending patches of trade kettles. On the First Terrace of Monks Mound, an historic Cahokia Illini burial was excavated with tinkling cones found on a stain from a fabric or buckskin garment (Walthall and Benchley 1987:71).

Copper Beads (n = 3; Figure 65 E-G). Three rolled tubular pieces of sheet copper in the surface collection may represent ornamental beads commonly worn by historic Indians. These specimens measured 2.75 cm, 2.8 cm, and 4.75 cm in length. The largest artifact has a small hole in one side near one end of the tubular piece.

Hair Pipe (n = 1; Figure 65 H). One fairly large, tubular artifact made of cut sheet copper was recovered from an excavation unit. This artifact is probably a hair pipe, an ornament worn by historic Indians. It measures 10.2 cm in length with a diameter ranging from 0.7 cm to 0.9 cm. The longitudinal junction of the rolled piece has been reworked into a fairly flush and smoothed plane. Several burials from the Dumaw Creek site, dating to 1605–1620 and located in western Michigan, were recovered with as many as 27 hair pipes still attached to the hair (Quimby 1966b:36–38). A hair pipe was also found with an historic Indian burial interred in a prehistoric mound at the Angel site in southern Indiana (Black 1967:251). This burial was reported to date to ca. 1800 (Black 1967:255).

Brass Tubular Ornament (n = 1; Figure 65 I). One rolled and worked piece of sheet brass was recovered from an excavation unit. It is a tubular artifact with some elaboration and possibly represents an ornament. It measures 4.95 cm in length. The smaller end has been shaped into a rectangular cross-section and measures 0.4 cm by 0.35 cm. The

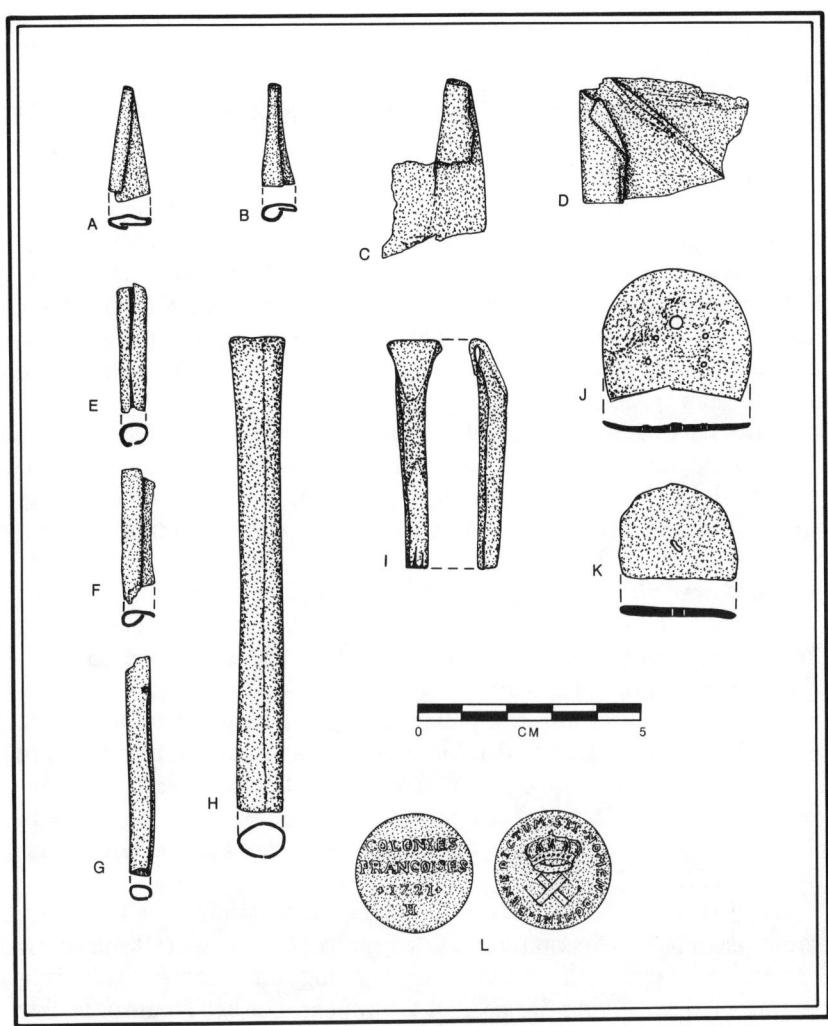

Fig. 65. A and B, copper tinklers; C and D, possible copper tinkler preforms; E-G, rolled copper beads; H, hair pipe; I, brass tubular ornament; J, metal disc ornament; K, lead whizzer; L, 1721 *Colonies Francoises* coin

midsection of the artifact is tubular and has not been extensively worked. The opposite larger end flares into a triangular shape with a width of 1.1 cm. This cut triangular end has been rolled over the top and attached to the opposite side of the tubular form, creating a lateral hole that could possibly have been for suspension or attachment. Several areas have been extensively worked with a metal tool, probably a file. With the exception of the elaborated, flared end and the lateral hole, this artifact is similar to the rolled copper or brass tubular beads of historic Indians. This artifact may have been made by the French for use in the Indian trade.

Metal Disc Ornament (n=1; Figure 65 J). One thin, flat piece of unidentified metal has been cut into a semi-circular shape. It was recovered in the controlled surface collection. The metal is very lightweight and silver to gray in color. It measures 3.2 cm by 2.7 cm, with a thickness of 0.1 cm. The surface has a hammered or pounded appearance, and all of the edges have been cut. One large punched hole, probably for suspension, is at the rounded edge of the piece, suggesting this is the top of the ornament. Four smaller holes, two located vertically below and on each side of the larger hole, appear to be decorations. The cut edges and the punched holes were produced by metal tools. This ornament may be of historic Indian or French manufacture and was probably of native use. The semi-circular shape and the arrangement of the perforations are similar to a gorget from the Trudeau site in Louisiana, although the gorget was larger and made of brass (Brain 1979:196).

Brass Brooch (n=1; Plate 23 A). One rectangular, brass artifact, from the surface collection, probably represents a brooch. It measures 3.35 cm by 2.3 cm, with a rectangular opening in the center measuring 2.4 cm by 0.9 cm, giving the artifact the appearance of a frame or buckle shape. What appears to be the top of the brooch is slightly convex, whereas the other sides are straight. The front of the artifact has an impressed or stamped floral design that is shown in negative on the reverse side. Located centrally on one of the short ends is a circular protrusion, which has the scar of an iron pin or tang that would have been used for attachment. The metal has an aged and weathered appearance. The shape and design are somewhat similar to shoe and knee buckles found on eighteenth-century colonial sites (Noel Hume 1970:84–87); however, the presence of the lateral tang indicates its use as a pin or brooch.

Religious Medallion (n=1; Plate 23 B; Plate 24 C). One religious medallion, identified as a *Miraculous Medal*, was recovered in the surface collection. The artifact is ovoid in shape, measuring 2.45 cm in

Plate 23. Metal artifacts. A, brass brooch; B, religious medallion; C, boot/shoe heel; D, unidentified brass ornament (top of blotting powder canister?); E, copper bracelet; F-H, brass mouth harp frames; I, iron mouth harp frame; J, zinc (?) harmonica plate; K, 1721 *Colonies Francoises* coin; L, Spanish 'piece of eight' coin

length, 2.05 cm in width, and 0.5 cm in thickness. It appears to have been cast in brass. A circular loop for suspension is at the top and flush with the body of the medallion. One side of the medallion has the figure of the Virgin Mary standing on the globe. Encircling the figure are inscriptions in French, which translate "Mary without sin, prays for you." The obverse relief design consists of a border design of twelve stars, encircling a large cross that rests on top of a rectangular bar interwoven with a large letter 'M'. Below this are two hearts representing Jesus and Mary. The relief design is heavily worn and the metal is corroded.

It has been recorded that in 1830 in Paris, France, the Virgin Mary appeared in a vision to St. Catherine Laboure and instructed her to "Have a medal struck . . . All who wear it will receive great graces . . ." (Catholic University of America 1967:894). Production of Miraculous Medallions was begun in June of 1832 in Paris, with the permission of Archbishop de Quelen. Societies devoted to the Blessed Virgin through the Miraculous Medal have continued to exist into the twentieth century. In Cahokia, sermons were still being conducted in French until 1912 (Illinois State Archives n.d.) and it is probable that French-inscribed religious items were also being used at least into the early twentieth century.

Copper Bracelet (n = 1; Plate 23 E). One fragment of a possible bracelet made of cut sheet copper was recovered from the surface collection. It has a ridged design and several perforations. The edges are rough and irregularly cut. Comparative examples have not been identified; however, this bracelet is dissimilar to the C-shaped bracelets commonly found on historic Indian and colonial sites (Wittry 1963:17; Good 1972:131; Stone 1974:135; Brain 1979:193–194).

Boot/Shoe Heel (n = 1; Plate 23 C). One fragment of a cast brass boot or shoe heel was recovered in the surface collection. It measures 5.8 cm in length with an estimated width of 5.5 cm. It has three interior projections with perforations for attachment, and if symmetrical, would have had a total of five projections. This artifact is dissimilar to typical shoe heel plates found on eighteenth-century sites (Stone 1974:87; Noble 1983:298).

Unidentified Brass Ornament (n = 1; Plate 23 D). One ornamental cast brass artifact was recovered from an excavation unit. It is a circular piece measuring 2.7 cm in diameter. Six perforations are incorporated into an elaborate, impressed floral design. Remnants of two iron tangs for attachment are present on the back of the piece. Two similar artifacts were reported from Fort Ouiatenon (Noble 1983:295) and it has been suggested that these artifacts may be lids for canisters of blotting powder which were used to dry writing ink (Vergil Noble, personal communication, 1988).

MUSICAL INSTRUMENTS

Brass Mouth Harp Frames (n = 3; Plate 23 F-H). Three cast brass mouth harp frames were recovered from the surface (n = 2) and from an excavation unit (n = 1). The shanks of the brass frames are square to diamond-shaped in cross-section, with a rounded frame head and tapered shanks. This type corresponds to Stone's (1974:141) Variety B1A brass mouth harp found at Fort Michilimackinac. Two of the mouth harp frames are complete, measuring 5.1 cm and 5.3 cm in length. The frame head width on both of these specimens measures 2.9 cm. The third brass specimen, with broken shanks, measures 3.0 cm in width at the frame head. The iron tongues are missing on the specimens, although iron stains are present within the notch in the frame head where the tongues would have been attached. File marks are present on all three artifacts.

Iron Mouth Harp Frame (n = 1; Plate 23 I). One iron mouth harp frame was identified in the surface collection. The fragmentary artifact has a flattened frame head and corresponds to Stone's (1974:141) Variety A1 mouth harp frame from Fort Michilimackinac. The maximum width of the frame head is 3.5 cm. The iron specimen is hand forged.

Brass mouth harps identical to the specimens from the Cahokia Wedge site were the most common type found at Fort Michilimackinac (Stone 1974:141). Comparative data by Stone (1974:144–145) indicate the temporal range for mouth harps is from 1640 to 1830 and that brass mouth harps appear to date primarily after 1740; however, at Fort Michilimackinac, brass mouth harps do occur as early as 1730. Similar brass and iron mouth harp frames were reported from the Guebert site (Good 1972:132).

Harmonica Pieces (n = 3; Plate 23 J). Three harmonica pieces, probably made of zinc, were recovered from the surface collection. The one complete specimen measures 11.1 cm in length, 2.8 cm in width, and 0.1 cm in thickness. Iron residue is present, indicating the attachment areas for the corresponding zinc bars inserted across the linear perforations. Identical harmonica pieces were recovered at the Alorton site (Anderson 1981:90).

Whizzer

Lead Whizzer (n = 1; Figure 65 K). One whizzer was recovered from the surface collection. It is a flat piece of lead that has been cut into a roughly semi-circular disc. The artifact was possibly reworked from a lead ball or lead waste. A roughly pierced perforation is centrally located. The diameter of the whizzer, prior to having one edge cut straight, is estimated as 2.6 cm to 3.0 cm. Lead whizzers, identified as toys or noise makers, are commonly found on historic Indian and eighteenth-century colonial sites. A string would have been threaded through the perforation, twisted and then released, making the disc rotate rapidly, producing a whizzing noise. Whizzers have been recovered from the Guebert site (Good 1972:154–155), the Kolmer site (Orser 1975:106), the Laurens site, Fort de Chartres I (Jelks and Ekberg 1984), and Fort Michilimackinac (Stone 1974:154).

Coins

Two coins dating to the eighteenth century were recovered from excavation units. One copper coin was minted in France for use in the French colonies and the other is a Spanish silver "piece of eight" probably minted in Mexico.

Colonies Francoises Coin (n = 1; Figure 65 L; Plate 23 K; Plate 24 A). This copper coin with a diameter of 2.55 cm and thickness of 0.2 cm, has the following inscriptions:

Obverse side: "COLONIES FRANCOISES"
"1721"
"H"

Reverse side: A circular inscription around the edge in Latin: "BENEDICTUM . SIT . NOMEN . DOMINI". Translation: "Be Praised the Name of the Lord".

The mint mark 'H' indicates manufacture in La Rochelle, France. The central design on the reverse side has two crossed L's and the crown of Louis XV.

The 1721 Royal Edict of Louis XV ordered the production of these coins for the French colonies because of the need for coins of small denominations (Zay 1894:52). The edict requested the production of three denominations, although only the 2 1/2c to a marc were put into circulation (Zay 1894:54). These were minted at La Rochelle (H) in 1721 and 1722 and at Rouen (B) in 1721. The edict also stated that these coins

Plate 24. A, 1721 *Colonies Francoises* coin; B, Spanish 'piece of eight' coin; C, religious medallion

were not to be used in France under penalty of a fine and confiscation (Zay 1894:52). In 1722, 20,000 of these coins were sent to Canada by the Company of the Indies and in 1724 there was a reduction in their value, apparently for circulation in Louisiana (Quimby 1957:137). Only 8,100 coins were placed into circulation in 1723, and the remaining coins were returned to France in 1726 (Quimby 1957:137).

A 1722 coin with a mint mark 'H', indicating manufacture in La Rochelle, was recovered from a refuse pit with historic Indian ceramics at the Bayou Goula site in Louisiana (Quimby 1957:137–8). A 1722 Colonies Francoises coin was found in the surface collection from the Guebert site (Good 1972:135). The mint mark on this coin has been obliterated; however, the 1722 date indicates it was minted in La Rochelle. These coins have also been found at Fort de Chartres (Margaret Brown, personal communication, 1987).

Spanish Piece of Eight (n = 1; Plate 23 L; Plate 24 B). A cut 1/4 or 2 bits of a Spanish silver coin has an approximate diameter of 3.8 cm and a thickness of 0.3 cm. The coin, although fragmentary, has the inscription on one side "CAROL", representing a portion of "CAROLLIS" for King Charles of Spain. The reverse side is obliterated. The silver coin was probably minted in Mexico City or one of the many mints in South America. The "CAROL" inscription probably represents King Charles III, who reigned from 1759 to 1788. The Mexico City mint continued producing King Charles III coins until 1790, because the dies representing the new king, King Charles IV, had not yet arrived from Spain (Hobson and Obojski 1983:285).

The eighteenth-century practice of cutting coins to make small change was common in the American colonies due to the lack of coins of small denomination. The eight reale Spanish coins were cut up into as many as eight pieces, with the quarter pieces (2 reales or 2 bits) being the most common. When the United States developed its coinage system in the 1790s, the silver dollar was modeled after the Spanish eight reale coins; however, Mexican coinage was still circulated until the 1850s (Hobson and Obojski 1983:285).

UTENSILS

Spoons (n = 3; Plate 25 A-C). Three metal spoons or spoon fragments were recovered from the surface collection. One complete spoon, possibly pewter or brass, measures 14.9 cm in length with a bowl width of 3.2 cm. The stem has a simple flared handle and a small, ornamental protrusion near the base of the spoon bowl. Impressed on the back of the stem is "HALL & ELTON". A fragmentary spoon bowl is similar in

Plate 25. Utensils. A-C, spoons; D, two-tined fork; E-G, bone-handled utensils; H, table knife; I and J, miscellaneous utensil handles; K-P, clasp knife blades; Q and R, sheath knife blades; S, butcher knife blade; T and U, razors

size and has identical ornamentation near the bowl base. The third spoon fragment is a fairly large spoon bowl made of iron. The spoon bowl measures approximately 7.0 cm to 7.5 cm in length, with a width of 4.7 cm.

Fork (n = 1; Plate 25 D). A two-tined fork fragment was recovered from the surface collection. The tines measure approximately 4.5 cm in length. The utensil is broken at the base of the tine element and the handle shape is unknown. Two-tined forks were common throughout the eighteenth century and the early nineteenth century (Stone 1974:175–176).

Bone-handled Utensils (n = 3; Plate 25 E-G). Three fragmentary bone-handled utensils were recovered from the surface (n = 1), from an excavation unit (n = 1), and from Feature 5 (n = 1). All three specimens have copper or brass posts to attach the bone handle to the central iron piece. Only one fragment has evidence for the upper portion of the utensil and it appears to be either a spoon or a fork.

Table Knife (n = 1; Plate 25 H). One nearly complete table knife was recovered from the surface. It is made of an unidentified metal and has a simple handle. It measures 21.3 cm in length.

Miscellaneous Utensils (n = 2; Plate 25 I, J). Two fragmentary iron stems and handles from unidentifiable utensils are present in the surface collection.

Clasp Knife Blades (n = 6; Plate 25 K-P). Six iron clasp knife fragments were recovered from the surface (n = 1), Feature 1 (n = 2), and Feature 4 (n = 3). One complete knife blade from Feature 4 measures 13.4 cm in length. The knife blade tapers to a point and the edge opposite the blade is angled. Manufacturer's marks are present on one side of the knife blade but could not be identified. A fragment of the proximal end of a clasp knife blade, also from Feature 4, has a portion of a manufacturer's mark (...M.LAM?..) (Figure 66 B). One large fragment from Feature 1 consists of a portion of the blade within a curved or crescent-shaped iron handle. The remaining three specimens are proximal or midsection fragments with no evidence of maker's marks. French clasp knives were common throughout the Early and Middle Historic periods (Quimby 1966a:68–69). The clasp knife fragments from the Cahokia Wedge site probably pre-date 1760.

Sheath Knife Blades (n = 2; Plate 25 Q, R). Two sheath knife blades were recovered from excavation units. These blades are made of one piece of iron, and a bone or wooden handle would have been attached to the proximal end. One specimen has a nearly complete blade measuring approximately 7.6 cm in length, and the narrow rat-tail or shaft

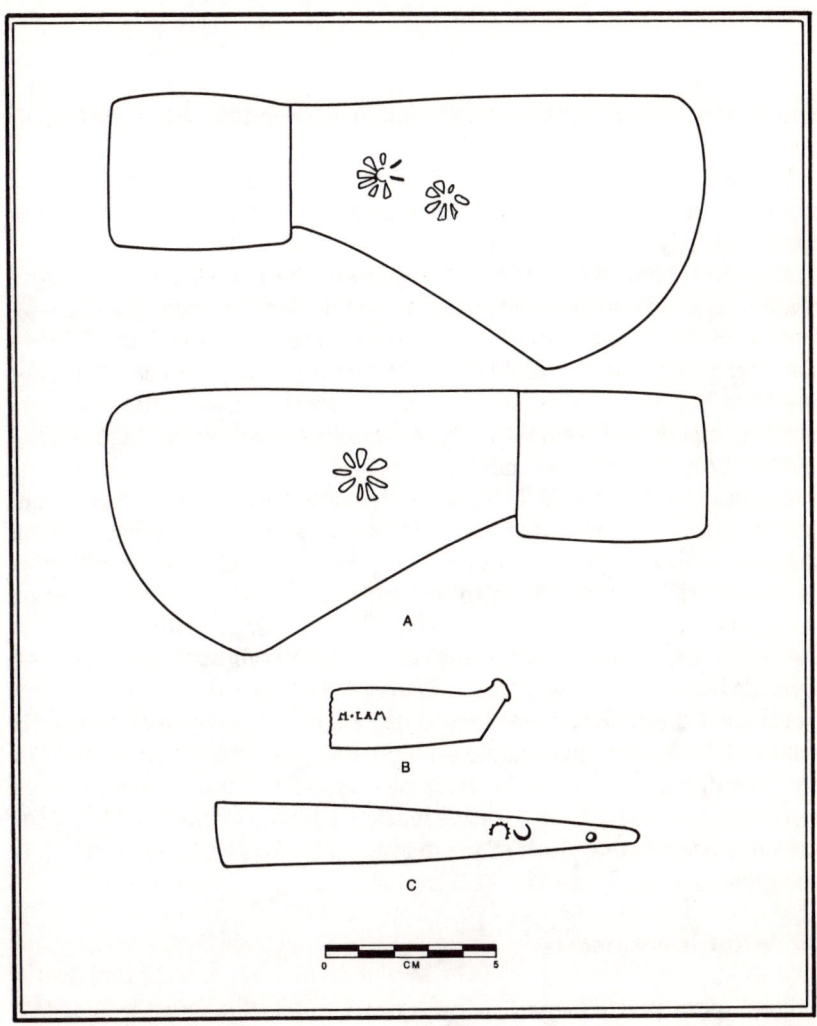

Fig. 66. Manufacturers' marks. A, trade axe; B, clasp knife blade; C, razor

handle portion is fragmentary. The other fragment is only a portion of the blade and the handle.

Butcher Knife Blade (n = 1; Plate 25 S). One nearly complete iron butcher knife blade was identified in the surface collection. It measures approximately 17.5 cm in length.

Miscellaneous Knife Blade Fragments (n = 15). Fifteen iron knife blade fragments were recovered from the surface collection (n = 4), from excavation units (n = 8), and from features (n = 3). Six of these blade fragments are possibly from French iron clasp knives, including one from Feature 7. Six other fragments are larger and probably from butcher knives. The remaining three specimens are very fragmentary and the type of knife was indeterminate.

Razors (n = 2; Plate 25 T, U). Two steel blade razors were recovered, one from the surface collection and one from an excavation unit. One specimen has a blade length of 7.7 cm, with the narrower handle portion measuring 5.4 cm, for a total length of 13.1 cm. A brass rivet or stud is located 1.4 cm from the end of the handle. The other razor has the blade edge and handle portion as one straight plane tapering towards the handle. The blade measures 7.8 cm and the handle portion measures 4.2 cm, for a total length of 12.0 cm. A steel rivet or stud is located 1.5 cm from the handle end. On one side of the handle portion are manufacturer's marks forming two semi-circular or horseshoe-like motifs (Figure 66 C). Comparative marks on razors or clasp knife blades have not been found. Both of these types of razors were found at Fort Michilimackinac (Stone 1974:139).

Trade Kettle Fragments

Cast Iron Kettle Legs (n = 2; Plate 26 A, B). Solid cast iron kettle legs were recovered from an excavation unit and from Feature 1. A complete kettle leg from Feature 1 measures 10.5 cm in length. The rounded front of the leg is vertically grooved and has an expanding base or foot. The back of the leg, which would be located underneath the kettle bowl, is flat and undecorated. Identical kettle legs found at Fort Michilimackinac were reported to be of British origin dating primarily after 1750 (Stone 1974:189). These types of kettle legs were also recovered at Fort Ouiatenon (Noble 1983:252–253)

The other specimen is a fragment of a leg with an expanded foot or base portion. The leg is roughly rectangular in cross-section and the back of the leg is slightly concave. These legs are from tripodal kettles which have a cylindrical body and an attached handle. Cast iron kettles were common trade items in the late seventeenth and eighteenth cen-

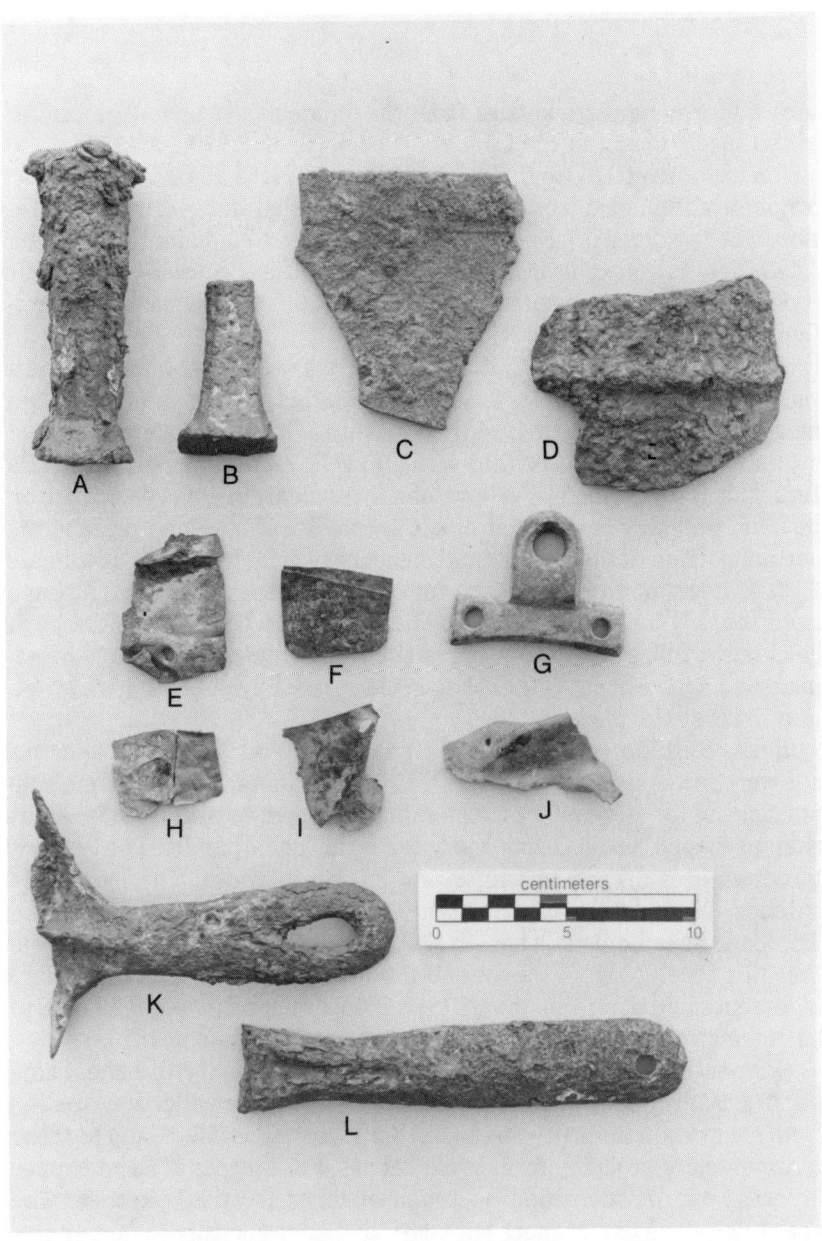

Plate 26. Trade kettle fragments. A and B, cast iron kettle legs; C and D, cast iron kettle bowl fragments; E and F, copper bail ears; G, brass bail ear; H-J, repair patches. Pan/skillet fragments. K and L, handles

turies. Many complete kettles from the Trudeau site have legs similar to the specimens from the Cahokia Wedge (Brain 1979:135–137).

Cast Iron Kettle Bowl Fragments (n = 2; Plate 26 C, D). Two bowl fragments from cast iron kettles were identified in the surface collection. One specimen is a lipped rim with an estimated diameter of 28 cm. The other fragment is from a bowl body and has a linear ridge that probably would have been located around the circumference of the kettle.

Copper Bail Ears (n = 2; Plate 26 E, F). Two copper bail ears were recovered from Feature 4. One bail ear is nearly complete and measures 5.5 cm in length by 4.0 cm in width. One perforation is located at the bottom of the piece that would have been attached to the kettle rim. The top is folded over and has a perforation covered with iron residue, probably from the iron kettle handle. The second piece is the bottom portion of the bail ear and measures 4.2 cm by 3.4 cm. It is made of two sheets of copper riveted together with copper studs that have been roughly hammered flush to the piece. The bottom corners have been cut off diagonally to remove the sharp edges. The top edge appears to have been cut rather than broken, possibly indicating an intention to reuse the piece.

Brass Bail Ear (n = 1; Plate 26 G). One cast brass kettle bail ear was recovered from an excavation unit. It is a rectangular bar with one hole at each end for attachment to the side of a copper or brass kettle. A circular or looped top piece has one hole for the kettle handle. The bar portion measures 6.7 cm in length and 2.0 cm in width. The loop piece extends 3.1 cm from the bar. One complete brass kettle from the Trudeau site in Louisiana has similar bail ears. Brain (1979:173) reports that this type of kettle was one of the latest varieties used in the late eighteenth and early nineteenth centuries, citing an example known to be of American manufacture and used by the Choctaw in 1833.

Copper/Brass Scraps (n = 75; Plate 26 H-J). Seventy-five sheet copper or brass scraps were recovered from the surface collection (n = 24), from excavation units (n = 36), and from features (n = 15). Many of these fragments are probably from trade kettles. Four pieces of sheet copper or brass can be identified as repair patches for trade kettles. The specimens have two or more cut edges and are generally square or rectangular in shape, with two or more rivet holes. None of the pieces have the rivets remaining. Four small fragments of sheet copper each exhibit at least one rivet hole. They possibly represent fragments of repair patches.

Fifty-eight fragments of sheet copper or brass have one or more cut edges. Most are rectangular or square in shape and may have been cut for use as repair patches, or are simply waste products. Nine pieces of scrap sheet copper or brass have been cut into long, narrow strips and are possibly waste pieces rather than repair patches.

Pan/Skillet Fragments

Pan/Skillet Fragments (n=2; Plate 26 K, L). Two handles from frying pans or skillets were recovered from the surface. One cast iron handle measures approximately 11.0 cm in length. It has a teardrop-shaped hole near the rounded end. A small portion of the skillet body is present and it appears to be very shallow (approximately 1.0 cm) with an estimated diameter of 21.0 cm. The other specimen, made of a less durable metal, measures 17.0 cm in length and has a small circular hole near the rounded end of the handle.

FURNITURE HARDWARE

Copper Hinge (n=1; Plate 27 A). One copper furniture hinge was recovered from an excavation unit. It measures 3.7 cm in length and 2.4 cm in width. The piece is fragmentary and appears to be one-half of the hinge. It is doubled in thickness (i.e., two pieces of sheet copper), rectangular in shape, and has two rivet holes located near the bottom two corners of the piece. On one long edge of the rectangular piece are two rolled appendages through which an iron or brass hinge pin would have attached. Iron stains are present on both sides of the rectangular plate, probably indicating the use of iron rivets for attachment. Similar small hinges were reported from Fort Michilimackinac and were interpreted as functioning as hinges for household furniture, such as a trunk or chest (Stone 1974:193–194).

Iron Hinge (n=1; Plate 27 B). One small, complete iron hinge was recovered from the surface collection. It has two holes on each side of the hinge pin and measures 3.7 cm by 3.9 cm. This hinge may have been used on a chest or trunk.

Drawer Handles (n=6; Plate 27 C-H). Six drawer handles or pulls were recovered from the surface collection. Four specimens are simple handles made of iron rods, which have been shaped into open rectangular or rounded handles. Three of the specimens have looped ends for attachment and the other handle is fragmentary. The lengths of these handles range from 8.5 cm to 15.0 cm. This type of simple drawer handle was also represented at Fort Michilimackinac (Stone 1974:204). A similar handle was from a burial chest excavated at the Cahokia Illini

Plate 27. Furniture hardware. A, copper hinge; B, iron hinge; C-H, drawer handles; I, triangular iron padlock; J, keyhole plate

cemetery on the First Terrace of Monks Mound (Walthall and Benchley 1987:66).

The other two handles from the Cahokia Wedge are different in form and are probably of a later date. One handle is made of a flat strip of metal, probably brass. It has been shaped into an open rectangular handle with projections on each end with holes for attachment. This handle measures 9.7 cm in length and 1.2 cm in width. The remaining drawer handle is made of cast brass. It is oval in shape, measuring 10.5 cm by 5.4 cm. The top portion of the handle is convex, creating a semicircular projection which acts as the pull element. Holes are located on each side of the oval handle for attachment.

Triangular Iron Padlock (n = 1; Plate 27 I). One complete triangular padlock made of iron with brass plating was recovered from Feature 7, a wall trench feature. The padlock measures 4.5 cm in length and 3.1 cm in width. The main body portion of the lock is covered with brass plating. This type of padlock, also in circular or ball forms with a sliding bolt to engage the hasp, was introduced in the fifteenth and sixteenth centuries in Europe (Noel Hume 1970:250). These padlocks were commonly found on seventeenth-century British colonial sites and are illustrated in Diderot's *Encyclopedia* in the eighteenth century (Noel Hume 1970:250). In the later part of the eighteenth century, padlocks became larger and different styles were introduced. The recovery of this padlock within the wall trench supports the interpretation of Feature 7 as a wall trench feature dating to the mid to late eighteenth-century Nicolle/Meunier structure. This relatively small padlock may have been used on a chest or trunk.

Keyhole Plate (n = 1; Plate 27 J). One cast brass keyhole plate was recovered from the surface collection. It is relatively small in size and was probably used on a chest, trunk, or other piece of furniture, rather than as a structural element. It is oval in shape, measuring 4.8 cm by 3.1 cm. At opposite ends are holes for attachment. A vertical, rectangular key hole, measuring 2.1 cm by 0.6 cm, is centrally located.

ARCHITECTURAL HARDWARE

Keys (n = 4; Plate 28 A-D). Four iron keys were recovered from the surface (n = 2), from an excavation unit (n = 1), and from Feature 1 (n = 1). A nearly complete key from Feature 1 is relatively large in size. The key shank measures 7.8 cm in length from the junction of the key handle to the distal end. The key blade (the actual lock mechanism) is flush to the distal end of the shank. It measures 2.2 cm in length below the shank and 1.8 cm in width. The key blade has three horizontal

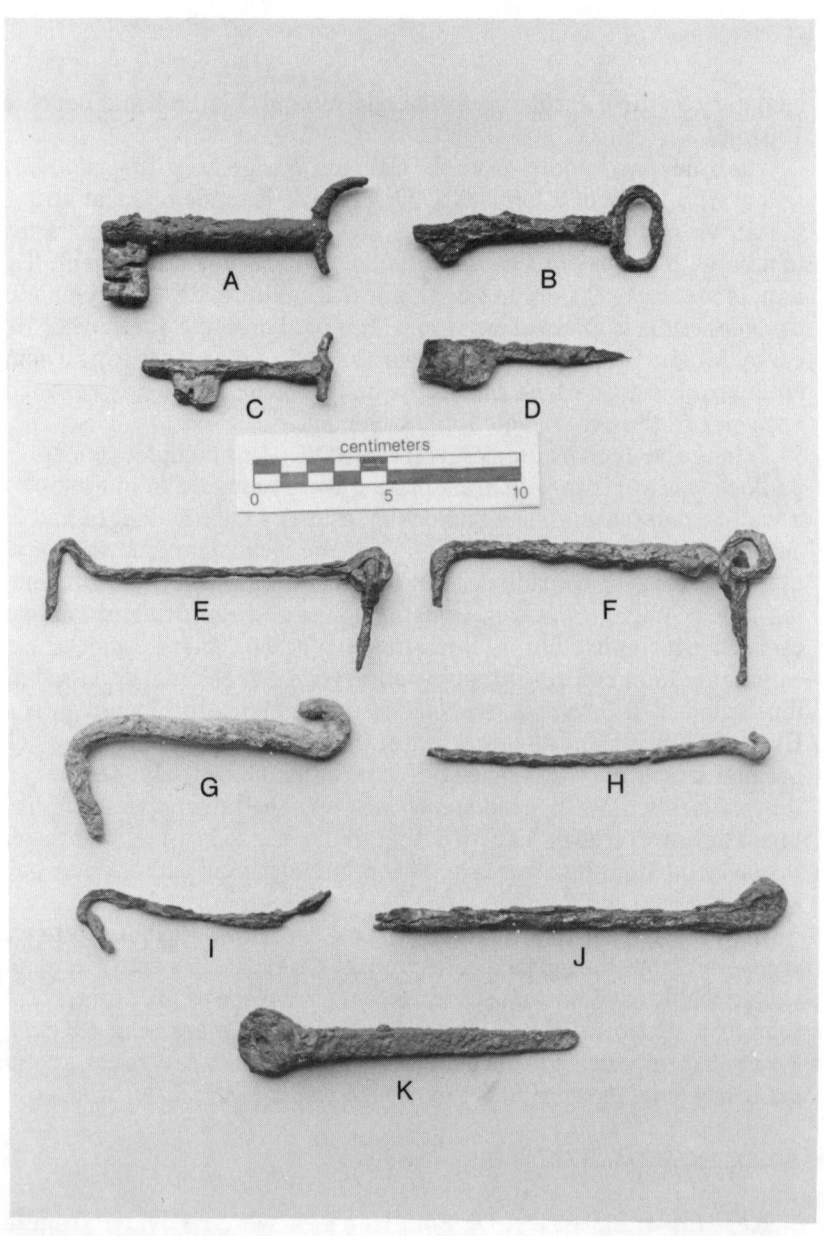

Plate 28. Architectural hardware. A-D, keys; E-J, L-shaped latch hooks; K, thumb lock catch

notches or slots, two extending from the distal end of the blade and one from the proximal end of the blade. Two smaller vertical notches are located on the bottom of the key blade. In cross-section, the key blade has a pronounced lip at the bottom of the blade. The key handle, although broken, has a small protrusion on the interior at the junction of the handle and the shaft, giving it a heart-shaped appearance. Another nearly complete key from an excavation unit also has a heart-shaped handle. The shank, measuring 6.6 cm, extends beyond the key blade, which has one vertical notch or slot extending from the blade bottom. Comparative examples have been found at numerous eighteenth-century sites, including Fort Stanwix (Hanson and Hsu 1975:62), Fort Michilimackinac (Stone 1974:225-229), Fort Ouiatenon (Noble 1983:259), and Fort Ligonier (Grimm 1970:95).

One complete key measures 9.3 cm in total length. It has a simple oval handle, and a shank that extends beyond the key blade. The specimen is corroded and the actual shape of the key blade is indeterminate. The fourth key is very fragmentary; it is only a portion of the shaft with the key blade. Both pieces are heavily corroded.

L-shaped Latch Hooks (n = 7; Plate 28 E-J). Seven L-shaped iron latch hooks were recovered from the surface collection (n = 4) and from excavation units (n = 3). These hooks may have been used on doors, gates, or window shutters. Three of the hooks are complete and measure 10.7 cm, 12.8 cm, and 13.0 cm in length. The two larger latches have the smaller eye hooks still attached to the proximal end. These eye hooks would have been emplaced in the supporting structural element.

Thumb Lock Catch (n = 1; Plate 28 K). One iron thumb lock catch or lift was recovered from Feature 1. This mechanism was part of a door handle or latch. The artifact measures 12.7 cm in length. It has a tapered shaft which is square in cross-section and measures 1.0 cm in maximum width. On the wide end is a flattened circular appendage on which the thumb would have been placed to operate the lock mechanism. The complete door handle/latch mechanism was illustrated by Diderot (see Stone 1974:210) and similar thumb lifts were recovered at Fort Michilimackinac (Stone 1974:242) and Fort Ouiatenon (Noble 1983:168, 171; Tordoff 1983:305).

Tapered Strap Hinges (n = 3; Plate 29 A-C). Three iron hinges or hinge fragments were recovered from the controlled surface collection. These hinges have tapered or triangular strap pieces attached to the central hinge pin. The smallest specimen consists of only the strap element, which has two holes. It measures 11.5 cm in length, with a maximum width of 4.8 cm at the hinge pin. This specimen, which probably dates to the eighteenth century, is similar to one found at Fort

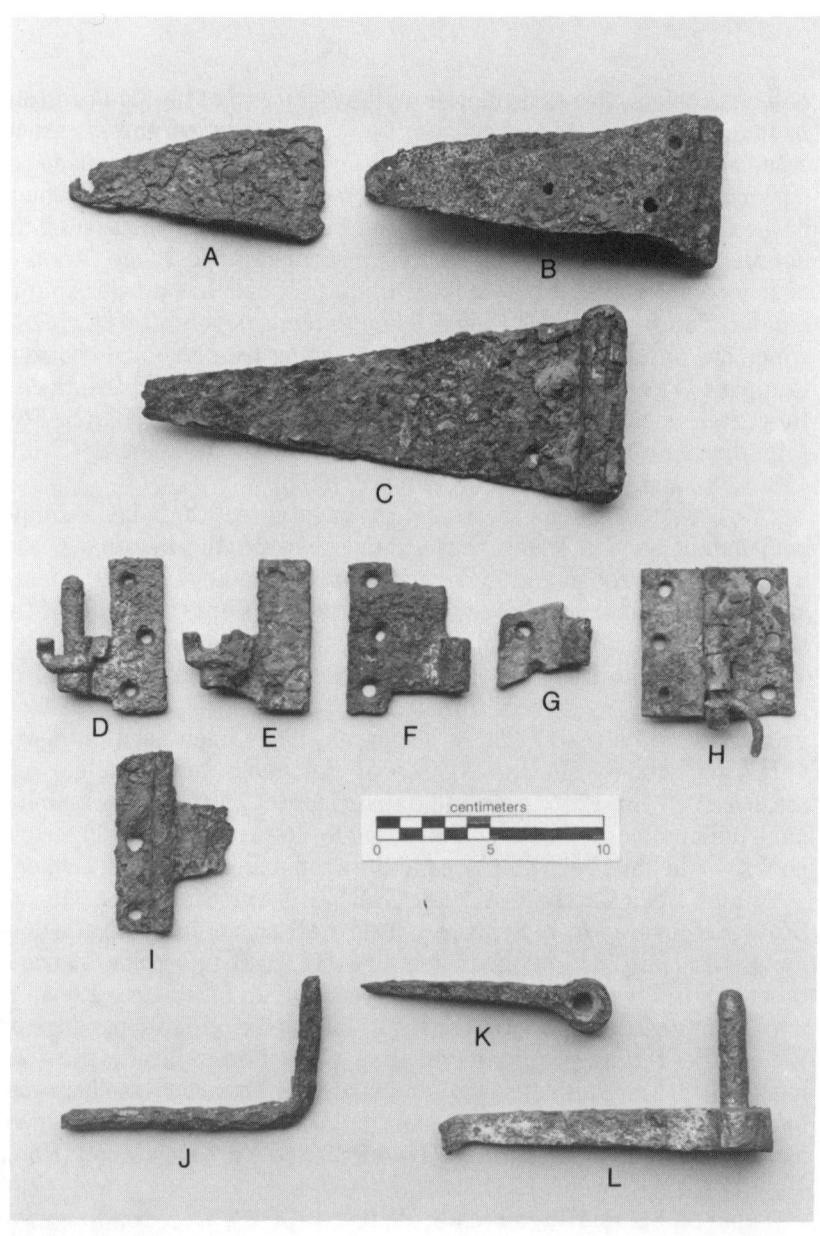

Plate 29. Architectural hardware. A-C, tapered strap hinges; D-I, square or rectangular hinges; J-L, pintles

Michilimackinac (Stone 1974:217–218). A complete hinge consists of the two tapered strap elements and the hinge pin. The strap elements each measure 15.0 cm in length, with a maximum width of 6.3 cm. Four irregularly-placed holes are located on each strap element. The largest strap hinge fragment measures approximately 19.0 cm in length with a maximum width of 7.5 cm and has evidence of only two holes.

Rectangular and Square Hinges (n = 7; Plate 29 D-I). Six rectangular or square iron hinges or hinge fragments were recovered from the surface collection (n = 6) and from an excavation unit (n = 1). Five of these hinges are similar in size and shape. The rectangular strap portions attached to the hinge pins measure 6.5 in length and 2.3 cm in width, and each side has three nail holes for attachment. A similar complete hinge is larger and has a square strap element measuring 6.5 cm by 6.5 cm. These types of hinges are dissimilar to eighteenth-century building hardware and most likely date to the nineteenth-century occupation at the site. One rectangular hinge is slightly different in form and possibly dates to the eighteenth century. It has one rectangular element, measuring 7.7 cm in length and 1.6 cm in width, attached to the hinge pin. On the opposite side of the pin is a smaller, fragmentary strap measuring 2.3 cm in length.

Pintles (n = 3; Plate 29 J-L). Two iron pintles were recovered from the surface collection, and another was recovered by construction workers on Route 157 along the northeast edge of the site. One specimen in the surface collection is a simple pintle made of a single piece of iron. The total length of the shank is 11.8 cm and the hinge pin measures 5.5 cm. Although corroded, in cross-section the pintle appears roughly rounded and the shank end is blunt. This pintle is similar to the B2 variety pintles identified from Fort Michilimackinac (Stone 1974:221).

The other two pintles have the shank and hinge pin as separate elements. The pintle from Route 157 construction is relatively small and the hinge pin is missing. The shank, measuring 11.0 cm in length, is rectangular in cross-section and tapers toward the distal end. The other pintle also has a rectangular and tapered shank, measuring approximately 14.2 cm in length, although the tip is broken. The hinge pin is rounded in cross-section and extends 5.0 cm from the shank. These pintles correspond to B1 variety pintles identified at Fort Michilimackinac (Stone 1974:221).

Nails (n = 2,789). A total of 2,789 nails was recovered from the surface collection (n = 1,828), from excavation units (n = 837), and from features (n = 124). The abundance of the sample and the poor condition of most nails dictated a general analysis. Nails were therefore separated into the following categories: rosehead, L-head, T-head, other square nails, round nails, and unidentifiable nails and nail fragments. Distinctions between handwrought and machine-cut square nails in the other square nail category could not be made because of the corroded condition of most specimens. Of the total assemblage, there were 214 rosehead nails, 13 L-head nails, five T-head nails, 725 other square nails, 358 round nails, and 1,474 unidentifiable nails and nail fragments.

It is noteworthy that, of the subtotal count of 957 handwrought rosehead, L-head, T-head, and other square nails, 637 or 66.6% were recovered in the Area A test excavation units and features; the remainder were from the controlled surface collection. In comparison, in the other categories (round and unidentifiable nails), out of the subtotal count of 1,832, only 329 or 17% were recovered in the excavations. These differences reflect on the poor condition of the surface artifacts. Nevertheless, it also substantiates the identity of Area A as an eighteenth-century occupational area, based on the abundance of handwrought and other earlier types of nails.

METAL TOOLS

Scissor Fragments (n = 5; Plate 30 A, B). Five fragments of scissors were identified from the surface collection (n = 1), from excavation units (n = 3), and from Feature 1 (n = 1). Four of the specimens are fragments of the handles or eyes. The largest handle fragment is oblong in shape with a length of 6.4 cm. Comparative examples suggest that the other handle would have been smaller and circular in shape (Stone 1974:160). The fragment from Feature 1 is a portion of a handle that appears to be fairly large. The two other handle fragments are very small and the handle shapes were indeterminate. The fifth specimen consists of the two scissor blades attached at the hinge element; however, the handles are missing. The blades appear to be nearly complete, measuring approximately 4.7 cm in length from the hinge element. This pair of scissors was relatively small.

Trade Axe (n = 1; Plate 30 C). One complete iron trade axe was recovered from an excavation unit. The axe was hand forged from a strip of iron that was doubled over a bar to create the looped haft element. The overall length of the axe is 17.4 cm, with the blade measuring 11.2 cm. The size of this axe fits within the medium-sized range identified for trade axes recovered from the Trudeau site (Brain 1979:141). On the axe blade near the haft is a maker's mark identified as the "3 rivers" cartouche (Stone 1974:297). This refers to the French

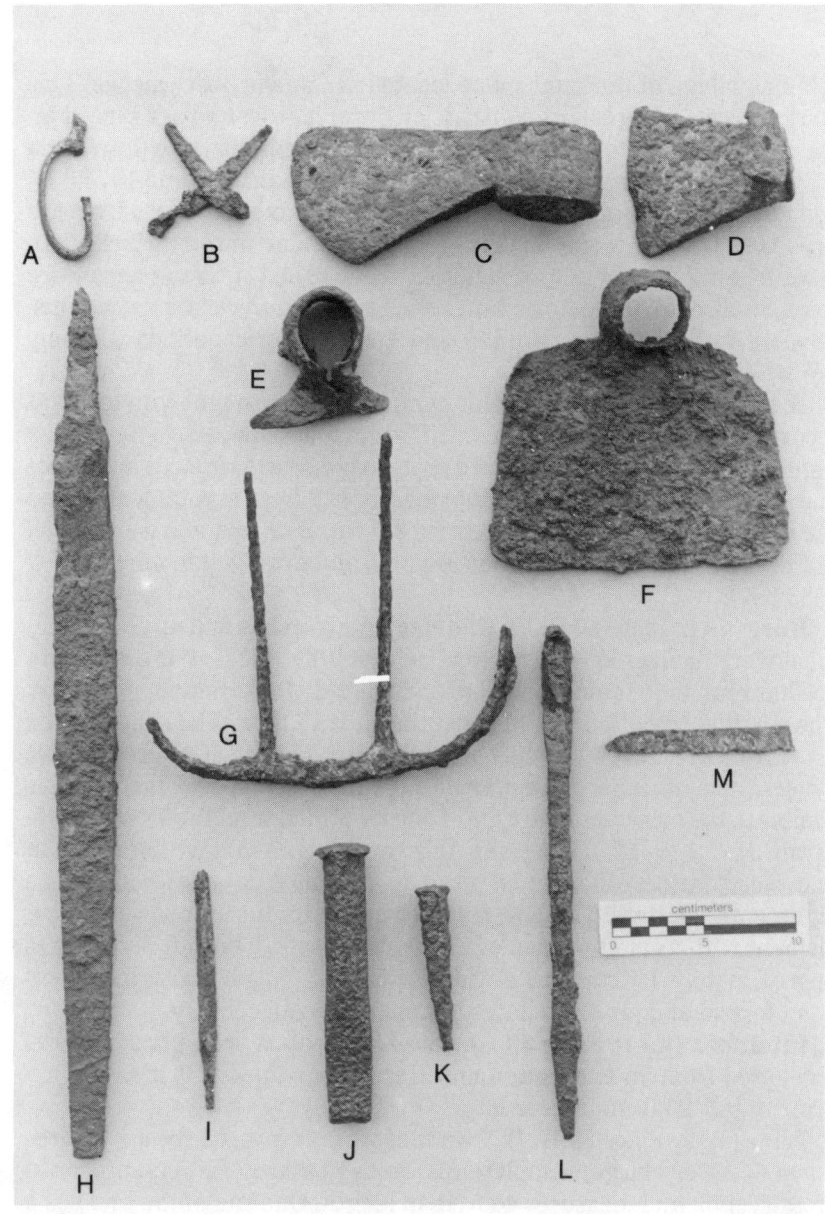

Plate 30. Metal tools. A and B, scissor fragments; C, trade axe; D, wedge; E and F, hoes; G, pitchfork; H and I, files; J, chisel; K, punch; L, gouge; M, saw blade

colonial village of the same name located in Canada near Quebec. This mark consists of circular geometric or floral motifs; two are placed on one side of the blade and one is located on the opposite side (Figure 66 A). Identical axes was found at Fort Michilimackinac (Stone 1974:301) and Fort Ouiatenon (Tordoff 1983:415). A trade axe recovered from the Gros Cap Cemetery site in Michigan has similar marks, which were identified as "blossoms" (Nern and Cleland 1974:11). Trade axes were common throughout historic times and stylistic differences are not discernible for the Early, Middle, and Late Historic periods (Quimby 1966a:69–71).

Wedge (n = 1; Plate 30 D). One complete handwrought iron tool was recovered from an excavation unit. This artifact appears to have been a small axe that had been utilized as a wedge. The haft element is split and extensively battered. The tool measures 9.5 cm in total length and the expanding blade or bit measures 8.5 cm. Similar tools were found at Fort Michilimackinac (Stone 1974:309) and Fort Ouiatenon (Tordoff 1983:360).

Hoes (n = 2; Plate 30 E, F). One complete iron hoe and one haft fragment were recovered from excavation units. The blade of the complete hoe has rounded shoulders and expands slightly to the square-ended bit. The maximum width of the blade at the bit is 16.5 cm. The length of the blade from the junction of the haft to the bit is 12.2 cm. The circular haft element has an inner diameter of 4.0 cm. The shape of the blade is similar to the most common type of hoe identified from the Trudeau site (Brain 1979:144–145). However, this hoe appears to have been cast in one piece, rather than hand forged, and may date later than the eighteenth century. The hoe fragment exhibits the complete hafting element with a small portion of the blade present. The haft diameter is approximately 4.5 cm with a width of 5.2 cm. This hoe fragment was hand forged and probably dates to the eighteenth century.

Pitchfork (n = 1; Plate 30 G). One fragmentary iron pitchfork was recovered from an excavation unit. It has four tines that measure approximately 23.0 cm in length.

Files (n = 2; Plate 30 H, I). Two files were recovered from Features 1 and 6. A very large, complete file, from Feature 1, is rectangular in cross-section and measures 46.5 cm in length. One end of the tool has a tapering tang. The file plane measures 3.4 cm in width and 1.6 cm in thickness. On the width portion are cross-hatched grooves and on the file edges are diagonal grooves.

The other file, from the Feature 6 structural basin, is much smaller, triangular in cross-section, and has a pointed tang on one end. The tool is nearly complete, and measures 12.8 cm in length. Both types of files have been recovered at Fort Ouiatenon (Noble 1983:172, 175; Tordoff 1983:363) and Fort Michilimackinac, where the larger type was reported to date from 1740 to 1780 (Stone 1974:304). The files from the Wedge were recovered in contexts dating to the early to mid-eighteenth century (Feature 1) and the mid to late nineteenth century (Feature 6).

Chisel (n = 1; Plate 30 J). One iron tool, which is probably a chisel, was recovered from the surface collection. The tool is complete and measures 14.6 cm in length. The upper portion of the shaft is rounded and it tapers into a slightly flared and flattened bit end. The head of the chisel is rounded and has evidence of battering. Similar tools have been identified from Fort Michilimackinac (Stone 1974:302), Fort Ouiatenon (Noble 1983:159), and Fort Stanwix (Hanson and Hsu 1975:108).

Punch (n = 1; Plate 30 K). One complete iron tool, recovered from Feature 1, was probably utilized as a punch. It measures 8.7 cm in length. The shaft is square in cross-section, measuring 1.4 cm in thickness, and tapers to a point. The head is rounded to square and has been heavily battered. Similar tools have been reported from Fort Michilimackinac (Stone 1974:303) and Fort Ouiatenon (Noble 1983:294; Tordoff 1983:365)

Gouge (n = 1; Plate 30 L). One complete iron gouge was recovered from the Feature 6 structural basin. It measures 27.2 cm in length and has a shallow "scoop" at one slightly expanding end. Similar gouges were recovered at Fort Ouiatenon (Noble 1983:195) and at from Fort Michilimackinac (Stone 1974:305). These artifacts are probably woodworking tools.

Saw Blade (n = 1; Plate 30 M). One fragmentary steel (?) saw blade was recovered from an excavation unit. The width of the blade measures 1.5 cm and the thickness is 0.1 cm. The blade edge has irregularly cut teeth. The opposite edge tapers toward the toothed edge, indicating one end of the tool.

BARREL PARTS

Barrel Hoop (n = 1; Plate 31 A). One nearly complete iron barrel hoop was recovered from Feature 1. The maximum hoop diameter is 24.5 cm. The vertical width of the hoop ranges from 2.4 cm to 2.6 cm. The area where the two ends of the hoop would have connected is heavily corroded and rivets are not visible. The hoop is beveled, indicating it would probably have been located at the top or bottom of the barrel rather than at the midsection. The diameter of the hoop is within the average diameter range recorded for iron barrel hoops from Fort

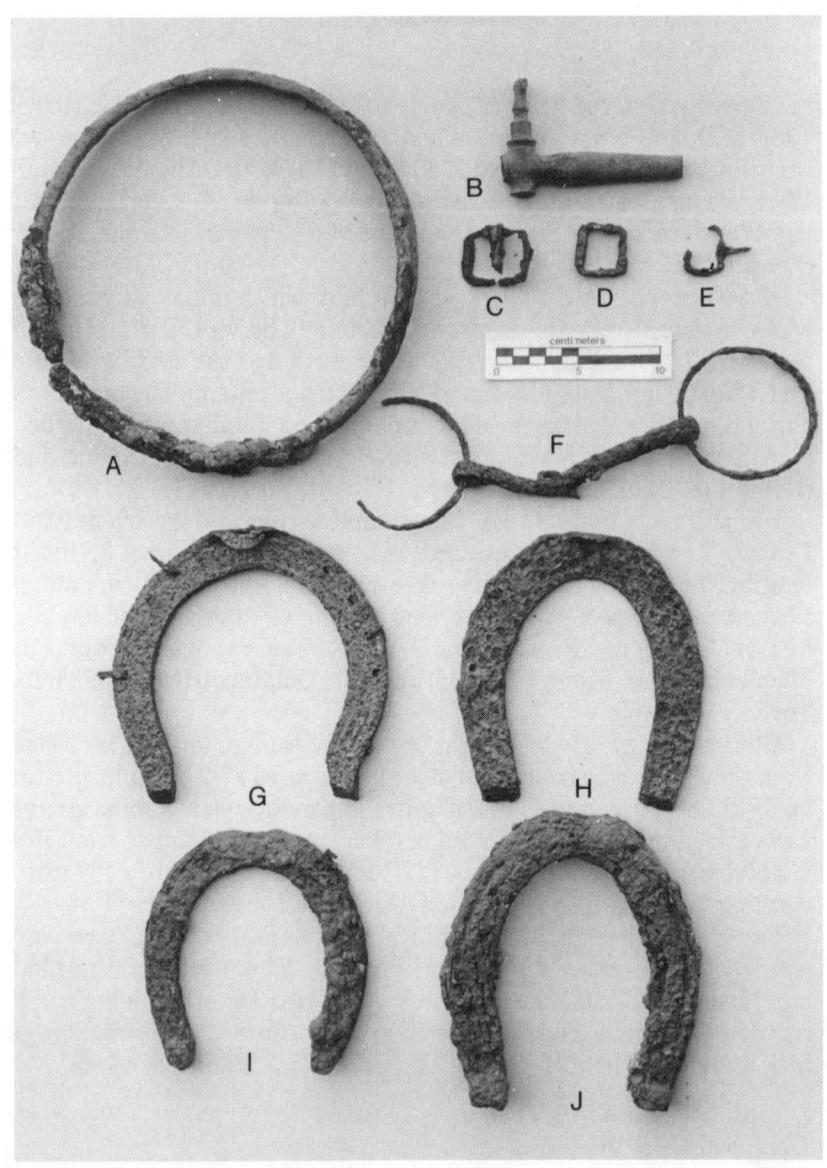

Plate 31. Barrel parts and equestrian items. A, barrel hoop; B, brass spigot; C-E, harness buckles; F, iron bit; G-J, horseshoes

Michilimackinac that date from 1750 to 1780 (Stone 1974:203). Numerous pieces of strap iron, often with rivets, were present in the Cahokia Wedge collection and some of these may be fragments of barrel hoops.

Brass Spigot (n=1; Plate 31 B). One nearly complete cast brass spigot was recovered in the controlled surface collection. Spigots were inserted into the sides or ends of wooden barrels and utilized as a dispensing mechanism. The neck end of the artifact is rounded to oblong in cross-section. It has longitudinal, incised or cut lines that may have been produced after casting. The neck end measures 9.1 cm in length, and has a distal diameter of 1.4 cm. The spout end, although broken at the junction of the cock, is also rounded in cross-section with a diameter of 1.6 cm. The cock end or handle has a simple flared top. Comparative examples were recovered at Fort Michilimackinac in feature contexts, primarily dating to the British occupation from 1761 to 1781 (Stone 1974:179). Similar spigots were also found at Fort Ouiatenon (Tordoff 1983:245).

EQUESTRIAN ITEMS

Bridle Boss (n=2; Figure 67 T, U). Two brass artifacts may represent ornaments or decorations, known as a boss, for the cheekpiece of a horse bridle. One specimen is oval in shape, measuring 2.8 cm in length and 2.2 cm in width. It has a convex face and concave back. The front surface is highly polished and the edges have striations probably produced by a file. Two pointed prongs for attachment have been soldered to the back.

The other artifact is rectangular in shape, measuring 2.0 cm by 1.6 cm. It has a convex face, concave back, and beveled edges. Two soldered and pointed prongs are located on the back at the edges of the length of the artifact. A similar artifact identified as a boss was recovered from the eighteenth-century Fort Independence in South Carolina. This boss is a circular piece, 3.0 cm in diameter, with two iron pins or prongs for attachment to the bridle or harness (Bastian 1982:106).

Harness Buckles (n=3; Plate 31 C-E). Three plain strap buckles were recovered from excavation units (n = 2) and from Feature 1 (n = 1). Two of the buckles are rectangular and one is square. The buckle from Feature 1 appears to be made of brass. The buckle frame is roughly square, measuring 3.1 cm by 3.4 cm, with rounded corners. The cross-section of the frame is square to rectangular. The tongue hinge is present on one side, but the tongue is missing. The smallest buckle, made of iron, is rectangular and measures 2.4 cm by 3.0 cm. A fragment of the tongue is attached to one side of the frame. The other iron rectangular buckle measures 3.4 cm by 4.3 cm. The cross-section of the frame appears to be square to rectangular. The tongue is present and heavily corroded. These buckles are dissimilar to the elaborately decorated buckles utilized in the eighteenth century as clothing and shoe adornment (Stone 1974:25–44; Grimm 1970:52, 54). Similar iron buckles were found at Fort Ouiatenon (Noble 1983:243; Tordoff 1983:423) and Fort Ligonier (Grimm 1970:117). The simple form of the Cahokia Wedge buckles suggests that they probably served a similar utilitarian function, rather than as clothing or shoe adornment.

Iron Bit (n = 1; Plate 31 F). An iron jointed-mouth bit was identified in the controlled surface collection. The symmetrical piece consists of two iron rings measuring 8.3 cm in diameter, which are attached at the ends of two iron bars to form the jointed mouthpiece. Each bar within the mouthpiece measures 10.0 cm in length and has looped ends for attachment. An identical bit was recovered from an eighteenth-century site in Virginia; however, it was suggested that this bit may date to a later occupation at the site (Noel Hume 1970:241)

Horseshoes (n = 5; Plate 31 G-J). Five handwrought iron horseshoes were recovered from the controlled surface collection. One of the shoes is very large. It measures 17.2 cm in width and was probably for a draft horse. Four nail holes are located on each side of the shoe, and remnants of two square, possibly handwrought, nails are present. The other four horseshoes are smaller. They have widths ranging from 14.0 cm to 15.0 cm, and appear to be for average-sized horses. All of the shoes have toe clips on the apex, an element which was introduced in the mid-nineteenth century (Noel Hume 1970:239). The heels of the horseshoes are turned slightly inward. This is indicative of the mid-nineteenth century, rather than the more U-shaped form of the later nineteenth century (Noel Hume 1970:238).

WEAPONS

by F. Terry Norris
District Archaeologist
United States Army Corps of Engineers
St. Louis District

GUN PARTS

A total of eight gun parts was recovered from the surface (n = 4), from excavation units (n = 2), and from Feature 1 (n = 2). With one exception, all of these are lock parts.

Lock Plates (n = 3; Plate 32 A-C). Three lock plates were recovered from the surface of the site. One exhibits an attached frizzen spring and flash pan. The craftsmanship exhibited on this specimen would suggest that it was once attached to a high quality fusil, dating to the first half of the eighteenth century. The remaining two lock plates are similar in quality to lock plates found on the more common, lower grade mid-eighteenth-century trade fusils.

Side Plate (n = 1; Plate 32 D). In addition to the lock parts, one iron side plate from a mid-eighteenth-century Type D trade gun was recovered from an excavation unit. A similar side plate was recovered by the Peabody Museum at Haynes Bluff, Mississippi (Hamilton 1980).

Cock Parts (n = 2; Plate 32 E and G). Also recovered from the surface of the site was a cock (hammer) similar to those observed on other mid-eighteenth-century trade guns (Hamilton 1980). An upper jaw of the cock, from Feature 1, probably represents a fragment from a mid-eighteenth-century fusil.

Sear Spring Fragment (n = 1; Plate 32 F). One sear spring fragment was identified from an excavation unit.

Frizzen (n = 1; Plate 32 H). One frizzen was recovered from Feature 1. This is also believed to represent a portion of mid-eighteenth-century fusils.

GUNFLINTS

Gunflints (n = 44; Plate 33). Forty-four gunflints were recovered from the controlled surface collection (n = 19) and excavation units (n = 30). This total includes 17 spall type, two undifferentiated blades, three British blades, 12 French blades, and 10 bifacial Native American flints. Percentages reflected in Table 7 suggest that the majority of gunflints, the balance of which are of spall type manufacture, probably

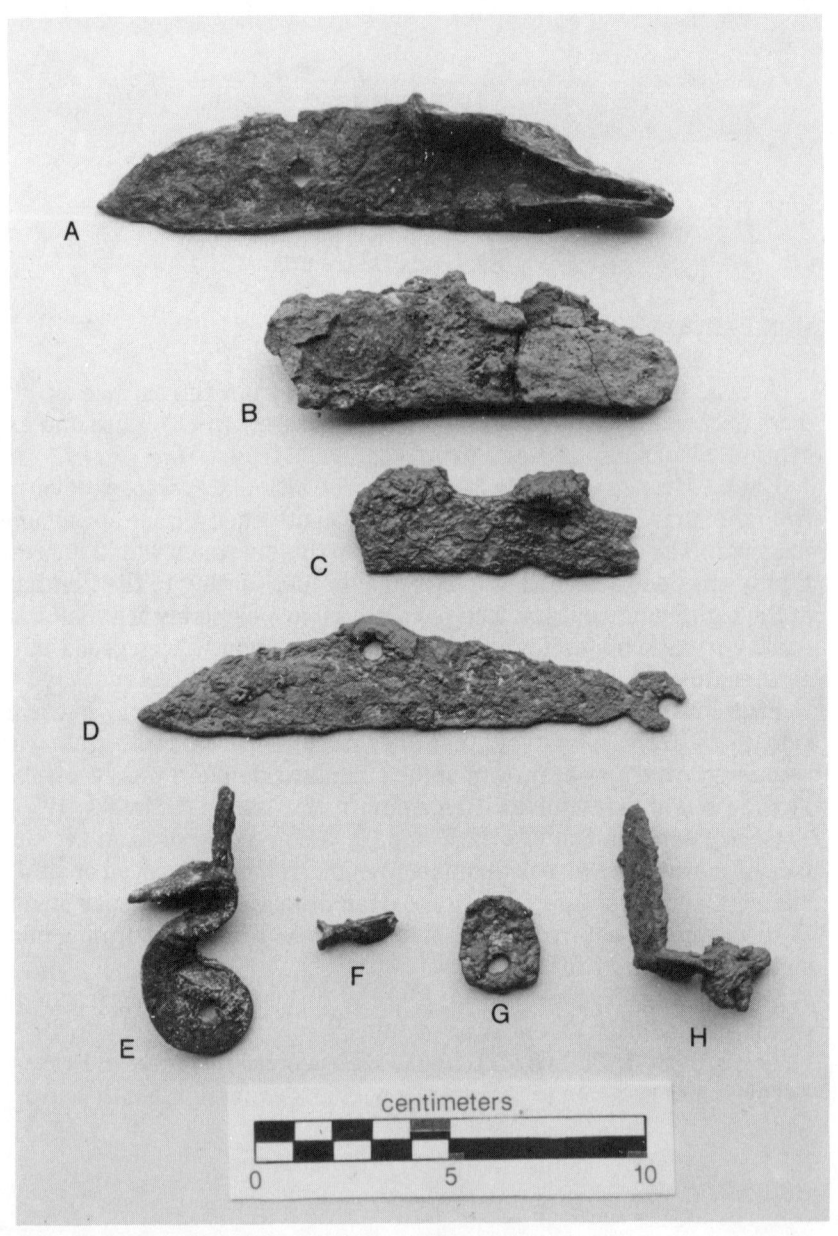

Plate 32. Flintlock gun parts. A-C, lock plates; D, side plate; E, cock (hammer); F, sear spring fragment; G, upper jaw of cock; H, frizzen

Plate 33. Gunflints. A, spall type; B, undifferentiated blades; C, English blades; D, French blades; E, bifacial Native American flints

TABLE 7

GUNFLINT TYPES AND PERCENTAGES

	Number of Specimens	Provenience	Chert Type/Color
Spall Type (n = 17)	1	CSC*	honey-colored
	1	CSC	tan/light brown
	1	CSC	light brown
	1	CSC	banded light brown
	2	CSC	light gray
	1	CSC	gray
	2	exc. unit	light brown
	2	exc. unit	grayish brown
	4	exc. unit	light gray
	2	exc. unit	mottled gray
Undifferentiated Blade (n = 2)	1	CSC	mottled gray
	1	exc. unit	light gray
English Blade (n = 3)	2	exc. unit	light gray
	1	exc. unit	gray
French Blade (n = 12)	1	CSC	honey-colored
	1	CSC	tannish gray
	1	CSC	mottled gray and white
	7	exc. unit	honey-colored
	2	exc. unit	light brown
Bifacial Native American (n = 10)	1	CSC	light gray
	1	CSC	banded light gray
	1	CSC	Burlington
	5	exc. unit	Burlington
	2 (spall type)	exc. unit	Burlington

*Controlled surface collection

	Counts	Percentages %
Spall Type	17	39
Undifferentiated Blade	2	4
English Blade	3	7
French Blade	12	27
Native American	10	23
Total	44	100

entered the archaeological record prior to A.D. 1750 (Hamilton 1960). French blade gunflints were not a regular article of trade until after 1740 (Good 1972). The three Prismatic English gunflints post-date the French period and probably date to the early nineteenth century. A total of 10 bifacially flaked gunflints of local chert are interpreted as being of Native American manufacture. The majority of these gunflints probably relate to an Illini Indian occupation at the site, and most likely entered the archaeological record during the late seventeenth or early eighteenth century.

LEAD

Lead Balls (n = 13; Plate 34 A). A total of 13 lead balls was recovered from the surface collection (n = 7) and excavation units (n = 6). A description of all spherical lead bullets is presented in Table 8. Comparison of the lead balls (bullets) recovered from the Cahokia Wedge site and the Guebert site is presented in Table 9. The Guebert site is located approximately 60 miles downstream from Cahokia and was occupied by members of the Kaskaskia Indian group. The similarity of bullet diameters, 0.5397 (Cahokia Wedge) and 0.5391 (Guebert), suggests that the residents of both the French village at Cahokia and the Kaskaskia Indian settlement at the Guebert site were utilizing similar firearms. Since the Kaskaskia lived amicably with and in close proximity to the French in the central Mississippi River Valley, this similarity is understandable.

Previous studies suggest that, on average, fusils (smoothbored, trade guns) of the late seventeenth and early eighteenth centuries tended to exhibit bore diameters less than 0.54 inches. In contrast, those of the late periods (mid-eighteenth to mid-nineteenth centuries) tended to average greater than 0.58 inch diameters (Hamilton 1960, 1980). This conclusion would suggest that the majority of bullets recovered from the Cahokia Wedge site entered the archaeological record prior to A.D. 1750.

Lead Waste (n = 36; Plate 34 B, C). A total of 36 pieces of lead waste was recovered from the surface collection (n = 9), from excavation units (n = 23), and from Features 1 (n = 2), and 4 (n = 1). Represented in this total are gang mold sprues, a possible weight or sinker, lead spatter, and sheet fragments. The 10 fragments of gang mold sprues were recovered from the test excavations; none were found on the surface of the site. The possible weight or sinker recovered from the surface is a small piece of spatter, which appears to have been folded into a cone-shaped artifact.

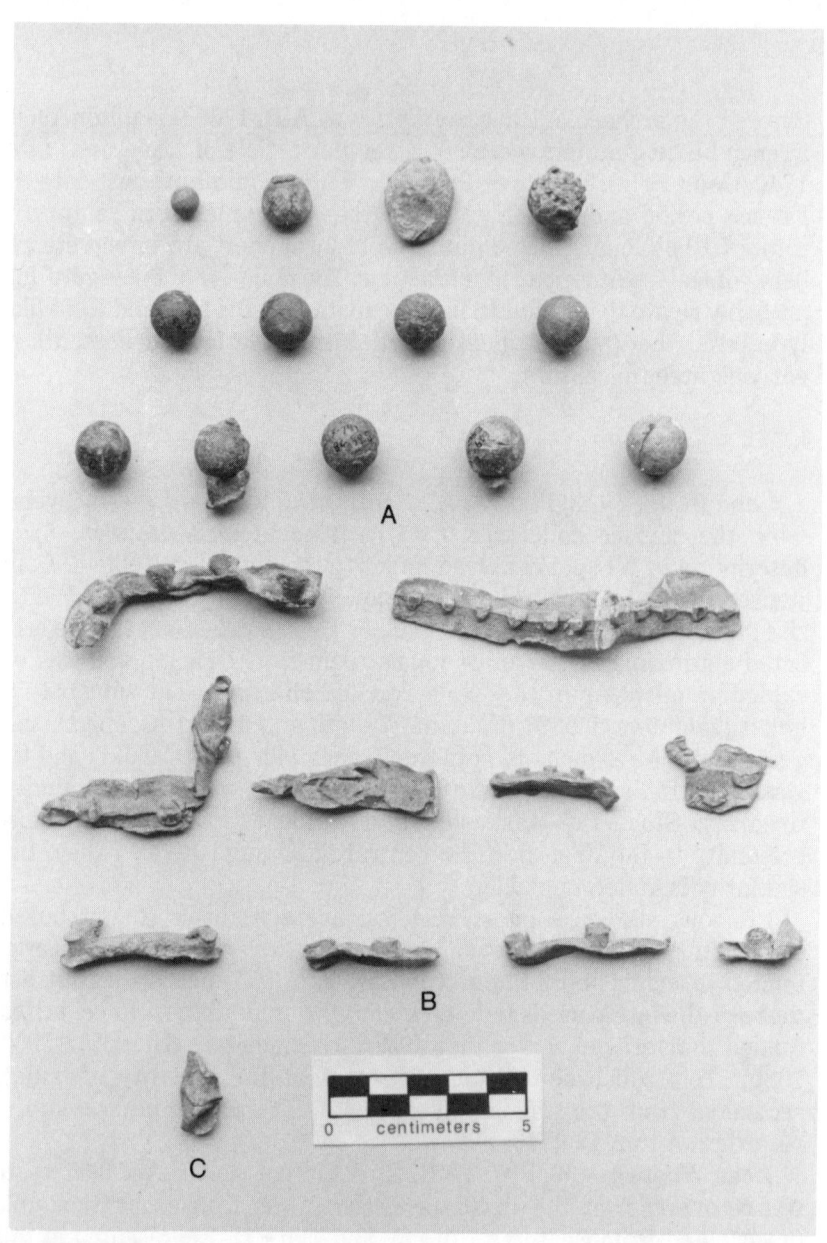

Plate 34. Lead. A, lead balls; B, gang mold sprues; C, possible lead sinker

TABLE 8

Lead Balls-Firearms Projectiles

Specimen	Provenience	Caliber	Wt.(g)	Comments
1	CSC*	-	9.0	Fired; flattened on one surface by impact
2	CSC	-	16.5	Fired; flattened on one surface by impact
3	CSC	.560	18.0	Unfired; sprue attached, chewed
4	CSC	.615	20.2	Unfired; portion of clipped sprue attached
5	CSC	.545	14.5	Unfired; portion of clipped sprue attached
6	CSC	.545 to .585	15.1	Unfired; deformed/chewed
7	CSC	.295	2.3	Unfired
8	exc. unit	.572	17.0	Unfired
9	exc. unit	.525	18.2	Unfired
10	exc. unit	.600	12.8	Unfired; chewed
11	exc. unit	.510	13.3	Unfired; chewed
12	exc. unit	.615	21.0	Unfired; sprue attached
13	exc. unit	.535	14.3	Unfired

Average diameter = 5397.54
*Controlled surface collection

Table 9

Comparison of Sizes of Lead Balls from the Cahokia Wedge Site and the Guebert Site

Caliber	Cahokia Wedge	Guebert site
.30	1	1
.33		1
.34		1
.36		1
.47		1
.48		8
.51	1	2
.52	1	
.53	1	10
.54	1	4
.55		8
.56	2	2
.57	1	5
.58		4
.59		3
.60	1	
.61	1	1
.61–.62		6
.62		2

Average diameter:
    Cahokia Wedge = .5397 caliber, n = 10
    Guebert site = .5391 caliber, n = 60

ARTIFACT DESCRIPTIONS

Galena (n = 1). One piece of galena was recovered from Feature 7, a wall trench of the eighteenth-century Nicolle/Meunier structure. Although galena is commonly found on prehistoric sites, the presence of galena within the fill of Feature 7 probably relates to the historic Indian, or more likely, French exploitation of the lead mines near Ste. Genevieve in southeastern Missouri in the eighteenth and early nineteenth centuries (Walthall 1981:20–21).

MISCELLANEOUS ARTIFACTS

Buttons

A total of 54 buttons was recovered from the controlled surface collection (n = 30), from excavation units (n = 19), and from features (n = 5). Button materials include brass, white metal, iron, bone, mussel shell, clay, and glass. When possible, comparisons are made with Stanley South's (1964) typology of buttons from eighteenth- and nineteenth-century sites in North Carolina.

Two-piece Brass/Copper Buttons (n = 4; Figure 67 A-D). One brass button is made of separately cast crown and back. These parts were brazed together, creating a hollow space within the button. The diameter is 1.1 cm. The crown is convex or dome-shaped, the back is slightly convex, and both surfaces exhibit circumferential striations. The wedge-shaped eye or shank was cast as part of the back, and the perforation was drilled after casting. This type of eye or shank is typical of eighteenth-century buttons (Luscomb 1967:220). Similar buttons have been recovered from Fort Ouiatenon (Noble 1983:120–121) and Fort St. Joseph (Hulse 1981:73). At Fort Michilimackinac, these button types were recovered in feature contexts dating from 1760 to 1780 (Stone 1974:53–54).

Another two-piece button of brass or copper measures 1.5 cm in diameter. Surrounding a central perforation on the button face is a stamped floral design with the petals outlined in relief and perforations or holes representing the petals. The button back has a cut strap eye that protrudes from the back piece.

The remaining two-piece brass buttons have diameters of 1.7 cm and 1.85. Both specimens are hollow with convex crowns and button backs. Iron stains are present on one side of each button, indicating the probable location of an iron eye or shank.

Metal Disc Buttons (n = 6; Figure 67 E-J). Six flat disc buttons have eyes or shanks soldered to the button backs. Four specimens have stamped decorations or inscriptions.

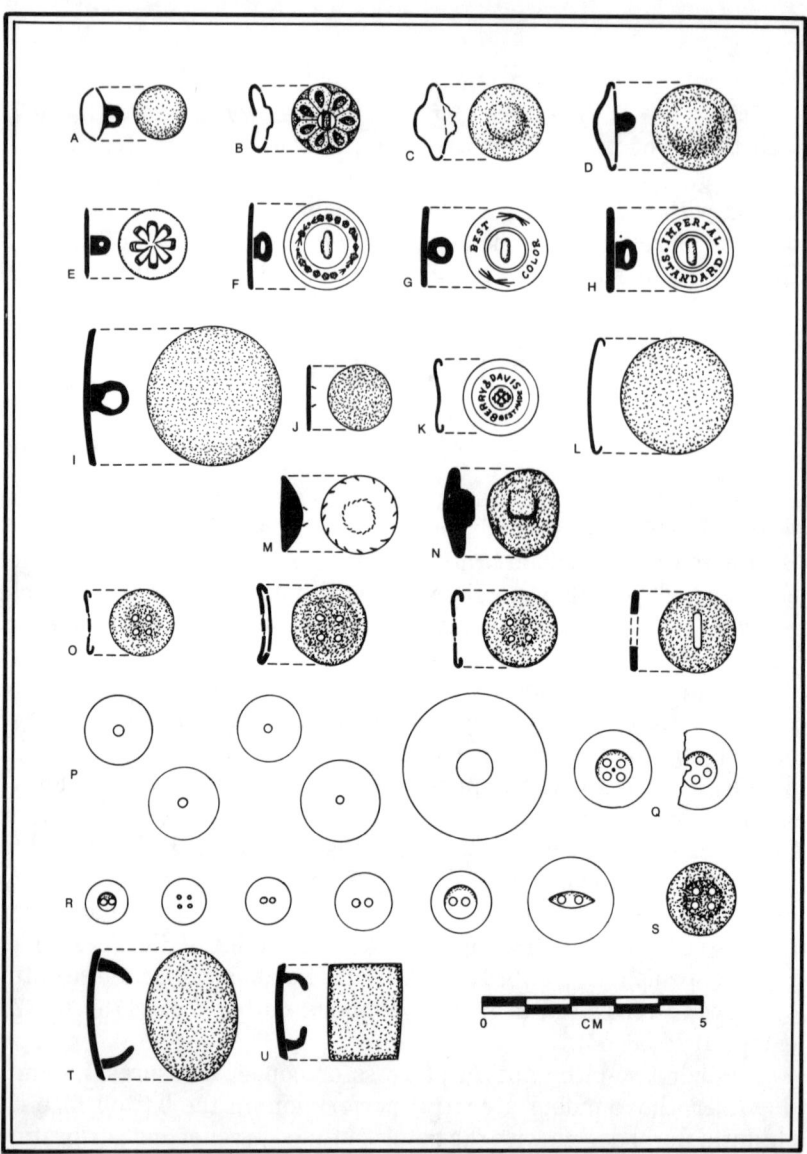

Fig. 67. Buttons and bridle bosses. A-D, two-piece brass/copper buttons; E-J, metal disc buttons; K and L, brass button faces; M and N, miscellaneous metal buttons; O, iron buttons; P, bone disc button backs; Q, four-holed bone buttons; R, shell buttons; S, clay button; T and U, brass bridle bosses

One disc button has beveled edges and a diameter of 1.55 cm. This button is dark gray in color and is probably made of a variety of white metal known as tombac. This metal was commonly used for buttons in the seventeenth and eighteenth centuries (Luscomb 1967:197). On the face is a symmetrical floral motif, which appears to have been scratched or incised by hand. The back of the button exhibits circumferential striations and has a wedge-shaped shank, both of which are characteristic of eighteenth-century buttons (Stone 1974:53–54).

One brass disc button measures 1.9 cm in diameter. It has a polished, plain face and a stamped, circular, floral motif on the back. A brass loop or wire eye is soldered to the back. This button is similar to South's Type 18 (1964:120–121), which has a temporal range of 1800 to 1865. A similar decorated button was reported from the Guebert site (Good 1972:133).

Two flat brass disc buttons have diameters of 1.8 cm. Each has a stamped inscription on the back, probably indicating the garment makers' names: "BEST COLOR" and "IMPERIAL STANDARD." Loop or wire eyes have been soldered to the backs. Similar buttons with inscriptions were grouped in South's Type 18 (1964:120–121), dating from 1837 to 1865. These types of buttons were probably used on work clothes and were manufactured in the United States throughout the nineteenth century (Luscomb 1967:224).

Two brass disc buttons are undecorated. The largest button measures 3.0 cm in diameter. It has a convex face and concave back, with an attached loop or wire shank. This button resembles one recovered at the Guebert site (Good 1972:132) and is similar to the type worn by the French military in ca. 1750 (Campbell 1965:4). Similar buttons have also been found at Fort Michilimackinac (Stone 1974:49), Fort St. Joseph (Hulse 1981:73), and Fort Ouiatenon (Noble 1983:120; Tordoff 1983:181). One small, flat disc button has a diameter of 1.4 cm. The wire shank is missing, although solder marks are evident.

Brass Button Faces (n = 3; Figure 67 K, L). Three brass button faces have crimped or lipped edges. These specimens would have been attached to a button back probably made of bone, metal, or wood. Diameters are 1.7 cm, 2.45 cm, and 2.6 cm. Two of the button faces are plain, and the smallest one has a circular stamped inscription "BERRY & DAVIS BEST MADE," identifying the manufacturer. Iron residue is present on the back of this button face, indicating that it was probably attached to an iron button back.

Miscellaneous Metal Buttons (n = 2; Figure 67 M, N). Two metal buttons of unknown construction were recovered from Feature 1 and Feature 5. A brass button from Feature 5 measures 1.65 cm in diameter. The flat button face has a stamped design. Notches occur along the button rim and a smaller, circular motif of dashed lines or notches is centrally located. The construction of the button back is indeterminate, although it is convex. A roughly circular to oval button, measuring 1.7 cm by 1.85 cm, was recovered from Feature 1. It is heavily corroded and the type of metal is indeterminate. The eye or shank on the button back appears to be square, and the button may have been made of one piece.

Iron Buttons (n = 10; Figure 67 O). Ten iron buttons have diameters ranging from 1.2 cm to 2.7 cm. Three of the buttons each have four central perforations and lipped or crimped edges, which indicate that these specimens were attached to a button back, probably made of bone, wood, or iron. One button has a centrally located, rectangular hole which measures 0.8 cm by 0.15 cm. Two of the buttons have scars on the button back, indicating the area for attachment of a wire eye. The remaining four buttons were heavily corroded and perforations were not apparent.

Bone Disc Button Backs (n = 5; Figure 67 P). Five bone discs represent button backs. Diameters range from 1.5 cm to 3.2 cm. The discs each have a single central perforation, where a wire eye would have been inserted, and tooled or lipped edges for attachment of the metal button face (South 1964:114). The bone button discs correspond to South's Type 4 (1964:114) with a suggested temporal range from 1726 to 1776. Similar bone discs were found at the Guebert site and were interpreted as non-utilitarian ornaments used by the historic Kaskaskia Indians (Good 1972:34). Buttons of this type were commonly found at Fort Michilimackinac, often with the metal button face still attached (Stone 1974:55-57).

Four-holed Bone Buttons (n = 2; Figure 67 Q). Two bone buttons measure 1.7 cm in diameter. Each button has four perforations within a central, depressed area on the button face. One of the specimens has a small pit located in the center of the perforations, which was possibly used for the attachment of the cutting tool. This type of bone button corresponds to South's Type 20 (1964:121), with a suggested temporal range of 1800 to 1865; however, they may date as early as 1750 (Cotter 1968:61). Similar bone buttons were found at the Guebert site (Good 1972:134), Fort de Chartres I (Jelks and Ekberg 1984:26), and in pre-1781 contexts at Fort Stanwix in New York (Hanson and Hsu 1975:89).

Shell Buttons (n = 9; Figure 67 R). Nine buttons were cut out of mussel shell and are possibly of local manufacture. Diameters range from 1.0 cm to 1.85 cm. Represented types are two-holed (n = 6), four-holed (n = 2), and lateral-holed on the back face (n = 1). The two- and four-holed buttons correspond to South's Type 22 (1964:121), ranging in time from 1800 to 1865, although production of shell buttons continued into the early twentieth century (Lopinot 1967).

Clay Button (n=1; Figure 67 S). One button appears to be made of a fired clay with an abundance of sand temper. It is dark gray in color. It has a diameter of 1.6 cm and four holes. The button face is slightly concave and the button back is slightly convex. The surfaces and edges are rough and slightly pitted, giving the appearance of having been made by hand.

Glass Buttons (n=14). Fourteen glass buttons are in the Cahokia Wedge collection. Six plain, white opaque glass buttons have four perforations each, located within a central depression. Diameters range from 1.1 cm to 1.7 cm. Two plain, white opaque glass buttons, with diameters of 1.0 cm and 1.1 cm, have ridged or fluted, circular designs on the edges of the button face. One odd specimen of white opaque glass is rounded with a maximum diameter of 1.2 cm. In cross-section, it has one flattened side. On the flat side are two small perforations which extend through to the opposite side, where there is one larger hole. One small, white opaque artifact with a diameter of 0.9 cm has one central pit, which does not go through to the opposite face. A metal eye was probably attached into this depression. Four glass buttons of different opaque colors, dark brown (n=1), medium brown (n=1), and medium blue (n=2), each has four perforations located within a central depression. Diameters of these specimens range from 1.0 cm to 1.45 cm. The manufacture of glass buttons began in the 1840s in the United States and continued throughout the nineteenth century (Luscomb 1967:80).

PENCILS

Lead Pencil (n=1; Plate 35 A). One cylindrical fragment of lead, probably a pencil, was recovered from an excavation unit. It has a maximum diameter of 1.0 cm. One end is flattened and the other appears to be broken. This artifact was probably locally produced, and may have been molded from a lead bullet or lead waste. Lead pencils are common artifacts at eighteenth-century sites (Stone 1974:154; Hanson and Hsu 1975:149–150).

Slate Pencils (n=8; Plate 35 B). Eight cylindrical slate pencil fragments were recovered from the surface (n=7) and from Feature 5 (n=1). Diameters range from 0.2 cm to 0.8 cm. Slate pencils are commonly found on nineteenth-century historic sites. Numerous pieces of thin, flat slate with very smoothed surfaces were also identified. Several of these fragments having parallel incised lines on one surface.

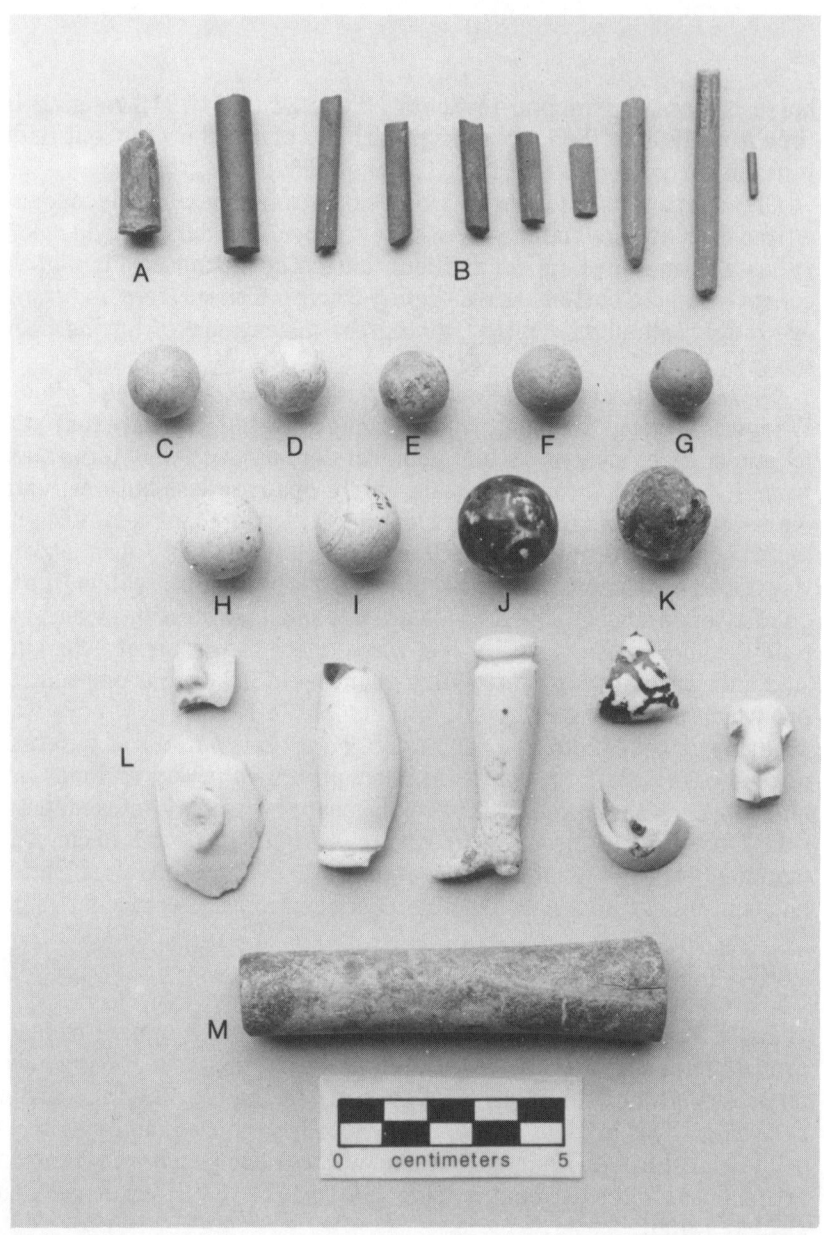

Plate 35. Miscellaneous artifacts. A, lead pencil; B, slate pencils; C-F, stone marbles; G, unglazed clay marble; H and I, china or porcelain marbles; J, glazed ceramic marble; K, blue glass marble; L, porcelain doll fragments; M, modified trumpeter swan humerus

ARTIFACT DESCRIPTIONS

Marbles

Eleven marbles were collected from the surface (n=8) and from excavation units (n=3). Marble materials include stone, clay, and glass.

Stone Marbles (n=4; Plate 35 C-F). Four marbles, with diameters of 1.5 cm to 1.6 cm, are made of limestone or marble. In the eighteenth and nineteenth centuries, Germany was the predominant producer of stone marbles for the export market. A decline in manufacture occurred during the 1870s when other materials, such as clay and glass, became popular (Randall 1971:102).

Unglazed Clay Marble (n=1; Plate 35 G). One unglazed, fired clay marble measures 1.4 cm in diameter. Numerous stone and clay marbles from various sites within Cahokia are in the artifact collections curated at the Cahokia Courthouse State Historic Site (personal observation).

China or Porcelain Marbles (n=2; Plate 35 H, I). Two china or porcelain marbles have diameters of 1.9 cm. One of the marbles is decorated with faint, orange, concentric circles, which is typical of this type of marble (Randall 1971:104). China and porcelain marbles were predominantly manufactured in Germany, beginning in the last third of the eighteenth century (Baumann 1970:32).

Glazed Ceramic Marble (n=1; Plate 35 J). One ceramic marble has a mottled brown glaze and a diameter of 2.2 cm. Production of this type of marble, often referred to as "Bennington," probably began in the 1840s when similar glazing techniques were produced on ceramic vessels (Randall 1971:104).

Glass Marbles (n=3; Plate 35 K). One fragmentary, dark blue, translucent glass marble has a diameter of 2.0 cm. It appears to have been made of handblown glass, due to the presence of a rough pit where the blow pipe would have been attached. The manufacture of handblown glass marbles began in the 1850s in Germany and in the 1880s in the United States, with production continuing until World War I (Randall 1971:104). Two glass "cats eye" marbles, with diameters of 1.5 cm and 1.6 cm, are machine-made marbles. These glass marbles were introduced in 1901 in the United States (Baumann 1970:84).

Porcelain Doll Fragments

Doll Fragments (n=11; Plate 35 L). Eleven porcelain doll parts were recovered from the surface (n=7) and from excavation units (n=4). Five fragments are bisque or unglazed doll faces that are hand-painted light pink or peach. Two doll legs have a ridge or groove above the knee for attachment to the cloth doll body. One hollow leg is of glazed china and has a handpainted garter near the broken foot. A solid leg is of bisque and has a black handpainted boot. Two doll fragments represent hair which is handpainted and shown in relief. One bisque shoe fragment, pink in color, has "2 1/4" impressed on the bottom. Production of porcelain dolls began in Europe in the 1750s, with the peak of popularity occurring in the 1850s (Coleman et al. 1968:118). One glazed, nude torso, measuring 2.25 cm in length, is probably a fragment of a "Frozen Charlotte" or "bathing baby," which were produced from the 1850s into the early twentieth century (Coleman et al. 1968:240).

CHAPTER 5:
ANIMAL REMAINS FROM THE CAHOKIA WEDGE SITE

by Terrance J. Martin
Associate Curator of Anthropology
Illinois State Museum

Excavations at the Cahokia Wedge site yielded a small but well-preserved collection of animal remains, the analysis of which provided a unique opportunity in which to view practices of subsistence and animal exploitation at a French colonial domestic site.

Previous studies of eighteenth-century faunal exploitation in the American Bottom (e.g., Cardinal 1977; Martin 1984; Parmalee and Bogan 1980) have been limited for the most part to habitation sites in the immediate vicinity of Fort de Chartres. Although considerable diversity has been noted among these faunal assemblages, white-tailed deer remained important to each group of inhabitants that were studied, i.e., Native American, French, and British. Considerable variety has been observed in the representation of domesticated animal species; e.g., at the Waterman site, a Michigamea/Kaskaskia habitation site near Fort de Chartres, faunal remains suggest limited reliance on domesticated animals in contrast to the European sites. Distinctive patterns are also apparent among the aquatic fauna and birds. Analysis of the faunal assemblages from the Cahokia Wedge site constitutes the first study of an eighteenth-century site in the American Bottom outside the immediate Fort de Chartres catchment zone. An attempt is made to discover whether inhabitants of domestic sites such as the Cahokia Wedge relied on domesticated animals and exploited wild animals as supplements or, alternatively, if the French selectively procured local resources on a seasonal basis in a pattern resembling the Native American adaptation. Participation in the fur trade might also be indicated.

Animal remains from the Cahokia Wedge site occurred in a variety of contexts that are broadly related to either an eighteenth-century or to a nineteenth-century occupation. Eighteenth-century features containing animal remains include two wall trenches from a *poteaux-en-*

terre (posts in the earth) structure (Features 7 and 8), a refuse pit (Feature 1), a limestone concentration (Feature 2), and a discrete midden area (Feature 4). Documentary evidence suggests that some of these features, particularly the wall trench features, are remnants of a domestic dwelling occupied from the mid-eighteenth century into the early nineteenth century. Nineteenth-century features yielding faunal remains include the remnant of a cellar or basement (Feature 6), a concentration of limestone mortar (Feature 5) that is part of a builder's trench adjacent to the cellar, and a refuse pit (Feature 9) observed in profile. This second group of features seems to be associated with a structure constructed sometime after 1841, and they include redeposited artifacts from the earlier French occupation. A large sample of bone fragments was also obtained during the controlled surface collection of the Cahokia Wedge site. Only materials obtained from excavated feature contexts were analyzed for this report.

The following study emphasizes subsistence adaptations and animal exploitation, but attention is also given to describing natural and cultural modifications on animal remains from both occupations.

Resource Setting

The resource catchment for the Cahokia Wedge site was dominated by the Mississippi River and its dynamic floodplain. The site is situated adjacent to and on a slight rise above Rigolet Creek, which prior to ca. 1800 was a former channel of the Mississippi River. Major abandoned meander scars of the river in the vicinity of the site include Lily Lake, Goose Lake, and the Grand Marais. Except for the bottomland forest along Rigolet Creek and on the island between the creek and the Mississippi River, vegetation in the vicinity of the site primarily consisted of prairie.

The location of the site provided an ideal setting for human exploitation of the Mississippi River and the varied bottomland environments. Not only would the river have provided fish, waterfowl, turtles, and freshwater mussels, but the large, backwater lakes were also rich in aquatic animal and plant resources. The floodplain forests along the creek and on the island were favorable for terrestrial and semiaquatic mammals as well as for various birds. Although lacking economically important animals when compared to forested areas of the American Bottom, the floodplain prairie near the Cahokia Wedge site would have supported prairie chickens and bison during the seventeenth and eighteenth centuries.

Methods

Faunal remains derived from dry-screening through 12.8-mm (one-half-inch) mesh were analyzed at the Illinois State Museum. Identifications were made by the author by direct comparison to modern specimens in the Museum's vertebrate and pelecypod collections. Both the eighteenth- and nineteenth-century faunal remains were examined for attributes related to provenience, biology, and condition. The following information was encoded on an IBM-compatible microcomputer using dBaseII software: (1) provenience (feature and lot designations); (2) class of animal (mammal, bird, reptile, fish, etc.); (3) taxon to the finest level possible, ideally genus and species; (4) anatomical element; (5) symmetry (left, right, or midline); (6) portion of element (e.g., proximal, distal, shaft, open or fused epiphysis); (7) completeness of element; (8) body size (8-cm size length class for identified fish; large, medium, or small for unidentified mammal and bird bones); (9) modifications (e.g., burning, cut marks, other human modifications related to artifact manufacture and use, staining, weathering, rodent or carnivore-gnawing). Length estimates for fish are based on standard length for all taxa except for bowfin and gar for which total length estimates are reported. Zoological nomenclature follows Jones et al. (1982) for mammals, American Ornithologists' Union (1982) for birds, Conant (1975) for reptiles and amphibians, and Smith (1979) for fish.

Summary calculations included tabulations of number of identified specimens (NISP) and minimum number of individuals (MNI) per taxon within a provenience unit. Two or more specimens were counted as one if they were fragments that could be refitted (e.g., an unfused epiphysis that fit to its corresponding shaft). MNI estimates were based on element, symmetry, portion, and body size. MNI are provided for gross level taxonomic categories, such as families, only if they are additive to more precise level identifications. Total MNI for each component at the site were estimated (1) on the basis of cumulative MNI calculated from separate features assuming that no individuals were disposed of in more that one feature (maximum distinction approach; see Grayson 1973), and (2) by ignoring feature designations (minimum distinction approach). MNI calculated by the maximum distinction approach are likely to be exaggerated, whereas estimates based on the minimum distinction approach are probably conservative.

Evaluation of relative importance of the various animal taxa is also attained by the use of allometric scaling, which provides an estimate of the amount of edible meat obtained from the various animals represented at the site. As described by Reitz and Scarry (1985:18), "The weight of the archaeological bone is used in an allometric formula to predict the quantity of biomass for the skeletal mass recovered rather that the total original weight of the individual animal represented by the recovered bone." Biomass estimates for the Cahokia Wedge site faunal assemblages were calculated for each feature from formulae presented by Reitz and Honerkamp (1983:15). This approach avoids the problem of whether or not the meat from entire animals was consumed at the site from which the archaeological sample was obtained. As true of other measures of species importance, the interpretive value of biomass estimates is not the *absolute* quantities projected for each taxa; instead, biomass is an alternative measure to NISP and MNI for evaluating the relative importance of various taxa in a given assemblage.

Discussion

Approximately 450 animal remains from excavated contexts were examined. From this total, 398 animal bone specimens and 12 freshwater mussel shell fragments were associated with eighteenth-century contexts (Tables 10 and 11). Except for shell, the earlier assemblage was well-preserved with approximately 54% of all specimens (92.4% by weight) being identified more specifically than class.

When 39 bones from one individual toad (probably intrusive) are excluded, the identified mammal bones comprise more than 86% of the identified vertebrate collection. White-tailed deer dominates with 45.9% of all identified specimens and 41.5% of the biomass from identified taxa. The deer body part assemblage reflects meat-bearing elements from the proximal forequarter and proximal hindquarter with ribs and vertebrae also being numerous. A doe is represented by a frontal bone from the cranium, and a buck was identified on the basis of an innominate bone.

Collectively, large bovids (i.e., cattle and bison) were of secondary importance with 10.0% of all identified bones and 40.8% of the biomass. Two specimens, a right distal humerus and a left proximal radius and ulna, are diagnostic of cattle (cf. Olsen 1960). Bison is represented by an astragalus from Feature 4. Although probably referable to cattle, the remaining 20 bovid specimens either lack diagnostic morphological characters or are too fragmentary to permit definite assignment to species. Consistent with deer, *Bos* and *Bos/Bison* skeletal portions best represented are the axial bones (vertebrae and ribs) and the proximal hindquarter and forequarter.

Additional mammals include pig, black bear, canid, and beaver. Pig bones consist of two mandibles, a fourth maxillary premolar, two distal humeri, a proximal tibia, and a calcaneus. At least two individual black bears were discerned on the basis of size differences among a thoracic vertebra, right proximal humerus, right proximal ulna, and two foot elements from a very large individual (all from Feature 4), and left proximal radius shaft from an average-sized bear (Feature 7). In addition, a human cranial bone (left *sphenoid*) came from the stripped ground surface in the vicinity of Feature 7. At least 14 human bones were noted in the controlled surface collection, primarily from the central portion of the site.

Bird bones are very sparse, and except for one domestic chicken bone, the specimens are from large-sized species such as trumpeter swan, cf. Canada goose, wild turkey, and sandhill crane. Considering the proximity of wet prairie and backwater lakes and sloughs, the underrepresentation of waterfowl is notable.

Exploitation of river and floodplain aquatic habitats is indicated by the presence of fish and turtle bones. Except for a snapping turtle coracoid, large red-eared (*Chrysemys scripta*) and smaller painted turtle (*Chrysemys picta*) elements consists of unmodified carapace and plastron fragments. The faunal samples suggest that large fish were selectively sought by the inhabitants of the Cahokia Wedge site. A blue catfish (*Ictalurus furcatus*) in excess of 100 cm standard length is represented by two pieces of the complex vertebra (Weberian apparatus). A buffalo fish (*Ictiobus* sp.) over 70 cm standard length was also identified. Fragments of freshwater mussel shell too small for identification were present in Feature 1. Interpretation of the bird and fish taxa is somewhat tenuous since recovery techniques may have introduced a bias against elements from small-bodied individuals. In addition, secondary deposition or sweeping by the site inhabitants may have resulted in only larger-sized items of refuse being deposited in the various features.

Modification of faunal remains by cultural or by natural agents was observed on relatively few specimens. Only two bones were altered by exposure to fire, a small portion of a deer femur head (caput) from Feature 4 and one unidentified medium to large mammal bone from Feature 8. The distal end of a deer scapula from Feature 7 was scored by a knife, probably the result of butchering when the shoulder was separated above the proximal end of the humerus. A right distal humerus shaft from a trumpeter swan was carefully modified into a tube (see Plate 35 M). This is reminiscent of the Waterman site in Randolph County (Parmalee and Bogan 1980) where the distal ulna of a trumpeter swan had been modified in a similar fashion. Five distal deer humeri were chewed by carnivores, as were two beaver bones, namely

TABLE 10.

Species Composition of Animal Remains from Eighteenth-century Contexts. MNI(Min) refers to minimum distinction approach; MNI(Max) refers to maximum distinction approach (i.e., MNI for each feature are added). Biomass refers to bone weight allometry calculated separately for each feature and combined.

	NISP	MNI (Min)	MNI (Max)	Wt. (g)	Biomass (kg)
MAMMALS					
Canis cf. *lupus*, Wolf	1	1	1	13.0	.265
Canis sp., Dog/Wolf/Coyote	14	1	1	54.2	.956
Castor canadensis, Beaver	5	1	3	22.0	.460
Ursus americanus, Black Bear	6	2	2	222.3	3.516
Sus scrofa, Pig	7	2	4	236.6	4.070
Odocoileus virginianus, White-tailed Deer	101	6	14	2067.6	29.108
Bison bison, Bison	1	1	1	90.5	1.517
Bos taurus, Cattle	2	1	2	546.9	8.195
Bos/Bison, Cattle/Bison	19	[2]	[5]	1313.8	18.925
Unidentified Medium/Large Mammal	165	-	-	369.5	6.437
Unidentified Medium-sized Mammal	5	-	-	2.8.071	
BIRDS					
Cygnus buccinator, Trumpeter Swan	3	1	1	31.6	.473
cf. *Branta canadensis*, Canada Goose	1	1	1	13.3	.215
Meleagris gallopavo, Turkey	2	2	2	9.5	.295
Gallus gallus, Chicken	1	1	1	.5	.011
Gallus/Meleagris, Chicken/Turkey	1	-	1	2.3	.044
Grus canadensis, Sand Hill Crane	1	1	1	17.3	.342
Unidentified Large-sized Bird	1	-	-	7.2	.123

TABLE 10 Cont.

REPTILES				
Chelydra serpentina, Snapping Turtle	1	1	2.1	.052
Chrysemys scripta, Red-eared Turtle	2	1	24.1	.333
Chrysemys picta, Painted Turtle	7	1	1.4	.185
Graptemys/Chrysemys, Map/Red-eared/ Painted Turtle	1	-	4.7	.089
AMPHIBIAN				
Bufo sp., Toad sp.	39	1	1.1	-
FISH				
Ictalurus furcatus, Blue Catfish	2	1	58.8	.957
Ictalurus/Pylodictis, Channel/Blue/ Flathead Catfish	1	-	.7	.014
Ictiobus sp., Buffalo sp.	1	1	3.4	.079
Catostomidae, Sucker	1	-	.6	.020
Unidentified Fish	1	-	.9	.027
VERTEBRATA				
Unidentified Vertebrate	5	-	4.1	-
PELECYPODA				
Unidentified Mussel	12	1	7.2	-
Totals	409	28	5130.0	76.779
Total Identified	220	27	4738.3	70.121

TABLE 11.

Animal Remains from Eighteenth-century Feature Contexts. Number of identified specimens is followed in parentheses by minimum number of individuals. MNIs in Totals column employs the minimum distinction approach by ignoring feature designations.

	F7	AREA NEAR F7	F8	F1	F2	AREA NEAR F2	F4	TOTALS
MAMMALS								
Canis cf. *lupus*, Wolf	-	-	-	1(1)	-	-	-	1(1)
Canis sp., Dog/Wolf/Coyote	-	-	-	14(1)	-	-	-	14(1)
Castor canadensis, Beaver	1(1)	-	-	2(1)	2(1)	-	-	5(1)
Ursus americanus, Black Bear	1(1)	-	-	-	-	-	5(1)	6(2)
Sus scrofa, Pig	2(1)	-	-	-	1(1)	1(1)	3(1)	7(2)
Odocoileus virginianus, White-tailed Deer	7(1)	3(1)	1(1)	29(3)	5(1)	12(3)	44(4)	101(6)
Bison bison, Bison	-	-	-	-	-	-	1(1)	1(1)
Bos taurus, Cattle	-	1(1)	-	-	1(1)	-	-	2(1)
Bos/Bison, Cattle/Bison	1(1)	-	-	3(1)	-	8(1)	7(1)	19(2)
Unidentified Medium/Large Mammal	31	5	4	63	7	15	40	165
Unidentified Medium-sized Mammal	-	-	-	3	-	-	2	5
BIRDS								
Cygnus buccinator, Trumpeter Swan	-	-	-	-	-	-	3(1)	3(1)
cf. *Branta canadensis*, Canada Goose	-	-	-	1(1)	-	-	-	1(1)
Meleagris gallopavo, Turkey	-	-	-	1(1)	-	-	1(1)	2(2)
Gallus gallus, Chicken	1(1)	-	-	-	-	-	-	1(1)
Gallus/Meleagris, Chicken/Turkey	-	-	-	-	-	1(1)	-	1(-)

TABLE 11 Cont.

BIRDS continued								
Grus canadensis, Sand Hill Crane	-	-	-	-	-	-	1(1)	1(1)
Unidentified Large-sized Bird	-	-	-	-	-	-	1	1
REPTILES								
Chelydra serpentina, Snapping Turtle	-	-	-	-	-	-	1(1)	1(1)
Chrysemys scripta, Red-eared Turtle	-	-	-	-	1(1)	1(1)	2(1)	2(1)
Chrysemys picta, Painted Turtle	-	-	-	7(1)	-	-	7(1)	7(1)
Graptemys/Chrysemys, Map/Red-eared/Painted Turtle	-	-	1(1)	-	-	-	-	1(-)
AMPHIBIAN								
Bufo sp., Toad sp.	-	-	-	39(1)	-	-	-	39(1)
FISH								
Ictalurus furcatus, Blue Catfish	-	-	-	-	-	-	2(1)	2(1)
Ictalurus/Pylodictis, Channel/Blue/Flathead Catfish	1(1)	-	-	-	-	-	-	1(-)
Ictiobus sp., Buffalo sp.	-	-	-	-	-	1(1)	-	1(1)
Catostomidae, Sucker	-	-	-	1(1)	-	-	-	1(-)
Unidentified Fish	-	-	-	-	-	-	1	1
VERTEBRATA								
Unidentified Vertebrate	1(-)	-	-	4(-)	-	-	-	5(-)
PELECYPODA								
Unidentified Mussel	-	-	-	-	12(1)	-	-	12(1)
Totals	46	9	6	181	16	39	112	409(28)
Total Identified	14	4	2	99	9	24	68	220(27)

a proximal radius and distal tibia. Only one rodent-gnawed bone, a distal deer femur, was observed.

Faunal remains associated with nineteenth-century features are presented in Tables 12 and 13. Discussion of this faunal assemblage must be cautious since (1) Features 5, 6, and 9 probably contain a mixture of redeposited eighteenth-century materials as well as nineteenth-century refuse, and (2) only 17 specimens were identified. Species composition is restricted to five taxa, but significant perhaps is the complete absence of black bear, beaver, waterfowl, turtles, and fish. The only sawed bones are a cow rib from Feature 5 and two unidentified round steak bones from Feature 6. Four unidentified medium or large mammal bones from Feature 6 were burned.

Conclusions

The faunal assemblage from the Cahokia Wedge site provides the first opportunity to perceive animal exploitation practices at a domestic habitation site in the American Bottom during the French colonial period. The present excavated sample, albeit small, reveals a distinct preference for wild animal resources, especially white-tailed deer. Domesticated animals include cattle, pig, and chicken, but in aggregate, these species contribute less than 14% of all identified bones (less than 5% if indeterminate *Bos/Bison* specimens are excluded) and less than 47% of the biomass (only 17.5% when indeterminate *Bos/Bison* bones are not considered). The early French subsistence pattern also incorporated bison, black bear, beaver, large birds, aquatic turtles, and fish. Although ducks, shorebirds, and marsh birds would have been especially abundant along the floodplain during their spring and fall migrations, these species are underrepresented at the Cahokia Wedge site. French disposal practices or archaeological recovery techniques might account for this as well as the absence of fish smaller than large river catfish and buffalo.

Faunal analysis of the Cahokia Wedge site supplements currently known information on the distribution of several species during the Neo-boreal climatic episode (Purdue and Styles 1986). Although constituting new records for St. Clair County for this period, the occurrence of bison, black bear, and beaver is compatible with animal distributions known from other archaeological sites in Illinois. Purdue and Styles (1986:7) observed that despite documentary evidence of bison in southern Illinois, archaeological data from the Zimmerman site (Parmalee 1961; Cardinal 1975; Rogers 1975a, 1975b) attest to a northern Illinois distribution for bison herds during the early historic period.

TABLE 12.

Species Composition of Animal Remains from Nineteenth-century Contexts. MNI(Min) refers to minimum distinction approach; MNI(Max) refers to maximum distinction approach (i.e., MNI for each feature are added). Biomass refers to bone weight allometry calculated separately for each feature and combined.

	NISP	MNI (Min)	MNI (Max)	Wt. (g)	Biomass (kg)
MAMMALS					
Sus scrofa, Pig	4	2	3	35.0	.676
Odocoileus virginianus, White-tailed Deer	5	1	3	47.7	.947
Bos/Bison, Cattle/Bison	6	1	3	81.6	1.520
Unidentified Medium/Large Mammal	19	-	-	71.6	1.348
BIRDS					
Meleagris gallopavo, Turkey	1	1	1	6.9	.118
Bonasa/Gallus, Grouse/Chicken	1	1	1	.1	.003
Unidentified Medium-sized Bird	1	-	-	.4	.009
Totals	37	6	11	243.3	4.621
Total Identified	17	6	11	171.3	3.264

TABLE 13.

Animal Remains from Nineteenth-century Feature Contexts. Number of identified specimens is followed in parentheses by minimum number of individuals. MNIs in Totals column employs the minimum distinction approach by ignoring feature designations.

	F5	F6	F9	Totals
MAMMALS				
Sus scrofa, Pig	1(1)	3(2)	-	4(2)
Odocoileus virginianus, White-tailed Deer	2(1)	2(1)	1(1)	5(1)
Bos/Bison, Cattle/Bison	4(1)	1(1)	1(1)	6(1)
Unidentified Med/Lg Mammal	4	14	1	19
BIRDS				
Meleagris gallopavo, Turkey	1(1)	-	-	1(1)
Bonasa/Gallus, Grouse/Chicken	1(1)	-	-	1(1)
Unidentified Medium-sized Bird	1	-	-	1
Totals	14	20	3	37(5)
Total Identified	9	6	2	17(5)

Recent analyses at the Illinois State Museum of animal remains from the site of the first Fort de Chartres (the Laurens site; Martin 1984) and from an early eighteenth-century Illini Indian occupation at the Naples-Abbott site, Scott County (Styles et al. 1987), have confirmed the presence of bison in the American Bottom and in the lower Illinois Valley. This is significant since bison was extirpated from the Illinois Country by the early part of the nineteenth century (Hoffmeister and Mohr 1972:205). The identification of black bear at the Cahokia Wedge is also consistent with recent records at Laurens, Fort de Chartres, Waterman, and Naples-Abbott. Bear oil, used widely as shortening and seasoning, was recognized as a delicacy by the French inhabitants of the Mississippi Valley (Ekberg 1985:303). Also in common with Fort de Chartres and the Laurens site is the presence of trumpeter swan, sandhill crane, and exceptionally large blue catfish. Ekberg (1985:303) recounts that Frenchmen in the region were impressed most by the catfish, and based on archaeological data, very large blue catfish were selectively sought.

Comparison to the refuse from French colonial sites in Randolph County, Illinois, indicates that a greater proportion of the meat diet of the various Fort de Chartres inhabitants was obtained from pigs and cattle. This is expected in light of the fort's function as a center for French government and the military in the central Mississippi Valley. Various historical accounts attest to the importance of these species elsewhere in the region as well (e.g., Belting 1948; Ekberg 1985). Despite this contrast to the Cahokia Wedge faunal assemblage, white-tailed deer was also an important supplement at the Laurens site and at Fort de Chartres. Perhaps the most surprising similarity, however, is between the Cahokia Wedge site and the Waterman site. At both sites, domesticated mammals and birds are underrepresented, wild species are plentiful, and present are examples of modified trumpeter swan wing bones. Although somewhat outside of the Illinois Country, another pattern of animal exploitation comparable to the Cahokia Wedge is that found at the Fort Ouiatenon site, a French fur trade post in the Wabash River valley of Indiana (Martin 1986). Not only are white-tailed deer, wild turkey, and waterfowl abundant in the archaeological faunal assemblage, but also noteworthy are numerous freshwater mussel shells and modified mammal bones that may be attributed to the ever present influence of various Indian groups that resided in the area.

The pattern that emerges is one in which French families that lived outside major French settlements (e.g., Kaskaskia or Fort de Chartres) were more self-sufficient regarding the acquisition of provisions. Even when domestic animals were maintained, the rich wildlife habitats present in the American Bottom were seemingly perceived as too bountiful to ignore. The pattern of animal exploitation that was adopted seems to have copied that followed by local Native American groups with the addition of cattle, pigs, and chickens as supplements. In addition, the French colonials exploited certain resources to a greater extent than local Indian residents; e.g., large blue catfish from the depths of the main river channel and sandhill crane from the wet prairies. A clear understanding of animal exploitation patterns represented by faunal assemblages at various French habitation sites must await additional analyses. Although large samples have been obtained from the Laurens site and Fort de Chartres, the complexity of archaeological deposits at these sites results in poorly understood contexts. Artifact analyses indicate that considerable mixture and redeposition of refuse by successive inhabitants may have taken place (especially at Fort de Chartres No. 3). As a consequence, small domestic sites such as those discovered at the Cahokia Wedge site are favorable for studies of behavior and subsistence because refuse deposits can more feasibly be assigned to specific groups of inhabitants, which in many cases, may be possible to identify from archival sources.

CHAPTER 6:
BOTANICAL REMAINS FROM THE CAHOKIA WEDGE SITE

by Neal H. Lopinot
Associate Coordinator
Contract Archaeology Program—SIUE

A total of 11 flotation samples was collected during the test excavations at the Cahokia Wedge site. The sediments comprising these samples were poured into 0.3 mm mesh nylon bags and partially submerged in a 55 gallon flotation drum filled with water. Following removal of the sediments by agitation, the contents of the bags were air-dryed. Separation of light and heavy fractions was undertaken with the aid of a South Dakota Type seed blower.

Four samples were selected for sorting and analysis of both the heavy and light fractions. These include three samples from Feature 1, two from Zone A and one from Zone B, and one sample from Feature 7, Zone A. All materials larger than 2.0 mm in diameter were sorted from the samples. The residual fractions, or those materials that passed through the 2.0 mm sieve, were scanned for seeds and other unique residues. The general contents of these samples are given in Table 14.

In addition to these four flotation samples, numerous charcoal concentrations were sampled during the field investigations. The contents of six charcoal samples also were analyzed and the results are presented below. These include three charcoal samples from Feature 1, and one each from Feature 4, Feature 6, and Feature 7.

Heavy Fractions

Bone and 11 classes of inorganic materials are present in the four flotation samples (see Appendix A). A total of 2,454 pieces of debris weighing 118.64 g was sorted from the four heavy fractions. Little can be stated about the probable function of the two features, since they do appear to contain diverse assortments of both light and heavy fraction debris. However, the samples from Zone A of Feature 1 and Zone A of Feature 7 do contain relatively abundant quantities of burned earth.

TABLE 14.

Flotation Sample Contents

Feature 1

Plant Remains	Samples								Totals	
	Feature 1-2 Zone A		Feature 1-6 Zone A		Feature 7 Zone A		Feature 1-7 Zone B			
	Ct.	Wt.(g)	Ct.	Wt.(g)	Ct.	Wt.(g)	Ct.	Wt.(g)	Ct.	Wt.(g)
Wood Charcoal	820	8.86	5509	191.42	328	8.49	3597	124.63	9926	324.91
Bark	228	1.91	1069	10.95	4	.05	473	5.24	1770	18.10
Twig	1	t	8	.08					9	.08
Grass Stem	5	.04					7	.08	12	.12
Maize Kernel	1	t	51	.93			1	.01	53	.94
Maize Cob			19	.28	2	.01	1	.01	20	.29
Coal			1	.01			1	.01	2	.02
Siliceous Masses			10	.07	33	.56			10	.07
Totals	1055	10.81	6667	203.74	367	9.11	4080	129.98	11802	344.53

They also contain the only specimens identified as clinkers, the by-product of intense heat on silica-bearing materials. Whereas other materials also are present in these two samples, it appears that the contents of the two zones represent either redeposited remains of an intense fire, or primary deposits of a fire pit or hearth of some type.

Few items of note are present among the heavy fraction materials. The chert flake in the sample from Zone B of Feature 7 may be aboriginal, but it is heavily patinated on all surfaces. This suggests that the flake represents an intrusive element from the prehistoric occupation of the site, rather than that from an early eighteenth-century Native American occupant. The glass fragment from Feature 1 appears to be from a clear window pane. It likely represents a contaminant as well. Two dark brown glass seed beads, one complete and one fragment, probably relate to the historic deposition of Zone A, Feature 7.

Light Fractions

A total of 12,169 specimens weighing 353.64 g was sorted from the four light fractions. Clearly, wood charcoal is the dominant element in the four samples, comprising 84.3% by count and 94.3% by weight of all plant remains. As with the heavy fraction materials, the dominance of wood charcoal also supports the inference that these features either contain redeposited residues from a fire or primary deposits of a fire or hearth. Bark fragments also are quite common in the samples and likely represent incidental inclusions with the fuel wood.

WOOD

Taxonomic identification of 25 randomly sampled wood charcoal fragments (total of 100 weighing 6.99 g) was performed for the flotation samples. In addition, a total of 76 pieces weighing 247.72 g was analyzed for the six charcoal samples (Tables 15 and 16). The spectrum of wood charcoal taxa indicates considerable selection from a quite disturbed environment. Woods from all the identified genera could have been obtained within close proximity to the village of Cahokia.

The flotation samples are dominated by charred wood fragments of red mulberry (*Morus rubra*), typically a pioneer species. Mulberry is recognized as a hardwood that has a high resistance to decay (e.g., Forest Products Laboratory 1955:45), and has been used historically for "... fence posts, barrels, boat building, and farm tools" (Steyermark 1981:562). Its resistance to decay appears to have been well recognized

TABLE 15.

Wood Charcoal Identification

Flotation Samples

	Feature 1-2 Zone A		Feature 1-6 Zone A		Feature 1-7 Zone B		Feature 7 Zone A		Totals	
	Ct.	Wt.(g)	Ct.	Wt.(g)	Ct.	Wt.(g)	Ct.	Wt.(g)	Ct.	Wt.(g)
Acer saccharinum/rubrum, Soft Maple	3	.05	4	.36	1	.03		3.23	11	.67
Carya spp., True Hickory Group							5	.14	5	.14
Celtis/Ulmus spp., Hackberry/Elm	3	.09					2	.17	5	.26
Fraxinus spp., Ash					1	.03			1	.03
Gleditsia/Gymnocladus spp. Honey Locust/Coffeetree	4	.16	1	.05					5	.21
Juglans spp., Waln	2	.05							2	.05
Morus rubra, Red Mulberry	10	.35	19	2.00	18	2.46	12	.42	59	5.23
Platanus occidentalis, Sycamore			1	.02					1	.02
Sassafras albidum, Sassafras	3	.10			2	.04	3	.14	8	.28
Ulmus cf. *rubra*, Slippery Elm					3	.10			3	.10
Totals	25	.08	25	2.93	25	2.66	25	1.10	100	6.99
Wood Charcoal Wt.(g)*	8.86		191.42		124.63		8.49		333.40	

*Total amount of wood charcoal present in 2.0 mm fractions of flotation samples.

by the French settlers in the Mississippi Valley (see Mereness, ed., 1916:75).

Wood charcoal fragments of soft maple (*Acer saccharinum/rubrum*), honey locust/Kentucky coffeetree (*Gleditsia triacanthos/Gymnocladus dioicus*), hackberry/elm (*Celtis/ Ulmus* spp.) and sassafras (*Sassafras albidum*) occur in considerably lower frequencies than that for mulberry, but all four taxa are represented in several samples. As a group, these taxa also occur most abundantly as successional species during all phases of forest regeneration.

MAIZE

Other types of plant materials than wood charcoal and bark are relatively few. Among the more notable materials are maize cob and kernel remains, present in all four flotation samples. The vast majority occur in the sample from Zone A, Feature 1.

Several of the cob fragments and kernels in this sample are sufficiently intact to permit measurement. The 19 cob fragments consist of a segment with two adhering cupules, two cupules with glumes, 12 cupule fragments, and four glume fragments. Measurements (not adjusted for carbonization shrinkage) for the intact specimens are as follows:

Row No	Cupule Width (mm)	Grain Thickness (mm)
8	10.4	3.7
8	8.2	4.0
10	6.2	4.2

A single whole cupule from the residual fraction of this sample has a cupule width of 4.9 mm and appears to be from an 8-rowed cob.

Maize grains occur in three of the samples but again are most abundant in the above-mentioned sample. The kernel remains from this sample include five whole kernels, 45 kernel fragments, and one embryo. Among the kernel fragments, three have very shriveled surfaces, perhaps representing either sweet maize or a flint/flour maize that was heated when immature. Measurements were obtained for the five whole grains as well as two large grain fragments. These measurements are as follows:

TABLE 16.
Wood Charcoal Samples
Features 1, 4, 6, and 7

	Feature 1-1 Zone A		Feature 1-3 Zone A		Feature 1-4 Zone A		Total	
	Ct.	Wt.(g)	Ct.	Wt.(g)	Ct.	Wt.(g)	Ct.	Wt.(g)
Acer saccharinum/rubrum Soft Maple	3	9.70					3	9.70
Gleditsia/Gymnocladus spp. Honey Locust/Coffeetree	1	15.30			2	37.88	3	53.01
Morus rubra Red Mulberry	5	14.98	6	42.34			11	57.32
Totals	9	39.81	6	42.34	2	37.88	17	120.03
Wood Charcoal Wt.(g)*		39.81		42.34		37.88		120.03

*Total amount of wood charcoal recovered in 1/2 inch screened feature fill.

TABLE 16 Cont.

	Feature 4 Zone A		Feature 6 Zone A		Feature 7-7 Zone A		Total	
	Ct.	Wt.(g)	Ct.	Wt.(g)	Ct.	Wt.(g)	Ct.	Wt.(g)
Acer saccharinum/rubrum Soft Maple	2	.60			3	.90	5	1.50
Carya cf. *glabra* Pignut Hickory					3	2.25	3	2.25
Celtis/Ulmus spp. Hackberry/Elm					4	1.56	4	1.56
Gleditsia/Gymnocladus spp. Honey Locust/Coffeetree					1	.56	1	.56
Morus rubra Red Mulberry	23	10.20	9	103.57	10	6.65	42	120.42
Sassafras albidium Sassafras					4	1.40	4	1.40
Totals	25	10.80	9	103.57	25	13.32	59	127.69
Wood Charcoal Wt.(g)*		92.12		103.57		119.29		314.98

*Total amount of wood charcoal recovered in 1/2 inch screened feature fill.

Shape	Row No.	Thickness (mm)	Width (mm)	Height (mm)
Pyramidal	10	6.0	8.1	8.1
Pyramidal	10	4.6	7.4	7.8
Crescentric	8	4.7	6.8	5.5
Crescentric	8	5.4	8.2	7.7
Crescentric	8	5.1	8.6	5.9
Crescentric	8	–	9.0	–
Crescentric	8	4.3	6.5	–

Two types of maize are indicated by these measurements: (1) a 10-rowed variety with pyramidal kernels; and (2) an 8-rowed variety with crescent-shaped kernels.

Unfortunately, the sample of maize is small and fragmentary. Nevertheless, the attributes are quite consistent with those found characterizing other maize collections from sites in eastern North America that date between A.D. 1600 and 1845 (see Blake 1986:Table 1.4).

SEEDS

Carbonized seeds are few but do occur in three of the four samples. Seeds of perhaps three cultigens are present, including wheat, tobacco, and perhaps apple. Two seeds that represent contaminants also are present in the flotation sample from Zone A of Feature 1. These include a whole beadgrass (*Paspalum* sp.) grain and a fragment from a trigonal knotweed (*Polygonum* sp.) achene.

Wheat grains are present in the three flotation samples from Feature 1. The grains are identifiable as breadwheat (*Triticum aestivum*). A total of 17 grains are represented. Measurements were obtained and include 15 lengths, 17 widths, and 17 thicknesses. The lengths range from 3.0 mm to 5.0 mm with a mean of 4.3 mm; the widths range from 2.2 mm to 3.3 mm with a mean of 2.7 mm; and the thicknesses range from 1.4 mm to 3.0 mm with a mean of 2.2 mm. Historic records indicate that wheat was extensively cultivated very early by the French in the Illinois Country (McWilliams 1953; Du Pratz 1975).

The possible cultivated apple (*Pyrus malus*) is represented by two nearly complete, but shriveled pips in Zone A of Feature 1. Du Pratz (1975:235), among others, clearly indicates that the European apple was being cultivated in French Louisiana minimally by the early 1700s.

The identification of tobacco (*Nicotiana* sp.) is based on the presence of at least four seeds embedded in a fused mass of plant tissue, possibly burned bits of leaves. This mass occurs in the sample from Zone B of Feature 1.

Summary

The study of archaeobotanical remains in flotation samples from the Cahokia Wedge site suggest that the early eighteenth-century occupants: (1) utilized woods of red mulberry and, to a lesser extent, a diverse assortment of other taxa for construction and fuel; (2) exploited these naturally available products from a very disturbed environment; (3) cultivated several different plants for both food and smoking purposes; and (4) probably practiced aboriculture, at least of apple, for domestic needs.

These results are based on relatively few samples. Nonetheless, they demonstrate the significance that should be attached to future collection and analysis of flotation samples from historic sites in the middle Mississippi River Valley. At present, the grains of breadwheat and tentatively of apple from early eighteenth-century deposits at the Cahokia Wedge represent the earliest records for these introduced crops in the Mississippi River Valley.

CHAPTER 7:
LIFE IN FRENCH COLONIAL CAHOKIA

The archaeological investigations at the Cahokia Wedge site yielded data relevant to the study of French colonial lifeways in the Illinois Country. Archaeological research involving French colonial sites in the American Bottom region has been relatively restricted to the military sites of Fort de Chartres and Fort Kaskaskia. The SIUE research effort in Cahokia represents a much needed investigation into domestic activities at a French colonial village. Furthermore, the excavations at the Cahokia Wedge site have underscored the potential for buried archaeological deposits within a modern urban area. It is possible that other remnants of the French colonial village are preserved in other areas of the modern town underneath residential yards and gardens.

Summary of Archaeological Investigations

The initial investigations recovered nearly 16,000 artifacts from the site surface. Utilizing numerous diagnostic artifacts and artifact types, surface distribution and density maps were produced. Six discrete artifact concentrations, Areas A through F, were identified. Correlating these maps with extant historical maps and land records, it was established that five of the concentrations, Areas A, B, D, E, and F, represented the remains of historic structures and associated activities. Documents providing physical evidence of historic structures on the Cahokia Wedge site included the following: (1) a 1766 map of Cahokia illustrating village lots and structures; (2) a 1790–1826 reconstructed map of lots and properties produced by the Works Progress Administration (WPA); (3) a ca. 1841 lithograph by J. C. Wild (Wild and Thomas 1841) illustrating the Cahokia Wedge and surrounding area, and; (4) a 1927 aerial photograph. The documents provided the partial reconstruction of the succession of owners and the relative time span of the occupations. The remaining artifact concentration, Area C, could not be corroborated by historic documentation. This concentration primarily contained lithic debitage and several historic trade items and was interpreted as a protohistoric/historic Indian habitational or activity area.

Area A, located in the southwest corner of the site, was the only artifact concentration that contained an abundance of eighteenth-century French colonial materials, particularly faience ceramics. This concentration corresponds to the location of the Nicolle/Meunier house as illustrated on the 1766 map and the WPA map. The subsequent test excavations in Area A uncovered 13 cultural features, including two structural remains: (1) portions of three wall trench features (Features 7, 8, and 10) of an eighteenth-century structure which is interpreted as the Nicolle/Meunier house; and (2) a portion of a nineteenth-century limestone and brick foundation (Features 5 and 6). Several other types of features were partially excavated (Features 2, 3, 4, 9, 11, 12, and 13). The feature density within the limited view of the excavation trench suggests the probability of other features relating to these two structures in this area.

Based on the interpretations of the surface artifact distributions and the documentary evidence, other subsurface deposits, including structural features, may also be preserved at the site. In Area B, located near the center of the site, the subsurface remnants of the Nicolle/Meunier barn, also illustrated on the 1766 map and the WPA map, may be present, particularly if the structure was of *poteaux-en-terre* (posts in the earth) construction, as was the Nicolle/Meunier house.

In Areas D and E, on the southeast corner of the site, the remnants of three limestone foundations were plowed to the surface. The documentary evidence indicates that these remains may date from the early nineteenth century to the early twentieth century. The 1841 lithograph shows a structural complex, including a two-story house and several outbuildings, in the vicinity of these artifact concentrations. The 1927 photograph clearly shows two houses including one of French colonial style and an outbuilding in Area E, and two outbuildings in Area D. Although these structures were demolished in the 1930s, the foundations of several of these structures are preserved at the site. Furthermore, although not revealed in the documentary evidence, it is also possible that subsurface features relating to the eighteenth-century colonial occupation may be present in these areas of the site.

Area F, located on the northeast corner of the site, probably contains the subsurface remains of the structure shown in the 1927 photograph. The documentary evidence, the physical appearance of the house, and the surface artifact concentration relating to this structure indicate that this house was probably constructed in the late nineteenth century. This house was also demolished in the 1930s. Although not the focus of this research, these later structures could provide an analysis and comparison of the eighteenth-century French colonial and the nineteenth-century American occupations of Cahokia.

Area C, the small concentration of Indian-related artifacts and trade items, was located near the center of the site and was relatively undisturbed by the later historic occupations. Area C may represent a habitational or activity area dating to the protohistoric/historic Indian use of the site. Human bone recovered from the surface in the vicinity of Area C may represent an associated burial or cemetery. However, some disturbance and possible destruction has already occurred as the result of cultivation. Other artifacts which may be attributed to the French and Indian trade were recovered from additional areas of the site, particularly in Areas E and F. However, the problematical context of surface artifacts does not provide interpretations of actual possession and/or use of some of these artifact types to the French, the Indians, or both.

In summary, the test excavations in Area A linked the interpretations of the controlled surface collection data and the documentary evidence with the presence of the Nicolle/Meunier house. Most of this structure, as well as the nineteenth-century limestone and brick foundation, remain preserved outside the limits of the test excavation trench. Furthermore, the test excavations substantiated the presence of abundant subsurface features within a small area of the Cahokia Wedge site. Soil stratigraphy in the test excavation trench indicated that the earliest features (i.e., the eighteenth-century house remains, Features 7, 8, and 10, the Feature 1 refuse pit, the Feature 2 limestone concentration, and the Feature 4 midden area) were located at a substantial depth (40–60 cm) below the present ground surface. Based on the historical documentation, the surface artifact distribution data, and the soil stratigraphy, it is assumed that several other subsurface structural remains are present within Areas B, D, E, and F. In addition, there is a potential for other types of non-structural features dating to both the colonial and Euro-American occupation at the site. The numerous protohistoric/historic trade items recovered from the site surface, particularly in Area C, is significant and may indicate the presence of features relating to an historic Indian occupation.

Historical and Archaeological View of French Colonial Life

A glimpse into the everyday lives of the Illinois French in the eighteenth century can be revealed through extant historical documents and the archaeological record. Historic written records can provide insights into the religious, social, and judicial aspects of colonial life at Cahokia. Unfortunately, the eighteenth-century documents specifically relating to Cahokia are somewhat limited. Many of the parish records were destroyed when the Church of the Holy Family burned in 1783, and various civic and court records from the early period at Cahokia have disappeared over the years (Alvord 1906).

The archaeological record provides data concerning colonial culture from the types and spatial occurrences of material remains. Aspects relating to individual socio-economic status, leisure activities, trade systems, dietary habits, and adaptations to local resources may be interpreted through examination of artifactual remains. Specifically, at the Cahokia Wedge site, the surface artifact distributions delineated the functional associations (i.e., domestic dwelling versus support buildings) of the historic structures. The artifacts collected from the excavations reflected certain aspects specifically relating to one eighteenth-century colonial household.

The various extant records (Alvord 1907; Boylan 1949) include estate appraisals listing the properties of individual households; contracts involving the sale and barter of household items, livestock, and farming equipment; and land titles describing the houses, barns, and other structures within the village. These descriptions provide information about the lifestyles of the inhabitants, the everyday appearance of colonial households, and the physical layout of the village.

The historical maps provide information concerning the evolution of the village plan of Cahokia. The village lots and street system, much of which exists today, were established early in the French colonial period. The congregated community plan was deemed necessary for the colonial villages in the American Bottom region, not only for social and religious activities, but also for protection against various elements of the frontier wilderness. The reconstructed WPA map for the years 1790–1826, has provided great detail as to visual appearance of the village lots. The palisaded house lots were fairly large and spacious, often containing orchards, garden plots, and numerous outbuildings, including barns, sheds, cook houses, and slave quarters. The commons and common fields surrounded the village proper, enclosed by fences which were often maintained collectively by the inhabitants. The agricultural fields were divided into long narrow tracts, a traditional land use system transplanted from France. This field system gave each owner access to the creek shoreline. This was the village pattern typically used at the French colonial settlements in the Illinois Country.

The French colonial houses were typically made of handhewn logs of locally available wood; generally those resistant to rot such as mulberry and cedar were sought. Building construction was predominantly of *poteaux-en-terre* (posts in the earth) or *poteaux-sur-solle* (posts on sill) styles. Usually the houses had whitewashed exteriors and porches or galleries on all four sides. The excavated Nicolle/Meunier structure was most likely a typical house in Cahokia and probably resembled those illustrated in the 1841 lithograph by J. C. Wild, as well as the numerous French colonial houses which are today located in the Historic District of Ste. Genevieve, Missouri. The recent investigations at the original village site of Prairie du Rocher (Safiran 1987) and at the Saline Springs near Ste. Genevieve (Michael Trimble, personal communication, 1987) have uncovered the archaeological remains of other domestic dwellings similar to the Nicolle/Meunier house.

The archaeological investigations at the Cahokia Wedge site were limited to only a small portion of the colonial settlement. The site represents approximately 10% of the village as it appeared on the 1766 map, and the test excavations consisted of less than 1% of the total site area. Most of the colonial village now remains underneath the modern town of Cahokia, and the feasibility of examining other portions of the historic village for archaeological remains is limited. However, these excavations have provided an examination of the cultural remains relating to one domestic colonial household, the Nicolle/Meunier house. Based on the available documents, the house was occupied by the Nicolle family from at least 1766 until 1779, had several short-term owners, and was later occupied by J. Meunier from 1794 to at least 1809. The structure apparently was no longer in existence by 1841. With this evidence it has been determined that this house was occupied for at least forty years.

The listings of the personal properties in the historic records give detailed descriptions of household items, including kitchen wares and furniture, personal items such as clothing, and farming equipment and tools. Luxury and imported items, such as French ceramics, tea services, porcelain, crystal goblets and wine glasses, and pewter and silver items, were mentioned frequently in the documents, reflecting a traditional way of life brought to the frontier village. These lists can provide comparative data for what types of materials are recovered in the archaeological record. As an example of the detail in the descriptions of personal properties, the 1773 estate appraisal of Jacques Compte (Boylan 1949:102–108) included the following kitchen items:

    one kitchen cupboard, estimated at thirty *livres*
    one bread box estimated at eight *livres*
    one large pot, one medium, and one small, estimated together at forty *livres*
    nine pewter plates, one large bowl of the same, and three medium-sized of pewter, seven spoons, six forks, good and bad, estimated at twenty-five *livres*
    three crocks, estimated at six *livres*
    two copper boilers, one tin ditto, estimated at twelve *livres*
    two smoothing irons, one old frying pan with skimmer, estimated at ten *livres*
    two pots of crockery and tin, one ditto of tin, one funnel and three bottles, estimated together at nine *livres*
    one small kettle, estimated at two *livres*

Numerous eighteenth-century artifacts from the site surface around the Nicolle/Meunier house and from the excavations attest to a substantial amount of material remains. Most significant perhaps is the eighteenth-century ceramic assemblage. The majority of this assemblage, which consists primarily of French faience and coarse earthenwares, appears to be associated with the Nicolle/Meunier structure. Of the nearly 1,000 sherds dating to the French period, approximately one-half represent tablewares, predominantly of faience but also including English delftware and Spanish majolica. A minimum of 50 vessels of tablewares may be associated with the occupation of this house. However, imported items, such as French ceramics, may have been considered luxury items in view of the frontier character of the village at Cahokia. Evidence of repair holes in many of the vessel sherds indicate a necessary adjustment to limited supplies.

Metal artifacts and tools from the Cahokia Wedge site include common trade items, such as the axe manufactured in Three Rivers, Canada, numerous blades from French clasp knives, and copper and brass kettle fragments. Construction hardware, such as handwrought nails, pintles and hinges, and handwrought tools may also have been imported to the Illinois Country, although some items may have been produced by local craftsmen. Among the earliest settlers at Cahokia with the Seminarian missionaries were two blacksmiths (Peterson 1949:8–9). Several artifact types, such as bottle fragments (probably for wine or a cheap rum known as *tafia*), smoking pipes, and musical instruments hint at the indulgence of leisure activities in French Cahokia.

A 1778 inventory of Charles Gratiot's store in Cahokia (Gieseker 1949:193) illustrates the varied assortment of items available to the French villagers:

88 yards cotton
1 2/3 yards grey frieze cloth
21 yards flowered flannel
16 1/4 yards Irish linen
6 yards common printed calico
2 pairs black knitted breeches
8 dozen muslin handkerchiefs
6 dozen cambric handkerchiefs
5 hats with piping
80 yards gold and silver lace
Silver, rose, red, black, yellow, green and flowered ribands [ribbons]
2 artificial flowers
42 assorted files
2 bridles
13 iron pots
31 razors
1 1/2 dozen combs for curling hair
25 pairs eye glasses
2 dozen big knives
3 pencils
Assorted buttons
10 pewter goblets
1 curry-comb
1 brush
14 pairs satin shoes
3 pairs shoes of woollen stuff
2 Candle sticks
1 sack of lead
1 seal

Inventories of personal items offer detail on the types of clothing worn by the French colonials. Fabrics, including linen, cotton, and muslin, and luxury goods, such as silk, taffeta, and velvet, were imported in large quantities (Van Ravenswaay 1956:235–238), consequential to the government forbidding the weaving of cloths in the colonies (Belting 1948:47). Imported cloth allowed the French to enjoy the luxury of high quality fabrics as opposed to undoubtedly limited varieties that locally produced cloths would have provided. Although such items as cloth and leather were not preserved in the archaeological record, numerous clothing adornments and accoutrements (e.g., buttons and jewelry), were recovered from the Cahokia Wedge site. The 1778 property description of Cahokia resident Charles Marois included the following clothing items (Alvord 1907:451-453):

> Item, thirteen handkerchiefs. red but small, at fifty *sols* per handkerchief
> Item, one hat with ornament and gold button at fifteen *livres*
> Item, one pair of breeches and one vest with silk drugget at thirty *livres*
> Item, one old vest of printed calico and one tafeta waistcoat at three *livres*
> Item, one vest and one pair of breeches of beaver at fifteen *livres*
> Item, one vest of brown cloth a *Beuillain* (?) black velvet at twelve *livres*
> Item, one cloak of brown *cade* (?) and one black waistcoat, both old, at seven *livres*
> One vest of green tafeta at twelve *livres*
> Item, one cloak of *cade* (?) with trimmings of crimson velvet at twelve *livres*
> Item, one coat and one pair of breeches of ash color, both old
> Item, two pairs of silk stockings, partly worn at the sum of twelve *livres*

Many of the goods found at French colonial forts and villages derived from an extensive trade network, primarily water transportation routes. In the early eighteenth century, this network extended from New France (French Canada) to the Illinois Country through various outposts in the Great Lakes region, such as the forts at Michilimackinac and St. Joseph. With the founding of New Orleans in 1718 and its subsequent development as a major port, many goods imported from France were shipped through New Orleans up the Mississippi River to the villages of the Illinois Country. The Illinois French supplied ". . . New Orleans and the lower parts of Louisiana . . . with flour, beer, wines, hams, and other provisions . . ." (Pittman 1770:52). The various settlements within the American Bottom (Cahokia, Fort de Chartres, Prairie du Rocher, St. Philippe, Kaskaskia, and Ste. Genevieve) maintained a smaller trade network, being dependent on one another for goods and foodstuffs. Early in the eighteenth century, a road crossing the upland bluff area was established, connecting Cahokia with the settlements in the southern portion of the American Bottom.

While many items were imported, locally crafted goods were also produced (Belting 1948; Van Ravenswaay 1956; Ekberg 1985). Historic records from the French villages in the Illinois Country list various craftsmen, including carpenters, masons, shinglers, blacksmiths, gunsmiths, locksmiths, master tool-makers, and coopers (Van Ravenswaay 1956:216). Other skilled laborers included tanners, tailors, wig-makers, and bakers (Belting 1948:61–63). Since it was impractical and difficult to import larger items, such as furniture, these items were more likely locally produced. Furthermore, local potteries developed in the late 1700s at Ste. Genevieve and St. Louis, providing for an increasing demand for these household items (Van Ravenswaay 1956:238–239).

Individual colonial households probably maintained a level of self-sufficiency with garden plots, the use of the village commons for livestock pasture, and individual tracts within the common fields for agricultural purposes. The major crops produced by the French colonials included wheat, corn, and tobacco, with cotton, flax, and hemp of lesser importance (Ekberg 1985:134–136). The fertile lands in the American Bottom enabled sufficient agricultural production for French farmers to have supplied the southern colonies with foodstuffs; for example, a recorded 300,000 pounds of flour were shipped from the Illinois Country to New Orleans in 1738 and 1739 (Surrey 1916:291–292).

Salt production, lead mining, and the fur trade further provided an economic base for the French colonies in the Central Mississippi River Valley. The salt springs by Saline Creek across the Mississippi near Ste. Genevieve, were being utilized by the French as early as 1700 (McDermott 1949b:3). Salt production continued throughout the colonial period since salt served as a curative for meat and animal hides (Ekberg 1985:158–161). Rumors of silver mines led to extensive mining operations during the 1720s, but only lead deposits were discovered. The mining of lead, which was used locally as well as exported south to New Orleans and north to French Canada (Ekberg 1985:147), continued throughout the eighteenth century and into the early nineteenth century (Walthall 1981:20–21).

Few historical accounts exist recording the lives and adventures of the early *coureurs de bois* in colonial Illinois. The fur traders, generally working independent of governmental jurisdiction (McDermott 1949:2), often traveled and bartered with the Indians. The preferred fur-bearing animals included beaver, deer, bear, wildcat, wolf, and fox (Belting 1948:66–67). As early as 1702, a tannery, although short-lived, was established at the confluence of the Mississippi and Ohio rivers (Pease and Werner 1934:286). Many artifacts from the Cahokia Wedge site may have been items used in the fur trade. It is probable that such interaction and bartering resulted in the local production of some items, such as ornaments and beads, for trade to the Indians. Additionally, the French may have enjoyed the use of Micmac pipes acquired through trade with the Indians. However, since most of these trade goods were recovered from the site surface, it is impossible to determine actual possession and use.

The faunal and botanical remains recovered from eighteenth-century features at the Cahokia Wedge site have allowed preliminary interpretations of subsistence and dietary habits. The apparent dependence on wild animal resources, particularly the white-tailed deer, reveals the French frontier adaptation to the wilderness environment and its abundant resources. Although cattle were introduced to the Illinois Country as early as ca. 1712 (Belting 1948:13), these domesticates, as well as pigs and chickens, appear to have served only as dietary supplements for the eighteenth-century villagers at Cahokia. In comparison, at the military outpost of Fort de Chartres, which maintained a much larger and diverse population, domesticates comprised a more evident role in the colonial diet. The other identified animal remains from the Cahokia Wedge, which included bison, black bear, beaver, and wolf or coyote, may be economically linked to the fur trade.

The recovered botanical sample, albeit small, contained the remains of corn, wheat, tobacco, and possibly apple, in addition to numerous types of wood utilized by the French. Environmental studies as well as historical documentation indicate that wild fruits and nuts such as grapes, plums, mulberries, blackberries, hickory nuts, pecans, and walnuts were also available and most likely consumed by the French. The colonists were known to make a "wine of the wild grapes, which is very inebriating, and is, in color and taste, very like the red wine of Provence" (Pittman 1770:51).

The historical documents provide a view of colonial lifeways during the French Regime of the eighteenth century. However, political events beginning in the 1760s soon changed the unique character of the French colonial villages in the Illinois Country. The French domination ended with the British victory in the Seven Years War in 1763, and with the Revolutionary War a decade later came an influx of Americans into the region. Throughout the nineteenth century, Cahokia remained a small semirural community with a mixture of French and European descendants and Americans. Although the archaeological record relating to the later history of Cahokia does not reveal the continuity of French culture, many social and religious traditions were maintained by the French descendants. As observed by Lewis Thomas (Wild and Thomas 1841:103);

> ... The lapse of nearly two centuries has not entirely destroyed the original impress upon this people of the manners, customs, and language of Old France.

Concluding Remarks

The controlled surface collection has yielded artifact assemblages associated with historic structures which have been functionally and temporally identified. The cultural materials recovered from the Nicolle/Meunier house appear to relate primarily to typical domestic and subsistence activities, such as food procurement and preparation. Although Etienne Nicolle and Jean Meunier are mentioned several times in the historic documents, neither are linked to a specific trade, skill, or occupation. Although trade and craft-related items were recovered from the site, discrete concentrations relating to the French occupation were not revealed.

In comparison, excavations at other historic sites, in particular, the numerous French colonial forts (e.g., Fort Michilimackinac, Fort Ouiatenon, and Fort de Chartres), have produced specialized activity areas and/or structures, which can be identified in the historic documents and in the archaeological record. A detailed functional analysis at the Cahokia Wedge site is not feasible at this time, due to a lack of archaeological comparison with other domestic dwellings in Cahokia or at other French village sites in this region. However, continued archaeological research at French colonial domestic sites, such as Prairie du Rocher and the Saline Springs settlement, would add to the data base relating to the everyday activities of a typical French household. Questions concerning the range of economic activities and the level of self-sufficiency of the colonial household could be examined. Furthermore, comparisons of French colonial domestic dwellings, commercial sites and/or structures, and military sites and/or structures should be included in future research.

Although much of the cultural remains from the Cahokia Wedge site were recovered from non-feature contexts (i.e., surface and excavation units), the artifact assemblage has revealed various aspects of the domestic, leisure, commercial, and subsistence activities. The lifeways of the French villagers as inferred by the material culture, represent traditions transplanted from France and adapted to a colonial frontier setting.

APPENDIX A

FEATURE ARTIFACTS
Counts and Weights

Feature 1: Zone A		Count	Weight(g)
Ceramics	Whiteware	1	.5
	Molded and green banded rim with gold luster	1	2.0
Bottle Glass	Dark green kick-up	1	66.0
Personal Items	Earthenware pipe bowl	1	84.0
Metal	Clasp knife blade	1	14.5
	Barrel hoop	1	816.0
	Cast iron kettle leg	1	431.0
	Square spike	1	53.0
	Lead mold waste with sprue attachment	1	2.0
	Lead waste	1	9.8
	Unidentified flat metal	10	12.2
	Unidentified iron clump	4	11.5
Building Hardware	Rosehead nail	6	67.0
	Other square nail	7	123.0
	Unidentified nail	4	45.0
	Thumb lock catch	1	8.4
	Square bolt	1	474.5
Building Materials	Brick	1	3.1
Faunal	Animal bone	115	333.7
	Mussel shell	1	.9
Botanical	Wood charcoal	12	77.0
Modified Rock	Triangular point	1	.5
	Ground limestone	3	580.5
Miscellaneous Materials	Burnt Clay	1	.5
	Limestone	34	805.0
	Igneous rock	1	132.5
	Hematite	2	6.5
	Subtotal	214	4160.6

APPENDIX A

Feature 1: Zones B and C		Count	Weight(g)
Other Glass	White opaque glass seed bead	1	.1
Personal Items	Iron button	2	12.0
	Brass buckle	1	12.0
Metal	Clasp knife blade	1	63.0
	Scissors fragment	1	11.5
	File	1	1169.0
	Iron punch	1	79.5
	Cut sheet brass/copper scrap	1	1.5
	Unidentified iron	5	115.5
Gun Parts	Frizzen	1	30.0
	Upper jaw of cock	1	6.0
Faunal	Animal bone	77	378.0
	Mussel shell	1	7.0
Botanical	Wood charcoal	4	43.5
Building Hardware	Rosehead nail	1	2.5
	Other square nail	3	33.5
	Unidentified nail	1	14.5
	Unidentified hardware	3	148.0
Miscellaneous Materials	Modified cobble	1	87.5
	Limestone	12	912.0
	Subtotal	119	3126.6
	Total	333	7286.6

Feature 1: Artifacts from Flotation Samples		Count	Weight(g)
Other Glass	Flat glass	1	p
Metal	Unidentified metal	10	.59
Building Materials	Plaster fragments	5	.02
Faunal	Bone fragments	41	3.57
Modified Rock	Chert flake	1	.01
Miscellaneous Materials	Limestone	30	3.45
	Sandstone	1	.04
	Gravel	17	.48
	Cinders/clinkers	8	.52
	Burned earth	1216	37.22
	Unidentified materials	20	.24
	Total	1350	46.14

APPENDIX A

Feature 2: Surface Artifacts		Count	Weight(g)
Ceramics	Coarse earthenware rim sherd	1	7.9
Bottle Glass	Dark green	1	2.8
Personal Items	Kaolin pipe stem fragment	1	1.3
Metal	Knife (clasp?) blade fragment	1	8.8
	Square iron spike	2	112.0
	Unidentified iron	4	41.5
Building Hardware	Rosehead nail	2	15.0
	Round nail	1	4.2
	Unidentified hardware	2	119.5
Faunal	Animal bone	21	569.5
Modified Rock	Worked catlinite	1	76.9
	Modified cobble	1	2128.5
	Total	38	3087.9

Feature 3: No artifacts collected

Feature 4: Surface Artifacts		Count	Weight(g)
Ceramics	Faience	1	6.2
	Coarse earthenware	7	159.7
	Westerwald stoneware	2	17.5
Metal	Clasp knife blade	2	38.0
	Copper scrap with hole	1	19.5
	Unidentified metal	1	15.0
Building Hardware	Rosehead nail	1	2.5
	Other square nail	2	30.0
	Subtotal	17	288.4

Feature 4: Test Trench		Count	Weight(g)
Ceramics	Porcelain	1	1.5
Bottle Glass	Blue-green kick-up	2	90.5
	Blue-green case bottle kick-up	2	44.7
Metal	Copper kettle bail ear	2	23.3
	Lead strip	1	28.0
	Iron clasp knife blade	1	10.0

258 APPENDIX A

		Count	Weight(g)
	Cut and riveted copper	1	8.5
	Unidentified iron clump	3	6.6
Building Hardware	Rosehead nail	1	11.0
	L-head square nail	1	11.0
	Other square nail	4	18.0
	Unidentified nail	1	2.0
	Unidentified hardware	4	214.5
Faunal	Animal bone	71	524.0
	Worked trumpeter swan humerus	1	14.0
Botanical	Wood charcoal	288	344.0
Modified Rock	Triangular point	1	1.0
	Utilized flake	1	2.9
	Whetstone fragment?	1	18.0
	Ground limestone	1	1950.0
Miscellaneous Materials	Burnt clay	2	34.3
	Sandstone	1	1.5
	Limestone	184	11673.0
	Cinders/clinkers	103	976.0
	Subtotal	678	16008.3
	Total	695	16296.7

Feature 5: Zone A		Count	Weight(g)
Ceramics	Creamware	4	6.5
	Pearlware	1	.8
	Pearlware blue shell edge	1	13.2
	Whiteware	5	12.5
Decorated Whiteware	Blue cord and hanging fern motif	2	52.4
	Blue transfer print	4	5.6
	Brown transfer print	1	1.5
	Polychrome transfer print	1	260.0
	Annular-banded	3	5.5
	Blue handpainted	1	1.3
	Polychrome handpainted	4	6.9
	Molded edge	1	2.8
	Indeterminate blue-decorated	1	1.0
Stoneware/Crockery	Brown glaze and orange paste	1	2.2
Bottle Glass	Dark green	2	11.0
	Medium green	1	8.5
	Blue-green	7	21.5

APPENDIX A

		Count	Weight(g)
	Blue fruit jar	1	5.3
	Clear	1	7.8
Other Glass	Milk glass liner	1	3.0
	Flat glass	18	29.0
Personal Items	Kaolin pipe stem	2	5.6
	Brass button with engraved design	1	3.5
	Slate pencil	1	3.0
Metal	Bone-handled knife	1	16.0
	Bottle cap	1	5.3
	Unidentified iron clump	1	5.5
Building Hardware	Rosehead nail	1	3.5
	Other square nail	6	35.0
	Unidentified nail	3	26.0
	Unidentified hardware	1	82.1
Building Materials	Limestone	55	–
	Mortar	1025	–
	Brick	10	439.5
Faunal	Sawed animal bone	2	22.4
	Animal bone	10	43.1
Miscellaneous Materials	Cinders/clinkers	6	4.5
	Pebble	1	3.1
	Subtotal (excluding limestone and mortar)	108	1156.4

Feature 5: Zone B		Count	Weight(g)
Ceramics	Creamware	1	.8
	Whiteware	1	1.5
Decorated Whiteware	Blue transfer	1	4.3
	Polychrome-banded handpainted	2	3.5
	Polychrome handpainted	2	6.3
	Green handpainted	1	2.0
	Annular-banded and swirled handpainted motif	1	3.4
	Unknown decorated	1	1.5
Bottle Glass	Blue	1	.8
Personal Items	Bone button	1	.5
Metal	Unidentified iron clump	1	4.5
	Unidentified (hardware?)	1	8.5

APPENDIX A

Building Materials	Limestone	15	405.5
	Mortar	53	44.5
	Brick	1	1.3
Faunal	Animal bone	2	24.0
	Snail shell	1	4.5
Modified Rock	Chert flake	1	.3
Miscellaneous Materials	Cinders/clinkers	1	2.6
	Subtotal	88	520.3
	Total	196	1676.7

Feature 6: Surface Artifacts		Count	Weight(g)
Ceramics	Faience	2	16.3
	Coarse earthenware	1	4.8
	Creamware	3	4.5
	Whiteware	4	24.2
Decorated Whiteware	Blue shell edge	2	1.6
	Blue dot and plume	1	3.0
	Blue cord and herringbone	1	6.5
	Blue cord and hanging fern/tassle	1	2.8
	Blue sponge/spatterware	2	9.2
	Polychrome transfer	1	44.5
	Blue handpainted	1	.8
	Annular-decorated	1	2.4
	Polychrome porcelain	1	3.8
Stoneware/Crockery	Brown saltglazed	1	69.5
Bottle Glass	Dark green	1	7.5
Other Glass	Flat glass	3	3.5
Personal Items	Kaolin pipe stem	1	2.8
Metal	Iron gouge	1	201.0
Building Hardware	Other square nail	3	31.7
Faunal	Animal bone	6	46.6
Miscellaneous Materials	Cinders/clinkers	1	16.2
	Subtotal	38	503.2

Feature 6: Excavated Trench		Count	Weight(g)
Ceramics	Faience	1	.4
	Coarse earthenware	2	6.0

APPENDIX A

	Creamware	1	1.0
	Pearlware-blue transfer	1	1.5
	Whiteware	6	13.0
	Yellowware	1	2.5
Decorated	Blue sponge/spatterware	1	2.0
Whiteware	Brown transfer	2	1.0
	Blue banded	1	96.5
	Polychrome handpainted	1	2.5
Stoneware/ Crockery	Saltglazed	3	12.5
Bottle Glass	Green soda bottle	1	461.5
	Clear bottle	1	36.3
	Dark green	1	.8
	Blue-green	25	96.5
	Blue fruit jar	17	197.5
	Brown	2	4.5
	Amethyst	1	2.0
	Clear	32	468.0
Other Glass	Flat glass	11	45.5
Personal Items	White opaque glass button	1	1.1
	Kaolin pipe stem	1	1.5
Metal	Knife blade	1	22.5
	Triangular file	1	37.0
	Iron spring	1	80.5
	Wire	1	22.5
	Bottle cap	1	6.0
	Unidentified iron clumps	16	101.0
	Unidentified flat metal	51	220.0
Building Hardware	Rosehead nail	1	28.0
	Other square nail	28	132.0
	Unidentified nail	15	50.5
	Bolt	1	57.5
	Unidentified hardware	2	42.5
Building Materials	Limestone	122	1957.0
	Mortar	160	1075.0
	Brick	82	2997.5
Faunal	Sawed animal bone	1	6.5
	Animal bone	12	59.7
Botanical	Charred and uncharred wood	7	109.5
Miscellaneous	Cinders/clinkers	39	164.0
Materials	Slate	3	18.0
	Shale	4	16.5

		Count	Weight(g)
Quartz		2	10.0
Chert gravel		32	243.0
	Subtotal	763	8910.8
	Total	801	9414.0

Feature 7: Surface Artifacts		Count	Weight(g)
Ceramics	Faience	2	7.0
	Coarse earthenware	1	8.7
	Creamware	3	10.5
Bottle Glass	Blue-green	2	4.2
Other Glass	Flat glass	1	1.5
Building Hardware	Bolt	1	39.7
Faunal	Animal bone	3	6.1
	Subtotal	13	77.7

Feature 7: Artifacts		Count	Weight(g)
Ceramics	Faience	13	37.2
	Delftware	1	.5
	Coarse earthenware	5	52.6
	Creamware	7	27.3
	Whiteware	4	11.1
Bottle Glass	Dark green kick-up	3	17.5
	Blue-green	2	3.7
Other Glass	Flat glass	5	3.5
Personal Items	Kaolin pipe stem	1	.3
Metal	Triangular padlock	1	20.0
	Square iron ring	1	44.0
	Cut pieces of sheet copper/brass	12	29.5
	Unidentified iron clump	1	17.5
	Unidentified flat iron	16	504.5
Faunal	Animal bone	20	72.0
Botanical	Wood charcoal	3	1.5
Building Hardware	Rosehead square nail	3	29.0
	Other square nail	10	53.0
	Unidentified nail	11	89.5
Modified Rock	Worked catlinite	1	7.2
	Chert flake	1	.1

Miscellaneous Materials	Limestone	10	157.0
	Cinders/clinkers	1	2.8
	Galena	1	6.5
	Subtotal	133	1187.8
	Total	146	1265.5

Feature 7: Artifacts from Flotation Samples		Count	Weight(g)
Other Glass	Brown seed bead	2	.02
	Unidentified glass	3	.53
Metal	Unidentified metal	219	23.09
Faunal	Bone fragments	52	4.44
Miscellaneous Materials	Limestone	348	33.36
	Sandstone	2	.03
	Gravel	4	.12
	Cinders/clinkers	24	10.53
	Burned earth	445	8.25
	Unidentified material	5	.14
	Total	1104	80.51

Feature 8 Artifacts: All Zones		Count	Weight(g)
Ceramics	Creamware	4	4.8
Decorated Whiteware	Blue shell edge	1	1.1
	Green handpainted	1	.5
	Brown handpainted	1	1.0
Bottle Glass	Dark green	1	2.5
Metal	Clasp knife blade	1	24.0
	Unidentified flat iron	1	2.3
Building Hardware	Other square nail	1	3.5
Building Materials	Limestone	25	214.0
	Mortar	4	7.0
	Brick	1	.5
Faunal	Animal bone	6	13.2
Miscellaneous Materials	Unidentified material	1	.3
	Cinders/clinkers	5	34.5
	Total	53	309.2

Feature 9: Artifacts from Profile		Count	Weight(g)
Ceramics	Whiteware	3	101.0
Decorated Whiteware	Blue-stamped	1	1.7
Stoneware/Crockery	Brown glaze and paste	1	34.2
Building Hardware	Other square nail	3	10.5
Building Materials	Brick	1	1.5
Faunal	Animal bone	3	50.5
	Total	12	199.4

Feature 10: No artifacts collected

Feature 11: Artifacts from Profile		Count	Weight(g)
Decorated Pearlware	Indeterminate blue-decorated pearlware (?)	1	.2
Building Hardware	Flat-head square nail	1	4.7
Faunal	Animal bone	1	.3
Miscellaneous Materials	Vitrified material	2	422.8
	Total	5	428.0

Feature 12: Artifacts from Profile		Count	Weight(g)
Glass	Clear glass rim (drinking vessel)	1	8.0
	Total	1	8.0

Feature 13: Artifacts from Profile		Count	Weight(g)
Ceramics	Creamware	1	1.0
Bottle Glass	Blue-green Pike's Peak figural flask	1	8.0
Other Glass	Flat glass	1	1.2
Metal	Unidentified flat metal	1	.8
Building Hardware	Other square nail	1	3.5
	Total	5	14.5

REFERENCES CITED

Alvord, Clarence W.
    1906   Eighteenth Century French Records in the Archives of Illinois. *Annual Report of the American Historical Association* 2:353–366, Washington D. C.

    1907   Cahokia Records 1778–1790. *Collections of the Illinois State Historical Library* 2, Springfield.

    1922   *The Illinois Country 1673–1818*. A.C. McClurg and Co., Chicago.

Alvord, Clarence W., and Clarence E. Carter
    1916   The New Regime 1765–1767. *Collections of the Illinois State Historical Library* 11, Springfield.

American Ornithologists' Union
    1982   Thirty-fourth Supplement to the American Ornithologists' Union Check-list of North American Birds. *The Auk* 99(3):1cc-16cc.

Anderson, Cynthia R.
    1981   Final Report of Historical Archaeological Investigations at the Alorton Site (11–S–331) on FAI Route 270, St. Clair County, Illinois. *FAI-270 Archaeological Mitigation Project Report* 36, Midwestern Archaeological Research Center, Illinois State University, Normal.

Armour, David A.
    1966   Made at Mackinac: Crafts at Fort Michilimackinac. *Mackinac History Leaflet* 8, Mackinac Island State Park Commission, Mackinac Island, Michigan.

Austin, Moses
    1900   A Memorandum of M. Austin's Journey. *American Historical Review* 3(4):518–542.

Bareis, Charles J., and James W. Porter (editors)
    1984   *American Bottom Archaeology.* University of Illinois Press, Urbana.

Barton, Kenneth J.
    1981   Coarse Earthenwares from the Fortress of Louisbourg. *National Historic Parks and Sites Branch, Parks Canada History and Archaeology* 55.

Bastian, Beverly E.
    1982   *Fort Independence, An Eighteenth-Century Frontier Homesite and Militia Post in South Carolina.* Russell Papers, Building Conservation Technology, Inc., Nashville, Tennessee.

Baumann, Paul
    1970   *Collecting Antique Marbles.* Mid-American Book Company, Leon, Iowa.

Bauxer, J. Joseph
    1973   The Historic Period. *Illinois Archaeological Survey Bulletin* 1, Urbana.

Belting, Natalia Maree
    1948   *Kaskaskia Under the French Regime.* University of Illinois Press, Urbana.

Benchley, Elizabeth D.
    1974   *Mississippian Secondary Mound Loci: A Comparative-Functional Analysis in a Time-Space Perspective.* Unpublished Ph.D. dissertation, Department of Anthropology, University of Wisconsin-Milwaukee.

    1981   Summary Report on Controlled Surface Collections of Ramey Field, Cahokia Mounds Historic Site, Madison County, Illinois. *Archaeological Research Laboratory Report of Investigations* 51, University of Wisconsin-Milwaukee.

Blake, Leonard W.
    1986   Corn and Other Plants from Prehistory into History in Eastern United States. In The Protohistoric Period in the Mid-South: 1500–1700, edited by David H. Dye and Ronald C. Brister, pp. 3–13. *Mississippi Department of Archives and History Archaeological Report* 18, Jackson.

Blasingham, Emily J.
1956   The Depopulation of the Illinois Indians. *Ethnohistory* 3(3):193-224, 361-412.

Bossu, Jean Bernard
1771   *Travels Through That Part of North America Formerly called Louisiana*. T. Davies, London.

Boylan, Rose Josephine
n.d.   *Report of the Cahokia Memorial Survey from August 1, 1938 to February 1, 1939*. Cahokia Historical Society of St. Clair County in co-operation with the St. Clair County Board of Supervisors. Works Progress Administration through the Illinois State Museum Extension Project. Report on file at Illinois State Historical Library, Springfield.

1949   Life as Illustrated by Legal Documents, 1772-1821. In *Old Cahokia*, edited by John F. McDermott, pp. 93-189. The St. Louis Historical Documents Foundation, St. Louis.

Black, Glenn A.
1967   *Angel Site: An Archaeological, Historical, and Ethnological Study*. Indiana Historical Society, Indianapolis.

Brain, Jeffrey P.
1979   Tunica Treasure. *Papers of the Peabody Museum of Archaeology and Ethnology* 71, Harvard University, Cambridge.

Brink, W. R.
1881   *History of St. Clair County*. Brink, McDonough and Company, Philadelphia.

Brown, James A. (editor)
1961   The Zimmerman Site. *Illinois State Museum Reports of Investigations* 9, Springfield.

Brown, Margaret Kimball
n.d.   *The Waterman Site: Archaeological Systematic Change*. Manuscript on file, Illinois State Museum, Springfield.

1971   Glass from Fort Michilimackinac: A Classification for Eighteenth Century Glass. *The Michigan Archaeologist* 17(3-4).

1976 The 1974 Fort de Chartres Excavation Project. *University Museum Archaeological Service Report* 14, Southern Illinois University, Carbondale.

Campbell, J. Duncan
1965 Military Buttons: Long-Lost Heralds of Fort Mackinac's Past. *Mackinac History Leaflet* 7, Mackinac State Park Commission, Lansing, Michigan.

Cardinal, Elizabeth A.
1975 Faunal Remains from the Zimmerman Site—1970. In The Zimmerman Site, by Margaret Kimball Brown, pp. 73–79. *Illinois State Museum Reports of Investigations* 32, Springfield.

1977 Faunal Remains from Fort de Chartres. In The 1975 Season of Archaeological Investigations at Fort de Chartres, Randolph County, Illinois, by Charles E. Orser, pp. 164–167. *Southern Illinois Studies, Research Records* 16, University Museum, Southern Illinois University, Carbondale.

Carter, Clarence E.
1910 *Great Britain and the Illinois Country 1763–1774.* American Historical Association, Washington, D. C.

Catholic University of America
1967 *New Catholic Encyclopedia* 9:894. McGraw-Hill Book Company, New York.

Chapman, Carl H.
1959 The Little Osage and Missouri Indian Village Sites. *The Missouri Archaeologist* 21(1).

Chmurny, William
1973 *The Ecology of the Middle Mississippian Occupation of the American Bottom.* Unpublished Ph.D. dissertation, Department of Anthropology, University of Illinois, Urbana.

Coleman, Dorothy S., Elizabeth A. Coleman, and Evelyn J. Coleman
1968 *The Collector's Encyclopedia of Dolls.* Crown Publishers, Inc., New York.

Conant, Roger
    1975   *A Field Guide to Reptiles and Amphibians of Eastern and Central North America*. Houghton Mifflin Company, Boston.

Cotter, John L.
    1968   *A Handbook for Historical Archaeology, Part I*. J. L. Cotter, Wyncote, Pa.

Deagan, Kathleen
    1987   *Artifacts of the Spanish Colonies of Florida and the Caribbean, 1500–1800*. Smithsonian Institute Press, Washington, D. C.

Denny, Sidney
    1974   *Survey of Cultural Resources of the Blue Water Ditch Area, East St. Louis and Vicinity, Illinois*. Report submitted to the Army Corps of Engineers, St. Louis District.

Donnelly, Joseph P., S.J.
    1949   The Founding of the Holy Family Mission and its History in the Eighteenth Century Documents. In *Old Cahokia*, edited by John F. McDermott, pp. 55–92. The St. Louis Historical Documents Foundation, St. Louis.

Du Pratz, Antoine Simon Le Page
    1975   *The History of Louisiana*. Edited by Joseph G. Tregle, Jr. Louisiana State University Press, Baton Rouge.

Ekberg, Carl J.
    1985   *Colonial Ste. Genevieve*. The Patrice Press, Gerald, Missouri.

Emerson, Thomas E., George Milner, and Douglas K. Jackson
    1983   The Florence Street Site. *American Bottom Archaeology FAI-270 Site Reports* 2. University of Illinois Press, Urbana.

Esarey, Mark E.
    1984   Historic Period. In *American Bottom Archaeology*, edited by Charles J. Bareis and James W. Porter, pp. 187–196. University of Illinois Press, Urbana.

Forest Products Laboratory
    1955   Wood Handbook. *U. S. Department of Agriculture, Agricultural Handbook* 72, Washington, D.C.

Fortier, Edward J.
    1909   The Establishment of the Tamarois Mission. *Transactions of the Illinois State Historical Society* 13:233–239.

Fowler, Melvin L.
    1959   Summary Report of Modoc Shelter 1952, 1953, 1955, 1956. *Illinois State Museum Reports of Investigations* 8, Springfield.

Garner, F. H.
    1949   *English Delftware*. Pitman Publishing Corporation, New York.

Garraghan, Gilbert J.
    1928   New Light on Old Cahokia. *Illinois Catholic Historical Review* 11:99–146.

Gieseker, Brenda R.
    1949   A Business Venture at Cahokia: The Letters of Charles Gratiot, 1778–1779. In *Old Cahokia*, edited by John F. McDermott, pp.190-231. St. Louis Historical Documents Foundation, St. Louis.

Goggin, John
    1968   Spanish Majolica in the New World. *Yale University Publications in Anthropology* 72.

Good, Mary Elizabeth
    1972   Guebert Site: An Eighteenth Century Historic Kaskaskia Indian Village in Randolph County, Illinois. *Central States Archaeological Society Memoir* 2.

Grayson, Donald K.
    1973   On the Methodology of Faunal Analysis. *American Antiquity* 39(4):432–439.

Gregg, Michael Lee
    1975   *Settlement Morphology and Production Specialization: The Horseshoe Lake Site, A Case Study*. Unpublished Ph.D. dissertation, Department of Anthropology, University of Wisconsin-Milwaukee.

Grimm, Jacob L.
    1970   Archaeological Investigation of Fort Ligonier: 1960–1965. *Annals of Carnegie Museum* 42, Pittsburgh.

Gusset, Gerard
    1980   Stoneware: White Salt-Glazed, Rhenish and Dry Body. *National Historic Parks and Sites Branch, Parks Canada History and Archaeology* 30.

Hamilton, Henry W., and Jean Tyree Hamilton
    1972   Clay Pipes from Pamplin. *The Missouri Archaeologist* 34(1-2):1–47.

Hamilton, T. M.
    1960   Indian Trade Guns. *The Missouri Archaeologist* 22.

    1980   *Colonial Frontier Guns*. The Fur Press, Chadron, Nebraska.

Hanson, Lee
    1971   Pipes from Rome, New York. *Historical Archaeology* 5:92-99.

Hanson, Lee, and Dick Ping Hsu
    1975   Casements and Cannonballs: Archaeological Investigations at Fort Stanwix, Rome, New York. *Publications in Archeology* 14, U. S. Department of the Interior, National Park Service, Washington, D. C.

Harrington, J. C.
    1954   Dating Stem Fragments of Seventeenth and Eighteenth Century Clay Pipes. *Quarterly Bulletin of the Archaeological Society of Virginia* 9(1):9–13.

Hess, Jeffrey A., Maricca J. Lutz, and Charles E. Peterson
    1982   *Restoration Inventory, Nicholas Jarrot Mansion, Cahokia, Illinois*. MacDonald and Mack Partnership, Minneapolis.

Hobson, Burton, and Robert Obojski
    1983   *Illustrated Encyclopedia of World Coins*. Doubleday and Co. Inc., Garden City, New York.

Hoffmeister, Donald F., and Carl O. Mohr
    1972   *Fieldbook of Illinois Mammals*. Dover Publications, Inc., New York.

How, Shu-wu
    1971   Catlinite on the Lasanen Site. In The Lasanen Site: A Historic Burial Locality in Mackinac County, Michigan,

edited by Charles E. Cleland, pp. 41–52. *Michigan State University Anthropological Series* 1(1), East Lansing.

Hulse, Charles A.
    1981   An Archaeological Evaluation of Fort St. Joseph (20BE23) Berrien County, Michigan. *The Michigan Archaeologist* 27(3–4).

Humphrey, Richard V.
    1969   Clay Pipes from Old Sacramento. *Historical Archaeology* 3:12–33.

Illinois State Archives
    n.d.   Narrative Reports. Cahokia Memorial Survey. Works Progress Administration (Illinois) and Illinois State Museum Extension Project.

Jelks, Edward B., and Rose Shun
    1975   *Archaeological Exploration at Cahokia Courthouse State Memorial.* Contract Archaeology Program, Illinois State University. Report submitted to Illinois Department of Conservation and Illinois Archaeological Survey.

Jelks, Edward B., and Carl J. Ekberg
    1984   *Archaeological Explorations at the Laurens Site (11–R–125), Randolph County, Illinois.* Midwestern Archaeological Research Center, Illinois State University, Normal. Report submitted to the Illinois Historic Preservation Agency, Springfield.

Jones, J. Knox, Dilford C. Carter, Hugh H. Genoways, Robert S. Hoffman, and Dale R. Rice
    1982   Revised Checklist of North American Mammals North of Mexico, 1982. *Occasional Papers of the Museum, Texas Tech University* 80, Lubbock.

Jones, Olive
    1971   Glass Bottle Push-ups and Pontil Marks. *Historical Archaeology* 5:62–73.

Karklins, Karlis
    1975   Seventeenth-Century Dutch Beads. *Historical Archaeology* 8:64–82.

Keene, David
   1986   Excavations at Fort de Chartres Answer Some Questions, Pose Others. *Historic Illinois* 9(2):5, 10–13.

Kelly, John E., Jean R. Linder, and Theresa J. Cartmell
   1979   The Archaeological Intensive Survey of the Proposed FAI-270 Alignment in the American Bottom. *Illinois Transportation Archaeology Scientific Reports* 1.

Kelly, John E., S. J. Ozuk, Douglas K. Jackson, D. L. McElrath, Fred A. Finney, and Duane Esarey
   1984   Emergent Mississippian Period. In *American Bottom Archaeology*, edited by Charles J. Bareis and James W. Porter, pp. 128–157. University of Illinois Press, Urbana.

Kenton, Edna (editor)
   1927   *Indians Of North America*. 2 vols. Harcourt, Brace and Company, New York.

Keslin, Richard O.
   1964   Archaeological Implications of the Role of Salt as an Element of Cultural Diffusion. *The Missouri Archaeologist* 26.

Koldehoff, Brad
   1980   An Inventory of Prehistory in Southwestern Illinois: The Russell Fischer Collection. *Rediscovery* 1:1–9.

Lindsey, Bessie M.
   1967   *American Historical Glass*. Charles E. Tuttle Company, Rutland, Vermont.

Lopinot, Al C.
   1967   The Illinois Mussel. *Outdoor Illinois Magazine* 6(3).

Lowrie, Walter, and Walter S. Franklin (editors)
   1834   *American State Papers, Documents, Legislative and Executive of the Congress of the Third Session of the Thirteenth Congress: Commencing November 27, 1809 and Ending March 3, 1815*, 29, Public Land Series 2. Gales and Seaton, Washington.

Lunn, John
   1972   Colonial Louisbourg and Its Developing Ceramics Collection. In *Ceramics In America*, edited by Ian M. G. Quim-

by, pp. 175–190. University Press of Virginia, Charlottesville.

Luscomb, Sally C.
    1967   *The Collectors Encyclopedia of Buttons.* Crown Publishers, Inc., New York.

Martin, Terrance J.
    1984   Animal Remains from Fort de Chartres I, Randolph County, Illinois: 1983 Excavations. In *Archaeological Explorations at the Laurens Site (11–R–125), Randolph County, Illinois, July 1983,* by Edward B. Jelks and Carl J. Ekberg. Midwestern Archaeological Research Center, Illinois State University, Normal. Report submitted to the Illinois Historic Preservation Agency, Springfield.

    1986   *A Faunal Analysis of Fort Ouiatenon, An Eighteenth Century Trading Post in the Wabash Valley of Indiana.* Ph.D. dissertation, Michigan State University. University Microfilms, Ann Arbor.

McDermott, John F. (editor)
    1949a   *Old Cahokia.* The St. Louis Historical Documents Foundation, St. Louis.

    1949b   Cahokia and Its People. In *Old Cahokia,* edited by John F. McDermott, pp. 1–54. The St. Louis Historical Documents Foundation, St. Louis.

McElrath, Dale L., Thomas E. Emerson, Andrew C. Fortier, and James L. Phillips
    1984   Late Archaic Period. In *American Bottom Archaeology,* edited by Charles J. Bareis and James W. Porter, pp. 34–58. University of Illinois Press, Urbana.

McWilliams, Richebourg G. (editor)
    1953   *Fleur de Lys and Calumet: Being the Penicaut Narrative of French Adventure in Louisiana.* Louisiana State University Press, Baton Rouge.

Mereness, Newton D. (editor)
    1916   Journal of Diron D'Artaguiette. In *Travels in the American Colonies, 1690–1783,* 2nd ed., pp. 15–92. Antiquarian Press, New York.

Miller, J. Jefferson, and Lyle M. Stone
  1970   Eighteenth Century Ceramics from Fort Michilimackinac. *Smithsonian Study in History and Technology* 4, Washington, D. C.

Milner, George R., Thomas E. Emerson, Mark W. Mehrer, Joyce A. Williams, and Duane Esarey
  1984   Mississippian and Oneota Periods. In *American Bottom Archaeology*, edited by Charles J. Bareis and James W. Porter, pp. 158–186. University of Illinois Press, Urbana.

Moorehead, Warren K.
  1929   The Cahokia Mounds. *University of Illinois Bulletin* 26(4), Urbana.

Munson, Patrick J.
  1971   An Archaeological Survey of the Wood River Terrace and Adjacent Bottoms and Bluffs in Madison County, Illinois. *Illinois State Museum Reports of Investigations* 21(1), Springfield.

Nern, Craig F., and Charles E. Cleland
  1974   The Gros Cap Cemetery Site, St. Ignace, Michigan: A Reconsideration of the Greenless Collection. *Michigan Archaeologist* 20(1).

Noble, Vergil E., Jr.
  1983   *Functional Classification and Intra-site Analysis in Historical Archeology: A Case Study from Fort Ouiatenon.* Unpublished Ph.D. dissertation, Department of Anthropology, Michigan State University.

Noel Hume, Ivor
  1970   *A Guide to Artifacts of Colonial America.* Alfred A. Knopf, New York.

Norris, F. Terry
  1979   *Old Town-Ste. Genevieve, Circa 1723–1785.* U. S. Army Corps of Engineers, St. Louis District. Report submitted to the Missouri State Historic Preservation Office.

  1984   Old Cahokia, An Eighteenth Century Archaeological Site Model. *Le Journal* 2(1):1–21.

Olson, Stanley J.
  1960   Post-Cranial Skeletal Characters of *Bison* and *Bos*. *Papers of the Peabody Museum of Archaeology and Ethnology* 35(4), Harvard University, Cambridge, Massachusetts.

Omwake, H. Geiger
  1955   Concerning TD Pipes. *Bulletin of the Nassau Archaeological Society* 1:26–28.

  1965   Analysis of 19th Century White Kaolin Clay Pipe Fragments from the Mero Site, Door County, Wisconsin. *Wisconsin Archaeologist* 26(2).

Orser, Charles E., Jr.
  1975   *The Kolmer Site: An Eighteenth Century Michigamea Village*. Unpublished Master's thesis, Department of Anthropology, Wayne State University, Detroit, Michigan.

  1977   The 1975 Season of Archaeological Investigations at Fort de Chartres, Randolph County, Illinois. *Southern Illinois Studies, Research Records* 16, University Museum, Southern Illinois University, Carbondale.

Orser, Charles E., Jr., and Theodore J. Karamanski
  1977   Preliminary Archaeological Research at Fort Kaskaskia, Randolph County, Illinois. *Southern Illinois Studies, Research Records* 17, University Museum, Southern Illinois University, Carbondale.

Palm, Sister Mary Borgias
  1931   *The Jesuit Missions of the Illinois Country, 1673–1763*. Cleveland.

Parker, James W.
  1982   Archaeological Test Excavation at 1 Su 7. The Fort Tombecbe Site. *Journal of Alabama Archaeology* 18(1).

Parmalee, Paul W.
  1961   Faunal Materials from the Zimmerman Site (Ls 13), La Salle County, Illinois. In The Zimmerman Site, edited by James A. Brown, pp. 79–81. *Illinois State Museum Reports of Investigations* 9, Springfield.

Parmalee, Paul W., and Arthur E. Bogan
   1980   Vertebrate Remains from Early European and Historic Indian Occupations at the Waterman Site, Randolph County, Illinois. *Transactions of the Illinois State Academy of Science* 73(3):49-54.

Pease, Theodore C., and Raymond C. Werner (editors)
   1934   The French Foundations 1680–1693. *Collections of the Illinois State Historical Library* 23, Springfield.

Peckman, Howard H.
   1947   *Pontiac and the Indian Uprising*. Princeton University Press, New Jersey.

Perino, Gregory
   1967   The Kaskaskia Indian Village Site 1700–1832. In *The Conference on Historic Site Archaeology Papers 1965–1966* 1:127–130.

Peterson, Charles E.
   1941   Early Ste. Genevieve and Its Architecture. *The Missouri Historical Review* 35:207–232.

   1949   Notes on Old Cahokia. *Journal of the Illinois Historical Society* 42(1–3):7–30, 193–209, 313–343.

   1965   The Houses of French St. Louis. In *The French in the Mississippi Valley*, edited by John F. McDermott, pp. 17–40. University of Illinois Press, Urbana.

Peterson, Eugene T.
   1963   Clay Pipes: A Footnote to Mackinac's History. *Mackinac History Leaflet* 1. Mackinac Island State Park Commission, Lansing, Michigan.

Philippe, Joseph S., and Mark E. Esarey
   1983   *Report of Preliminary Archaeological Assessment at FAI-270 Borrow Pit 55, Monroe County, Illinois*. Midwestern Archaeological Research Center, Illinois State University, Normal.

Pittman, Philip
   1770   *The Present State of the European Settlements on the Mississippi River*. Facsimile edited by John F. McDermott. Memphis State University Press.

Porterfield, Neil H.
    1969   Ste. Genevieve, Missouri. In *Frenchmen and French Ways in the Mississippi Valley*, edited by John F. McDermott, pp. 141–175. University of Illinois Press, Urbana.

Price, Cynthia R.
    1979   Nineteenth Century Ceramics in the Eastern Ozark Border Region. *Center for Archaeological Research Monograph Series* 1, Southwest Missouri State University, Springfield.

Puckett, William Touches Deer
    1979   Settlement History Development of the Cahokia Canal Drainage Area. *Bulletin of the Illinois Geographical Society* 21(2):15–27.

Purdue, James R., and Bonnie W. Styles
    1986   Dynamics of Mammalian Distribution in the Holocene of Illinois. *Illinois State Museum Reports of Investigations* 41, Springfield.

Quimby, George I.
    1957   The Bayou Goula Site, Iberville Parish, Louisiana. *Fieldiana: Anthropology* 47(2), Chicago Natural History Museum.

    1966a   *Indian Culture and European Trade Goods*. The University of Wisconsin Press, Madison.

    1966b   The Dumaw Creek Site: A Seventeenth Century Prehistoric Indian Village and Cemetery in Oceana County, Michigan. *Fieldiana: Anthropology* 56(1), Field Museum of Natural History, Chicago.

Randall, Mark E.
    1971   Early Marbles. *Historical Archaeology* 5:102–105.

Reitz, Elizabeth J., and Nicholas Honerkamp
    1983   British Colonial Subsistence Strategy on the Southeastern Coastal Plain. *Historical Archaeology* 17(2):4–26.

Reitz, Elizabeth J., and C. Margaret Honerkamp
    1985   Reconstructing Historic Subsistence with an Example from Sixteenth-century Spanish Florida. *Society for Historical Archaeology, Special Publication Series* 3.

Reynolds, John
  1852   *A Pioneer History of Illinois*. N. A. Randall, Belleville.

Rogers, Karel
  1975a Faunal Remains from the Zimmerman Site--1971. In The Zimmerman Site, by Margaret Kimball Brown, pp. 80–85. *Illinois State Museum Reports of Investigations* 32, Springfield.

  1975b Faunal Remains from the Zimmerman Site--1972--Grid B. In The Zimmerman Site, by Margaret Kimball Brown, pp. 86–91. *Illinois State Museum Reports of Investigations* 32, Springfield.

Safiran, Edward T.
  1987   *Archaeological Investigations at the Louvier Site: Part of the Original Settlement of French Colonial French Prairie du Rocher*. Manuscript on file at the Midwestern Archaeological Research Center, Illinois State University, Normal.

Sauer, Carl O.
  1980   *Seventeenth Century North America*. Turtle Island Foundation, Berkeley.

Schlarman, J. H.
  1929   *From Quebec to New Orleans*. Buechler Publishing Company, Belleville.

Schnell, Gail S.
  1974   Hotel Plaza: An Early Historic Site with a Long Prehistory. *Illinois State Museum Reports of Investigations* 29, Springfield.

Shea, John Gilmary (editor)
  1861   *Early Voyages Up and Down the Mississippi*. Joel Munsell, Albany.

Smith, Hale G.
  1965   Archaeological Excavation at Santa Rosa, Pensacola. *Florida State University Notes in Anthropology* 10.

Smith, Philip W.
  1979   *The Fishes of Illinois*. University of Illinois Press, Urbana.

South, Stanley
    1964   Analysis of Buttons from Brunswick Town and Fort Fisher. *Florida Anthropologist*, 7(2):113–133.

Spielbauer, Ronald H.
    1976   *Chert Resources and Aboriginal Chert Utilization in Western Union County, Illinois*. Unpublished Ph.D. dissertation, Department of Anthropology, Southern Illinois University, Carbondale.

St. Clair Title Company
    1956   *An Atlas of St. Clair County, Illinois*. Belleville.

Stearns, Raymond Phineas
    1936   Joseph Kellogg's Observations on Senex's Map of North America (1710). *The Mississippi Valley Historical Review* 23:345–354.

Steyermark, Julian A.
    1981   *Flora of Missouri*. Iowa State University Press, Ames.

Stone, Garry Wheeler
    1973   Ceramics from the John Hicks Site, 1723–1743: The Material Culture. In *Ceramics in America* edited by Ian M. G. Quimby, pp. 103–140. University Press of Virginia, Charlottesville.

Stone, Lyle M.
    1974   Fort Michilimackinac 1715–1781; An Archaeological Perspective on the Revolutionary Frontier. *Michigan State University Anthropological Series* 2. East Lansing.

Styles, Bonnie W., Terrance J. Martin, and Mary Carol Masulis
    1987   Middle Woodland and Historic Faunal Remains from the Naples-Abbott Site, Scott County, Illinois. *Illinois State Museum Society Quarternary Studies Program Technical Report* 87-329-8.

Surrey, N. M. Miller
    1916   The Commerce of Louisiana During the French Regime 1699–1763. *Studies in History, Economics and Public Law* 71(1), Columbia University, New York.

Sussman, Lynne
    1978   British Military Tableware, 1760–1830. *Historical Archaeology* 2:93–104.

Temple, Wayne C.
   1966   Indian Villages of the Illinois Country. *Illinois State Museum Scientific Papers* 2(2), Springfield.

   1975   Indian Villages of the Illinois County. *Illinois State Museum Scientific Papers* 2(1), Springfield.

Thwaites, Reuben G. (editor)
   1959   *The Jesuit Relations and Allied Documents; Travels and Explorations of the Jesuit Missionaries in New France 1610–1791.* 73 vols. Pageant Book Company, New York.

Tordoff, Judith Dunn
   1983   *An Archaeological Perspective on the Organization of the Fur Trade in Eighteenth Century New France.* Unpublished Ph.D. dissertation, Department of Anthropology, Michigan State University.

Toulouse, Julian
   1968   Empontilling-A History. *The Glass Industry* Part I:137-142.

Tucker, Sara Jones
   1942   Atlas of Indian Villages of the Illinois Country. *Illinois State Museum Scientific Papers* 2(1), Springfield.

Van Ravenswaay, Charles
   1956   The Creole Arts and Crafts of Upper Louisiana. *Bulletin of the Missouri Historical Society* 12(3):213–248.

Walitschek, David
   1986   *Report of Monitoring for Archaeological Remains Along Illinois Route 3 (FAP 14) from Illinois Route 157 to Fifth Street in Cahokia, St. Clair County, Illinois.* Midwestern Archaeological Research Center, Illinois State University, Normal. Report submitted to Illinois Department of Transportation, Springfield.

Walker, Iain C.
   1967   Clay Pipes from the Fortress of Louisbourg. *Archaeology Magazine* 20(3):187–193.

Wallace, D. L.
   1978   *Soil Survey of St. Clair County, Illinois.* U. S. Department of Soil Conservation Services in cooperation with Illinois Agricultural Environment Station.

Walthall, John A.
   in press *Ceramics in French Colonial Illinois*. Illinois State Museum, Springfield.
   1981   Galena and Aboriginal Trade in Eastern North America. *Illinois State Museum Scientific Papers* 17, Springfield.

Walthall, John A., and Elizabeth D. Benchley
   1987   The River L'Abbe Mission. *Studies in Illinois Archaeology* 2, Illinois Historic Preservation Agency, Springfield.

Walton, Clyde C. (editor)
   1962   *John Francis Snyder: Selected Writings*. Illinois State Historical Society, Springfield.

Waselkov, G. A., B. M. Wood, and J. M. Herbert
   1982   Colonization and Conquest: The 1980 Archaeological Excavation at Fort Toulousa and Fort Jackson, Alabama. *Auburn University Archaeological Monograph* 4.

Weymouth, John, and William I. Woods
   1984   Combined Magnetic and Chemical Surveys of Fort Kaskaskia and de Chartres Number 1, Illinois. *Historical Archaeology* 18(2):20–37.

White, William P., Sissel Johannessen, Paula G. Cross, and Lucretia S. Kelly
   1984   Environmental Setting. In *American Bottom Archaeology*, edited by Charles J. Bareis and James W. Porter, pp. 15–33. University of Illinois Press, Urbana.

Wild, J. C., and Lewis Thomas
   1841   *The Valley of the Mississippi; Illustrated in a Series of Views*. Chambers and Knapp, St. Louis.

Wilderman, A. S., and A. A. Wilderman
   1907   *Historical Encyclopedia of Illinois and History of St. Clair County, II*. Munsell Publishing Company, Chicago.

Williams, Joyce, and Richard B. Lacampagne
   1982   Final Report on Archaeological Investigations at the Adler Site (11–S–64). *FAI-270 Archaeological Mitigation Project Report* 43, Department of Anthropology, University of Illinois, Champaign-Urbana.

Wittry, Warren L.
    1963   The Bell Site, Wn 9, an Historic Fox Village. *Wisconsin Archaeologist* 44(1):1–57.

Wray, Donald E.
    1952   Archeology of the Illinois Valley: 1950. In *Archeology of Eastern United States*, edited by James B. Griffin. University of Chicago Press, Chicago.

Yarbrough, Ronald E.
    1974   The Physiography of Metro East. *Bulletin of the Illinois Geographical Society* 16:12–28.

Zay, E.
    1892   *Histoire Monetaire Des Colonies Francais*. Typograpchie de J. Montorier, Paris.